Tomáš Vinař, Martin Holeňa, Matej Lexa,
Ladislav Peška, Peter Vojtáš (Eds.)

ITAT 2013: Information Technologies—Applications and Theory
Workshops, Posters, and Tutorials

Conference on Theory and Practice of Information Technologies
Donovaly, Slovakia, September 11-15, 2013

ITAT 2013: Information Technologies—Applications and Theory
(Workshops, Posters, and Tutorials)
Donovaly, Slovakia, September 11-15, 2013
Tomáš Vinař, Martin Holeňa, Matej Lexa, Ladislav Peška, Peter Vojtáš (Eds.)
Cover design: Róbert Novotný
Publisher: CreateSpace Independent Publishing Platform, 2013
ISBN 978-1490952086

http://www.itat.cz/

Introduction

This volume contains workshop papers, poster abstracts, and tutorial materials of the 13th ITAT conference, which took place on September 11-15, 2013 at Donovaly, Slovakia. ITAT is a computer science conference with the primary goal of presenting new results of young researchers and doctoral students from Slovakia and the Czech Republic. The conference serves as a platform for exchange of information within the community, and also provides opportunities for informal meetings of the participants in a mountainous regions of the Czech Republic and Slovakia. The traditional topics of the conference include software engineering, data processing and knowledge representation, information security, theoretical foundations of computer science, computational intelligence, distributed computing, natural language processing, and computer science education. The conference accepts papers describing original previously unpublished results, significant work-in-progress reports, as well as reviews of special topics of interest to the conference audience.

The conference program this year included the main track of contributed papers, workshops, posters, and three invited lectures. Overall, 44 papers and abstracts were submitted to all conference tracks. This volume contains papers from the three conference workshops:

- Data Mining and Preference Learning on the Web
  (organized by Ladislav Peška, Peter Vojtáš)

- Bioinformatics in Genomics and Proteomics (organized by Matej Lexa)

- Computational Intelligence and Data Mining (organized by Martin Holeňa)

Refereeing standards differed between the workshops and are described separately for each workshop in each section of this volume. The volume also contains poster abstracts and tutorial materials. The papers from the main track were published as a separate volume.

I would like to thank all workshop chairs, workshop program committees, organizers, and all contributing authors for helping to create an exciting scientific program of the conference.

Tomáš Vinař
Comenius University in Bratislava
Chair of the Program Committee

Contents

Poster Abstracts   119

Tutorial Materials   127

Workshop on Data Mining and Preference Learning on the Web

Workshop "Data Mining and Preference Learning on the Web" aims to help users with increasing information overload on the contemporary web. The workshop combines areas of data mining, preference learning and semantical web.

The amount of information on the web grows continuously and processing it directly by a human is virtually impossible. Number of tools was designed to aid users with information searching, filtering, aggregating or processing such as search engines, recommender systems, information aggregators etc. An integral part of such systems are different forms of data mining i.e. textual data mining, mining semi-structured data records, aggregation of machine-readable data, usage of Linked Open Data, Named Entities, relational data mining, etc.. Personalization and related problems of preference learning, user feedback, machine learning or Human-Computer Interaction represent a further extension of such tools allowing to focus on the needs of individual user.

Each submission was evaluated by at least two reviewers from the Program Committee. The papers were evaluated for their originality, contribution significance, clarity, and overall quality.

Peter Vojtáš
Ladislav Peška
Charles University in Prague, Czech Republic
Workshop Progam Chairs

Workshop Program Committee

Peter Vojtáš, Charles University in Prague, Czech Republic
Ladislav Peška, Charles University in Prague, Czech Republic
Tomáš Horváth, Pavol Jozef Šafárik University in Košice, Slovakia
Štefan Pero, Pavol Jozef Šafárik University in Košice, Slovakia

ITAT 2013: Workshops, Posters, and Tutorials, pp. 2–4
ISBN 978-1490952086, © 2013 J. Hlaváčová

Special domain data mining through DBpedia
on the example of Biology

Jaroslava Hlaváčová

ÚFAL MFF UK
hlava@ufal.mff.cuni.cz

Abstract: Wikipedia is not only a large encyclopedia, but lately also a source of linguistic data for various applications. Individual language versions allow to get the parallel data in multiple languages. Inclusion of Wikipedia articles into categories can be used to filter the language data according to a domain.

In our project, we needed a large number of parallel data for training systems of machine translation in the field of biomedicine. One of the sources was Wikipedia. To select the data from the given domain we used the results of the DBpedia project, which extracts structured information from the Wikipedia articles and makes them available to users in RDF format.

In this paper we describe the process of data extraction and the problems that we had to deal with, because the open source project like Wikipedia, to which anyone can contribute, is not very reliable concerning consistency.

1 Introduction — machine translation within the Khresmoi project

Khresmoi[1] is the European project developing a multilingual multimodal search and access system for biomedical information and documents. There are 12 partners from 9 European countries. The languages involved are English, Czech, German and French. The Czech part is responsible for machine translations between English and one of the other languages.

Machine translation is processed by means of statistical methods. For achieving good results, big amounts of language data are needed. They are used especially for training the system and afterwards for evaluations. The whole process of machine translation is nicely described in Czech in [3].

There are two types of data needed for the statistical machine translation task:

- parallel data — the same text in two languages, aligned on the sentence level
- monolingual data — for creating language model that is needed for the correct sentence creation in the target language

Both types of data is necessary to collect and preprocess. There are sets of data already prepared for various purposes, but for every special task it is usually necessary to collect more data or special sort of data.

In our case it was the need for data from the special domain — namely biomedicine. In the following text we will call them in-domain data. Apart from existing in-domain databases and registers we decided to extract in-domain data from a large general source — Wikipedia, especially its superstructure DBpedia.

2 DBpedia as a source of linguistic data

DBpedia[2] [2, 1] is a large multi-lingual knowledge base of structured information extracted from Wikipedia articles. The data is stored in RDF format putting together different entities, categories, languages. The data in DBpedia are divided into two datasets:

- **Canonicalized** — data having an equivalent in English.

- **Localized** — data from non-English Wikipedias.

As English was a central target language, we used the canonicalized data sets for our experiments.

The DBpedia has its own ontology, which is however not complete and in its recent shape is not possible to use for our purpose, namely the biomedical domain. Nevertheless, there are files in DBpedia (skos_categories_XX.ttl, where XX stands for abbreviation of a language (en for English, cs for Czech, fr for French, de for German).) putting together names of articles and their Wikipedia categories. The relations between the categories use the SKOS[3] vocabulary, namely the link *skos:broader* indicating that one category is more general (broader) than the other. We used this relation for extracting chains of Wikipedia subcategories for all the languages mentioned above. As the top category, we used the category *Biology*, as it appeared that all the medical categories are transitively subcategories of the category *Biology*.

3 Wikipedia categories and their relations

The categories are assigned to Wikipedia articles by their authors. Thus, the assignments are to a considerable extent subjective which has the troublesome consequence: the system of Wikipedia subcategories is not properly ordered. There are cycles, which means that one category

---

[1] http://www.khresmoi.eu
[2] http://dbpedia.org/About
[3] http://www.w3.org/2004/02/skos

might be transitively subcategory of itself. We present an example from the Czech category with the name *Endemité* (*Endemic*). There are two paths from the top category *Biology* leading to that category. The number at the beginning of each path represents number of levels from the top category:

44 Biologie Život Evoluce Strom_života Eukaryota Opisthokonta Živočichové Strunatci Obratlovci Čtyřnožci Synapsida Savci Placentálové Primáti Hominidé Člověk Lidé Profese Inženýrství Teorie_systémů Ekonomie Ekonomika Služby Zdravotnictví Lékařství Lékařské_obory Biomedicínské_inženýrství Lékařská_diagnostika Klinické_příznaky Psychologické_jevy Psychické_procesy Myšlení Abstraktní_vztahy Systematika Systémy Sluneční_soustava Planety_sluneční_soustavy Země Vědy_o_Zemi Geografie Geografické_disciplíny Fyzická_geografie Biogeografie Endemité

2 Biologie Endemité

In French, there is only one path of the length 7 leading to the category *Endémique*, English category Endemism (as the Wikipedia counterpart of the Czech category name) is not a subcategory of *Biology*, German category of that name does not exist. From this small example, we can get an idea of the extent of the inconsistency within Wikipedia categories.

There are even the cycles leading to the top level category *Biologie* in Czech and French (but not in English and German). They have the same length, but it is only an accident, as we can directly see from the paths — the individual levels do not correspond between the languages:

Czech (36) *Biologie* Život Evoluce Strom_života Eukaryota Opisthokonta Živočichové Strunatci Obratlovci Čtyřnožci Synapsida Savci Placentálové Primáti Hominidé Člověk Lidé Profese Inženýrství Teorie_systémů Ekonomie Ekonomika Služby Zdravotnictví Lékařství Lékařské_obory Biomedicínské_inženýrství Lékařská_diagnostika Klinické_příznaky Psychologické_jevy Psychické_procesy Myšlení Znalosti Věda Přírodní_vědy *Biologie*

French (36) *Biologie* Discipline_de_la_biologie Zoologie Animal Phylogénie_des_animaux Vertebrata Gnathostome Tétrapode Mammalia Eutheria Epitheria Boreoeutheria Euarchontoglires Euarchonta Primate Haplorrhini Simiiforme Catarrhini Hominoidea Hominidé Homininae Hom"minini Humain Sciences_humaines_et_sociales Économie Branche_de_l'économie Économie_publique Administration_publique Service_public Travail_social Éducation Association_ou_organisme_lié_à_l'éducation Académie Discipline_académique Sciences_naturelles *Biologie*

We present some more statistics about the cycles in the category systems of individual languages — see table 1. In all the languages except English, the shortest cycles are only 2 levels long, similarly as in the previous example with Czech *Endemité*. In English, the shortest cycles have 8 levels.

We can see that the ratio of cycles to all biological subcategories is very high. It suggests that almost one half of categories may be reached via more than one path from the top category of *Biology*. Only German has significantly less cycles. We might only guess the reason, there might be better checking team for the German Wikipedia.

The longest paths are usually cycles, but it is not always so. For instance in German, there are paths of the length 16, that are not cycles. Also in Czech, among the 5 longest paths, there are only four cycles. The fifth path leads to a category unambiguously.

The examples demonstrate that there is not possible to use the category structure for parallel mapping between the languages. Every languages has its own category system, they are not related. It even happens that articles with the same meaning are incorporated in different categories for different languages.

Table 1: Number of cycles in Wikipedia categories for individual languages. (Cycles means number of cycles, All subcat. is number of transitive subcategories of *Biology*, the column Longest presents the length of the longest cycle.)

	Cycles	All subcat.	Ratio	Longest
Czech	56 061	113 376	49,45%	54
English	374 357	782 325	47,85%	166
French	170 000	344 359	49,37%	62
German	1 219	6 186	19,71%	12

To avoid cycles during the processing the data is not difficult. The more problematic is the scope of the transitive subcategories. Table 2 shows that the subcategories cover almost all the Wikipedia categories, especially in case of Czech and French. The German Wikipedia again appears to be mantained more carefully.

Table 2: Ratio of in-domain categories to all the categories for different languages.

	All categories	In-domain subcateg.	Ratio in-domain/all
Czech	58 329	57 315	98,26%
English	865 900	407 968	47,11%
French	206 324	174 359	84,51%
German	144 876	4 967	3,43%

It was the reason why we tried to use the German in-domain categories as a basis. In DBpedia, there are files (interlanguage_links_same_as_XX.ttl) mapping names of all titles, including categories, among all the languages, where such a mapping appears in Wikipedia. The relation sameAs is used to link pairs of titles between two languages. As the relation is symmetric and for our purposes, English is always one member of the language pair, we could use only the file for English (namely interlanguage_links_same_as_en.ttl).

Resulting number of categories in other languages is shown in table 3. The result is not satisfactory, the number of in-domain categories for other languages is about one third of the number of German ones, which seems to be too few. When we collected all the titles of Wikipedia articles from those categories, we missed a lot of relevant terms.

Table 3: In-domain categories based on Germann

		Ratio to German
Czech	1 174	0.24
English	1 981	0.40
French	1 496	0.30
German	4 967	1

The reason was simple — the system of subcategories does not match among the languages. Moreover, the same terms are often put into a different category in different languages. For instance the article *Plodová voda Amniotic fluid* belongs only to one Czech category *Těhotenství Human pregnancy*, which is not a category for the German Wikipedia. That is why this term did not appear in the result.

Our findings confirm the way how the Wikipedia is created and mantained. There is no (or not satisfactory) coordination among the languages involved.

4   Combination with other sources

We had to find another way how to extract the in-domain data from Wikipedia.

For every language, we used other DBpedia source files for selection all titles belonging to in-domain categories acquired through German in-domain categories. Then, we used files interlanguage_links_same_as_XX.ttl providing translations of all Wikipedia titles and made translations for all pairs among our four languages. It did not help much, there were still missing many useful terms.

We decided to take all the terms acquired so far, find all categories they belong to, and add all the rest titles from those categories. We got again into trouble with inconsistency of categories and had to adopt a limit of at least two terms in a category to be accepted as in-domain. Thus, we took titles of every category that contained at least two terms selected as in-domains in previous steps.

The last decision was to add data from external source, namely MeSH. MeSH is the abbreviation for Medical Sub-

ject Headings[4]. It is a vocabulary thesaurus mantained by the U.S. National Library of Medicine. It has translations into many languages and is used for indexing medical articles all over the world. We used the list of MeSH terms in all languages the same way as the last step described above; we tried to find all categories that included at least two MeSH terms. Then, we copied all the terms from those categories into the final lists.

The last step was building in-domain dictionaries with English. The final table 4 presents number of in-domain term pairs. We made a small manual evaluation of indomainness for the Czech-English pair. We randomly selected 200 pairs and manually checked those belonging to the domain of biomedicine — they were only 14. However, we did not evaluate personal names that constitute almost 50% of the selection. A next evaluation should probably exclude the personal names. We will make a similar evaluation for other languages.

The result is not very impressive. Nevertheless, our selections present reasonably big and consistent in-domain dictionaries that can be used as a basis in further processing toward using in statistical machine translation.

Table 4: Sizes of final dictionaries

	Number of terms
Czech-English	69 598
French-English	379 830
German-English	310 203

Acknowledgments

The research leading to these results has received funding from the European Union Seventh Framework Programme (FP7/2007-2013) under grant agreement n° 257528 (KHRESMOI).

References

[1] Pablo N. Mendes, Max Jakob and Christian Bizer. DBpedia for NLP: A Multilingual Cross-domain Knowledge Base. Proceedings of the International Conference on Language Resources and Evaluation, LREC 2012, 21–27 May 2012, Istanbul, Turkey.

[2] Christian Bizer, Jens Lehmann, Georgi Kobilarov, Sören Auer, Christian Becker, Richard Cyganiak, and Sebastian Hellmann. 2009. DBpedia - A crystallization point for the Web of Data. Journal of Web Semantics: Science, Services and Agents on the World Wide Web, (7):154– 165.

[3] Bojar Ondřej: Čeština a strojový překlad. Studies in Computational and Theoretical Linguistics. Praha, ÚFAL 2012

---

[4]http://www.nlm.nih.gov/mesh/

ITAT 2013: Workshops, Posters, and Tutorials, pp. 5–9
ISBN 978-1490952086, © 2013 J. Hajič jr., K. Veselovská

ITAT

Developing Sentiment Annotator in UIMA – the Unstructured Management Architecture for Data Mining Applications

Jan Hajič, jr.
Charles University in Prague
Faculty of Mathematics and Physics
Institute of Formal and Applied Linguistics
Malostranské nám. 25, 118 00 Prague
Czech Republic

Kateřina Veselovská
Charles University in Prague
Faculty of Mathematics and Physics
Institute of Formal and Applied Linguistics
Malostranské nám. 25, 118 00 Prague
Czech Republic

Abstract. *In this paper we present UIMA – the Unstructured Information Management Architecture, an architecture and software framework for creating, discovering, composing and deploying a broad range of multi-modal analysis capabilities and integrating them with search technologies. We describe the elementary components of the framework and how they are deployed into more complex data mining applications. The contribution is based on our experience in work on the sentiment analysis task for IBM Content Analytics project. Note that most information on UIMA in this paper can be obtained from UIMA documentation; our main goal is to give the reader an idea whether UIMA would be helpful for her or his task, and to do this in less time than reading the documentation would take.*

1 Introduction

UIMA is an acronym standing for Unstructured Information Management Architecture. "Unstructured information" means essentially any raw document: text, picture, video, etc. or a combination thereof. Unstructured information is mostly useless – a string of five digits will not tell us much unless we know it's a ZIP code and not a price tag. In order to make an unstructured document useful, we must first discover this type of meaning in the unstructured document and make this additional information available for further processing.

The process of making sense of unstructured information is in UIMA called annotating. Components that discover the hidden meanings and store them as annotations are, predictably enough, called annotators. The point of UIMA is to provide a common framework so that multiple components can be linked to create arbitrarily rich annotations of the unstructured (semantically "flat") input. This is the most important contribution of UIMA: a very flexible way of passing analysis results from one component to another, and so gradually discovering and making use of more and more information contained within the unstructured document.

The interoperability of various components is achieved by defining the Common Analysis Structure, CAS, and its interfaces to various programming languages (most notably JCAS for Java). The CAS is the tumbleweed that cascades through the various annotators, each of which adds its annotation results to the CAS. The CAS can also pass more information than annotations of document regions: the

representation scheme for analysis results is very general and supports such information as "the annotation span 43-47 and 55-59 are references to the same company".

The component that houses an annotating pipeline is called an Analysis Engine. An Analysis Engine at its simplest contains just one annotator and is called a *primitive* AE. AEs that house more annotators are called *aggregate* engines. Also, an Analysis Engine can be composed of multiple other AEs. The Analysis Engine is the component that is actually *run* by the framework. The simplest AE is just this runnable wrapper of an annotator.

Individual annotators are usually used for small-scale, granular tasks: language identification, tokenization, sentence splitting, syntactical parsing, named entity recognition, etc. Analysis Engines are typically used to encapsulate "semantic" tasks on raw documents (or on somehow meaningful levels of document annotation, such as a document after linguistic analysis or a picture after segmentation), such as document-level sentiment analysis. Both annotators and Analysis Engines are easily re-usable in various UIMA pipelines.

UIMA is currently an Apache project, meaning it can be freely downloaded at http://uima.apache.org. (Previously, the architecture was proprietary to IBM. IBM still uses UIMA extensively in its applications like Content Analytics and Enterprise Search.)

The architecture also provides facilities to wrap components as network services and scale up to very large volumes by running annotation pipelines in parallel over a networked cluster. This is done through a server that provides analysis results as a REST service.

A number of annotators and other components is available as a part of the UIMA Sandbox from the Apache project. Others are lying around the internet.

UIMA is not oriented towards data mining research, although it is universal enough to be used as such. There are no built-in facilities for evaluating data mining performance.

For our sentiment analysis project, we have not worked with other media in UIMA than text, so we will limit ourselves to text analysis in this paper. However, UIMA is capable of multi-modal analysis as well.

Apache UIMA is very well-documented, from our experience significantly better than the IBM applications using it.

2   UIMA Components Overview

UIMA is a software architecture which specifies component interfaces, data representations, design patterns and development roles for creating multi-modal analysis capabilities.

The *UIMA framework* provides a run-time environment in which developers can plug in their component implementations and with which they can build and deploy unstructured information management applications. The framework is not specific to any IDE or platform; Apache hosts a Java and a C++ implementation of the UIMA Framework.

The *UIMA Software Development Kit (SDK)* includes the UIMA framework, plus tools and utilities for using UIMA. Some of the tooling supports an Eclipse-based (http://www.eclipse.org/) development environment. These tools (specifically the Component Descriptor Editor and JcasGen, see below) proved to be extremely useful for orienting ourselves in the complex interfaces of annotation components.

There are two parts to a *component*: the code and the *component descriptor*, which is an XML document describing the capabilities and requirements of the component. The descriptor holds information such as the input and output types, required parameters and their default values, reference to the class which implements the component, author name, etc. The Component Descriptor Editor for Eclipse IDE is a tool for creating component descriptors without having to know the XML. The descriptor of a component serves as its declared interface to the rest of UIMA.

2.1   Types, CAS and SOFAs

A subject of annotation is called a SOFA. SOFAs can be texts, audio, video, etc. Annotations are anchored to the SOFAs. An annotator may work with any number of SOFAs it gets, even create new ones. Typically, SOFAs going through the pipeline together will be of more modalities, like a news story and an associated picture, or any other group of unstructured documents that we wish to process together to discover relevant information.

Discovered structured information about the SOFAs are kept in *types*. A type is anything: Company, Name, ParseNode, etc. Types are domain-, application- and (unless some coordination/sharing is involved) developer-specific. Each type has an associated *feature structure*. The feature structure holds additional information about the annotated span; for instance, the Company type may have a feature structure that holds whether the company is publicly traded, who its CEO is, where is it based, etc. The feature structure also may be empty. A type can also be a subtype: the type class can inherit from another (multiple inheritance is not allowed).

Types that are associated with a specific region of the SOFA are called *annotation types*. These types have a

span, a start and end feature which delimit the annotated region.

A non-annotation type could be a Company, a type describing all there is to know about a company mentioned in the various SOFAs. Annotation types could be then various   CompanyNameAnnotation, CompanyCEOAnnotation, etc. Our analysis goal could be to recover whatever there is to know about companies mentioned in a collection of SOFAs; we would gradually annotate the SOFAs by the annotation types and finally put all the pieces together into the Company type.

For working with type systems, the UIMA SDK provides a Type System Descriptor Editor within the Component Descriptor Editor tool. Defining types then becomes more or less a point-and-click operation. Additionally, once the type system descriptor is done, the JCasGen utility (also a part of the UIMA SDK for Eclipse) automatically generates the appropriate classes for the annotation types themselves, so that the user never needs to do anything with the types but define them in the Descriptor Editor.

The whole bundle of SOFAs, annotations and whatever else goes through the pipeline is housed inside a *Common Analysis Structure* (CAS). This class is passed from one annotator to another, from one AE into another and is available at the end for some consumer to use the discovered information however it wishes. The CAS class provides iterators to each annotation type and allows annotators to do whatever they wish to them (an annotator may even clear results of previous annotators, so as to keep the CAS uncluttered with intermediate steps that never get used later). An example of an UIMA multi-modal processing pipeline is in Fig. 1:

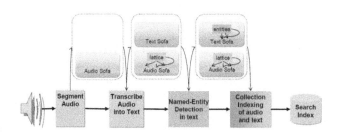

Fig. 1: multi-modal processing pipeline

2.2   Annotators

Annotators are the innermost components in an UIMA processing pipeline. They are the components that actually discover the information from the unstructured document: all the "interesting" things happen in annotators.

UIMA provides the base class for an annotator. At its simplest, all one needs to do to implement an UIMA annotator is to override the *process(...)* method of the base class.

Annotating in UIMA means attaching UIMA annotation *types* to certain spans of text (more precisely, creating the annotation type with attributes that denote which region in the associated document is "responsible" for this particular piece of information). The definition of input and output types – the annotator *type system* – is the critical decision in designing an annotator.

Annotators have two sources of information they can work with: the CAS that runs through the pipeline, from which an annotator gets the document and previously done annotations, and the UIMA Context class, which contains additional information about the environment the annotator is run in: various external resources, configuration parameters, etc. All the inputs an annotator needs to run are described in its component descriptor.

An example annotator could be a tokenizer, an annotator responsible for segmenting text into tokens. It may simply delimit tokens, or it may also add features such as lemma, part of speech, etc. The simpler annotator will require nothing and output the type, let's say, TokenAnnotation with only the span defined and no associated features. The more complex tokenizer will require no input types and maybe an outside resource with a trained statistical model for lemmatization and POS tagging; it will output the type ComplexTokenAnnotation with a feature structure containing the lemma and part of speech features. Maybe the annotators should require an input LanguageAnnotation type that is associated with the whole document and its feature structure has a *language* feature, containing some pre-defined language code, so that the tokenizer knows which statistical model to load. This LanguageAnnotation might be the output of a language recognition algorithm implemented by another annotator further up the pipeline. There can instead be a LanguageSpanAnnotation type can also be designed to allow for multi-lingual documents, by actually giving it a span. The Tokenizer will then iterate over those LanguageSpanAnnotations and will load a different model for each of them, etc.

This example only illustrates the flexibility and ease of use for UIMA: other than the type system, there is no restriction on what the components actually do inside. The input and output of annotators is standardized by the UIMA framework, so that if you think you have a better language identifier which uses a completely different algorithm, you can plug it in and as long as it keeps outputting the LanguageAnnotation type, nothing needs to be changed for the tokenizer. This is no magic – any good programmer knows how to keep things modular – but the point is, UIMA already does this for free, and with a great amount of generality.

2.3 Analysis Engines

The basic blocks in the UIMA architecture that "do something" are the analysis engines. At their simplest, an Analysis Engine simply wraps an annotator so that the UIMA framework can run the annotator inside. Analysis Engines with a single annotator are called *primitive* AEs. An *aggregate* Analysis Engine links more annotators together into a pipeline:

Fig.2: Aggregate Analysis Engine

Analysis Engines provide encapsulation: the only thing a developer needs to know is its input and output types (and some technical information), described in its component descriptor. This enables the developer to aggregate AEs into a more complex UIMA application, perhaps a hierarchical one where top-level AEs consist of multiple sub-engines. These sub-engines are called *delegate AEs*. Generally, Analysis Engines can be thought about as CAS-in, CAS-out processing components and any two where the outputs and inputs in the CAS match can be linked together.

Starting from UIMA 2.0, there is a *flow control* facility of UIMA which can even make decisions, based on what the processing pipeline has come up with so far, as to which analysis engine to use next. (We have no experience with this, though.) The UIMA framework, given an aggregate analysis engine descriptor, will run all delegate AEs, ensuring that each one gets access to the CAS in the sequence produced by the flow controller.

The UIMA framework is also equipped to handle different deployments: the delegate engines, for example, can be tightly-coupled (running in the same process) or loosely-coupled (running in separate processes or even on different machines). The framework supports a number of remote protocols for loose coupling deployments of aggregate analysis engines, including SOAP (which stands for Simple Object Access Protocol, a standard Web Services communications protocol).

3 Scenarios of UIMA Applications

How the components described in the previous section can be fit together to actually do something and what is the "division of labor" between the UIMA framework and the developer is best described in images.

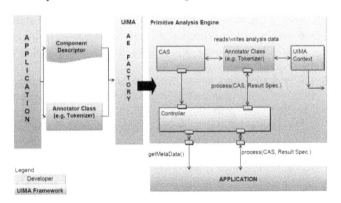

Fig. 3: An elementary UIMA application

This is the elementary deployment scenario. The developer determines what she or he wants to annotate, creates the appropriate Type System descriptor and incorporates it into the Component Descriptor, implements the annotator itself and passes this information to the UIMA Analysis Engine factory. This factory is a part of the UIMA framework. The factory then takes the information from the Component Descriptor and the class and instantiates the Analysis Engine.

The UIMA framework provides methods to support the application developer in creating and managing CASes and instantiating, running and managing AEs. However, since our work is only to implement the annotator class and provide the descriptor into an IBM application, we have no experience with actually using an Analysis Engine.

3.1 Collection Processing

Typically, the application will be processing multiple documents, a *collection*. This presents additional challenges in creating a *collection reader* and managing the iterative workflow (distributed processing, error recovery, etc.) Almost any UIMA application will have a source-to-sink workflow like in Fig. 3:

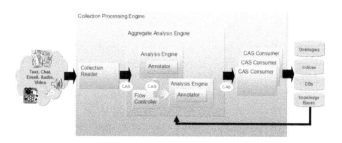

Fig. 4: UIMA collection processing workflow

UIMA supports this larger operation through its *Collection Processing Engines*. This support is through two additional components: the *Collection Reader* and the *CAS Consumer,* and a Collection Processing Manager. The Collection Reader is responsible for feeding documents into the Analysis Engine. The CAS consumers are, predictably enough, responsible for processing the output CASes – for instance, indexing them for a semantic search application, or in a sentiment analysis setting, track opinion trends. The CPEs, as any UIMA component, need an associated Component Descriptor.

UIMA provides some CAS consumers for semantic search and a simple consumer for storing the data into an Apache Derby database.

Creating a CPE is a process analogous to creating an Analysis Engine; of course, the sum of what needs to be configured is different. The following figure illustrates the analogy:

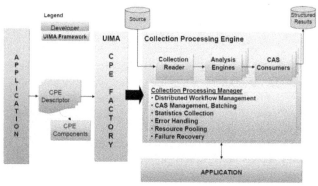

Fig. 5: An UIMA application with a Collection Processing Engine

The descriptor for a CPE specifies things like where to read from, how to do logging, what to do in case of error or what the control flow among various Analysis Engines inside the CPE should be.

Collection processing is the "final step": this is UIMA at its fullest.

4   Annotating Sentiment with UIMA

We are working on a Sentiment Analysis annotator for Czech for IBM Content Analytics (ICA). The task of Sentiment Analysis is currently two-fold. First, we determine whether a segment of the input document contains an evaluative statement: whether a sentence says something nice or bad about about something. Second, we determine the orientation of the segment – whether the statement is positive, or negative.

We work with lexical features using statistical methods, essentially estimating the precision of individual words in predicting a sentiment class (negative/neutral/positive).

How to implement sentiment analysis in UIMA? We are only creating an annotator, so we do not need to concern ourselves with application deployment. All that needs to be done is defining the inputs and outputs. We have determined the input type system from an IBM Content Analytics developer tool that was provided to us through the IBM Academic Initiative. The output types are ours to define. There is one external resource our annotator will need to access: the statistical model of lexical units' precision.

4.1   Creating the Component Descriptor

Since we used lemmatization to increase feature recall, we need lemmatized input. Also, we need some sentence segmentation, in order to determine which segments our classifier should operate on. The ICA standard UIMA pipeline has a lexical analysis component that outputs types *uima.tt.TokenAnnotation* and *uima.tt.SentenceAnnotation* (this component is available in the ContentMaker component from the UIMA Sandbox). We will need the *lemma* feature of *TokenAnnotation*.

On output, we will provide both the token sentiment annotations and the sentence annotations. We named the corresponding types *UFALSentimentToken* and *UFALSentimentSentence*. The token's feature structure consists of the Lemma, the lexicon tag for negation and various precision statistics for the polarity classes. The sentence annotation type contains cumulative statistics over the tokens that span regions contained within the sentence span and a final classification statement.

Our external resource is a CSV file that we pack in one JAR together with the annotator. The default parameter value for the UIMA Context, through which the annotator can access this resource, is provided in the Component Descriptor as well.

Creating the component descriptor using the Component Descriptor Editor did not take more than several minutes. Aside from the type system and the external parameter specification, we only needed to provide the relative path to the annotator class.

4.2 Code

Creating the annotator code then consisted of running the JCasGen utility to generate from the type system the classes that go into the CAS as annotations and writing the algorithm itself. The only UIMA-specific code that had to be written raw was reading from the CAS and adding annotations to it (no more than some 10 lines of code). On the UIMA side, development was easy; on the IBM side, we are still encountering interoperability issues.

5 Conclusions

Our experience with UIMA is not very extensive: currently, our task is simply to implement a sentiment annotator for the IBM Content Analytics application. However, according to our up-to-date knowledge of the system, we are convinced that UIMA is a very thorough, flexible and robust framework. Moreover, the documentation of UIMA is *extremely* good.

The UIMA SDK does its utmost to relieve the developer of tedious, repetitive tasks through utilities like the JCasGen and the Component Descriptor Editor, as long as the Eclipse IDE is used. These utilities make it easy to start working with UIMA. The SDK does its best to help the developer focus on the meaningful parts of the task at hand only: on implementing the algorithms that discover information inside the unstructured data.

This is, we feel, the greatest contribution of UIMA: standardizing and automating the common parts of more or less any data mining application and providing an easy enough way of filling in the "interesting bits", while at the same time being flexible enough to meet most application demands (multi-modality, complex control flow, etc.) At the same time, it also provides robust runtime capabilities.

Also, UIMA aggregate AEs enable and encourage granularity, so individual annotators can be designed so that they do not require more than one person to implement them reasonably fast. Therefore, once the component descriptors are agreed upon, teamwork should be easy.

A weak point may be flexibility on the programmer side: as soon as one strays from a development scenario where the UIMA SDK tools are useful, the amount of work necessary to get an UIMA application up and running increases dramatically. We also do not know how complicated it is to administer an UIMA application.

UIMA might not be the framework of choice in an academic, experimental setting, since it provides no facilities for evaluating the performance of the data mining algorithms inside and is probably unnecessarily complex for most experimental scenarios. Implementing such an evaluator, however, might not be too difficult, either as an external application operating on the database one of the available CAS consumers generates, or as an UIMA component, using some of the semantic search CAS consumers. Furthermore, given UIMA flexibility, modularity and re-usability, if such an evaluation component was present, an UIMA CPE could be a great way of testing data mining algorithms in various complex settings.

We are convinced that UIMA is worth knowing about.

Acknowledgment

The work on this project has been supported by IBM Academic Initiative program. Text and images from the UIMA documentation (http://uima.apache.org/documentation.html) have been used. The sentiment analysis research is also supported by the GAUK 3537/2011 grant and by SVV project number 267 314.

ITAT 2013: Workshops, Posters, and Tutorials, pp. 10–14
ISBN 978-1490952086, © 2013 S. Vojíř

Transformation of GUHA association rules to business rules for implementation using JBoss Drools

Stanislav Vojíř

Department of Knowledge Engineering
University of Economics, Prague
W. Churchill Sq. 4, Prague 3, 130 67, Czech Republic

Abstract. *Data mining of association rules is one way of finding interesting relationships in data - especially in the case of using GUHA method. These rules have not been used only to description but also to learn the preferences of users and used like decision rules in the form of business rules. The following paper presents a transformation from GUHA association rules to DRL form of business rules and using of them in business rules system JBoss Drools. The paper also outlines some possibilities of interpretation of association rules in the form of business rules and possible solving of transformation problems (with uniqueness, entity identification and best results selection).*

1 Motivation and problem definition

If we consider the environment of information systems, we cannot ignore their growing complexity and integration. With the increasing complexity it grows also the efforts to better separation of business logic from application code itself. For this purpose some specialized formats for saving and exchange of business logic get more and more popular. These formats are collectively called "business rules".

Business rules may be stored in many forms (text, structured data, diagrams…) and formats. We can find quite a lot of specifications of them – SBVR, SWRL etc. (see 2.2) These specifications have different expressive power, but it is possible to say, that all the final formats are quite easy to understand. The disadvantage of business rules is that in most cases they have to be written manually. For example it is necessary to have an expert for the domain of "client preferences".

On the other side, many companies usually have quite much data about behavior of their clients. With a little exaggeration it could be said that almost every bigger company collects data about its own customers (clients). The behavior of clients is driven by their preferences and these preferences should in an ideal case be the same preferences, which are hidden in the domain knowledge written in business rules.

The author of this paper believes that it is possible to extract the domain knowledge (described above) from data using descriptive method of data mining – association rules. Association rules may be not only concerned on the problem of shopping cart. We can use the GUHA method, more precisely the GUHA association rules [4] extracted using software LISp-Miner [2][3].

GUHA Association rules have a great expressive power, but they are quite difficult interpretable. And of course, these rules cannot be directly executed – they only describe the reality. The data mining expert usually has to write a long analytical report with information of data preprocessing, particular questions and finally about founded association rules and their impact on the business. Then there must be a domain expert, which reads the

results of analytical report and "rewrites" some of the results into domain knowledge base (in any form of business rules).

It would be very useful if we could semi-automatically convert founded association rules into the form of business rules.[1] But this problem is not so easy how it could look out. It is not possible to write a simple transformation from association rules to business rules. It is necessary to solve some partly problems, which have to be solved during the transformation process.

The following text is divided into these sections: 2 – Business rules in information systems, 3 – Execution of business rules based on GUHA association rules, 4 – The uniqueness of entities and their relationships, 5 – Problem of conflicting rules and 6 – Conclusion and future work.

2 Business rules in information systems

2.1 Business rules – in general

"Business rule" in a general meaning is a rule for business, but in informatics (and of course in this paper, too), we use extended definition. Business rules are a way of separation of business and application logic of an information system or business application. These rules are used for two different purposes: for saving and exchange of "business know how" and for "decision making and reactions to events" in an application.

We can speak about three different types of business rules [6]:

- declaration business rules – term (entity, relation…) declarations
- descriptive business rules – declaration of relations between terms and term derivation
- action business rules – execution of actions like reaction on change in inference base (inference tree in business rule system)

2.2 Format of business rules

Business rules can be created and saved in different forms and their relevant formats. Regarding the forms we can nominate: text form (semi-natural language like Simple English in SBVR), structured text form (mostly used, specialized dialects like DRL, Jess etc.), diagrams (UML form of SBVR), XML or ontology (SBVR, SWRL and more others) and decision tables (used by many rule engines). And we can complete the previous list with the rules written in some programming language.

---

[1] The suitability of this conversion was also syndicated on the occasion of presentation of tool I:ZI Miner on conference ECML-PKDD 2012. [5]

Too many forms, too many formats and dialect – it is a big problem for selection of one "best" language for business rules. When we look at business rules engine and components for their inclusion (or connection) into information systems, we have to say, that fast each rule engine uses another form of rules. And some business rule formats are very well described but there is no existing implementation.

For example the language Semantics of Business Vocabulary and Business Rules (SBVR) [1] is a standard, which has four possible forms. These forms are described in one document, but they are not fully compatible and have different expression power. And for some of them there are no existing execution engines.

2.3 Choise of business rule language and execution engine

Performed background researches of business rules execution and management system gave us a closer range of languages and engines for selection.

The author wants to use as the main execution engine JBoss Drools. [7] This business rules engine is distributed as open source and written in java. It supports basic operations for adding rules to the derivation rule base and execution of them on a set of entities saved in inference tree. The entities could be changed during the evaluation and each activated rule could work with java objects. The rules are (a little simplified) in the form (in DRL language):

rule <name of rule>

when <condition>

then <some action> end.

JBoss Drools as a base component does not support management of the rules themselves. It could be an advantage for modification of management for using in combination of data mining results. [8]

For administration of business rules by lay users (management of a company etc.), rules in DRL form are still too complicated. For this purpose the author would like to use "Simpler English" form of SBVR. [1]

For connection to ontologies (for example for deriving on the semantic web) could be a good choice the language Semantic Web Rule Language (SWRL). [10]

When we want (or have to) combine more languages of business rules, which are not directly convertible between themselves, we must be able to map entities with values from each form to another one. It is necessary to use unique entity names etc. – more in the section 4.

2.4 Generation of business rules

The main idea of business rules deals with the think, that business rules should be defined by domain (business) experts. The definition could be made by writing of definition of business rules, setting-up business rules in the form of parameters of business processes (in BPEL etc.), using graphical definition tools, or in tables in Excel spreadsheets.

But the domain of business rules is currently being quite much studied (world-wide) and one of the targets of the research is automatic generation of business rules. Other groups which are interested in generation of business rules on the base of collected data are working for example in IBM (at least according to interviews with some of their members). Some research teams try to extract business rules from plaintext (textual description of business processes), other from data mining results. But the author has not found publications about generation of business rules from association rules.

3 Execution of business rules based on GUHA association rules

If we want to speak about conversion of GUHA association rules into business rules in DRL form (for JBoss Drools), we have to introduce the both types of these rules. For simplification we could use an example of association rule:

$$age\ ([35\text{-}45)) \wedge income(big) \sim bought(BMW)$$
(where "~" means an GUHA quantifier)

This descriptive association rule could be interpreted as "If the customer had age 35-45 years and big loan, he bought a BMW." This could be useable for example for targeted advertising. When we know, that we have a potential customer in the appropriate age and income category, we should offer to him information about new BMWs.

The described business rule (described in previous paragraph) could be executable using the JBoss Drools system. We could check if an object (converted to appropriate set of entities, which characterize attributes of the object) correspondents to the left side of association rule. So it is the condition of business rule. When it will be true, the business rule system fires the corresponding rule – and it could answer with the right side of the rule.

One complication is the need of conversion from categorized value (in example written [35-45)) to condition with comparisons only using ">", "<" and "=".[2] We use the transformation of each entity to an instance of "generic" java object called "Attribute". The condition is than like:

(Attribute.name = "income") AND (Attribute.value = "big")

In case of comparison of value in an interval or nominal enumeration, the condition is divided into a set of partly conditions.[3]

Using this approach, we encounter a problem in case of rules with different decisions (recommendations). Maybe when the customer will be a woman, she probably wants other car than BMW. JBoss Drools does not solve this problem [7] so we have to manage it in the wrapping application, or add rules for selection of the best corresponding rule. See the section 5.

---

[2] It is true that under the JBoss Drools system we could define an own function or object for comparison of intervals or enumerations, but it would cause complications in case of conversion to other language of business rules.

[3] The author has implemented a set of XSLT transformations from data mining results (in PMML format) to DRL form.

4 The uniqueness of entities and their relationships

A problem of transformation of real-world data into exchangeable form is that there are many names for entities with the same meaning. In this part of the article we focus on some possible approaches to solving this problem.

4.1 Entity name and identification

Almost all formats of business rules are based on some entities (objects extracted from real-world). These entities have some attributes, which can be compared with the specification saved in business rules. When we work with standardized data from one dataset, everything should be OK. The domain expert should use one data vocabulary and every entity should have the same meaning in every rule, in which it is used, etc. But we want to generate business rules from data-mining results. And these data can have various names and categories of values. The best is to put the problem in the example:

We have data-table with column "age". This column contains values of age of people. (It does not matter in what context with other columns.) We want to save one business rule containing: "**Customers under 15 years usually buy <something>.**" The domain expert could know this preference and knows that age must be specified in years as a number. Also he should write something like "**age < 15**". But the data-table was used for data-mining and the domain expert receives some underlying association rules with contents (entities) "**80% of children**" and "**young customers**" What does it mean? The domain expert have to read the full content of the analytical report and look out, how old are the "young customers" and what was meant by the entity "children".

In some formats (languages) of business rules, these named entities can be described in a separate set of rules and after that the entities can be used in other business rules. But if we apply this approach often, it will result in too complex set of business rules (because of the large number of labels for similar entities).

The better approach is using of only one label (name) for each entity. We could easily say that the domain expert (or semi-automatic system) should do re-preprocessing of data-table and use the original column name and values for expression of the rule. The prize will be an extending of processed rules and it does not solve the problem of more analytical reports based on different data-tables. The domain or analytical expert should use only entity names from a "company vocabulary"?

It would be nice when the domain expert could use his own preferred set of entities in connection with entities used in data-mining results, dataset and other business rules in the domain knowledge base.

4.2 "Dictionaries" of entity names

As outlined in the preceding paragraphs for using of business rules it is necessary to use only one set of entities, which are used in conditions or actions of business rules. Event when using of "class definition" in SBVR or SWRL, the business rules engine must be able to translate the entities used in business rules to their base form with unique names.

4.2.1 Relational database

If we look at the world of relational databases (because the data-tables used for data mining are usually saved in relational databases), one solution could be very easy. We could create one table for names of entities. This table could have a column (primary key) for "name" and other column for alternative name. The same could be done for relational-connected table (or tables) for mapping of values.

This approach should work, it could be useable for transformation from association rules or data values for using in business rules engine. The disadvantage of this approach could be the big growth of size of this mapping tables and this solution would be only hardly administrable.

4.2.2 Entities from an ontology

Other approach for identification of entities used in rules could be "matching to entities in any ontology". Ontologies are currently one of the popular topics related to semantic in information systems. They help their users to unify the concepts used in communication and data exchange.

In the world of languages and formats for business rules, we can find the Semantic Web Rule Language (SWRL), which is based on ontological expressions [11]. It expects to use entities defined as concepts in any ontology. The author of this paper believes that it could be useable for solving of the problem of ambiguity of names of entities. We could extend this approach for mapping of values (and categories of them) used in data-table, rules etc. This extension could be connected with a knowledge base used for data-mining – see the following chapter.

4.2.3 Background knowledge for data mining

In the SEWEBAR Project, we deal with background knowledge base for data mining. We collect information about data formats and their preprocessing. We are using a proprietary format called BKEF[4] (based on XML). We know that it is necessary to have information about each type of entity (column in data table) - in connection with BKEF, we call it "meta-attribute". Each meta-attribute could have more formats with different scales of values and each format could have more definitions of preprocessing for data mining. [15] We are working with semi-automatic mapping of these meta-attributes and their formats to data-tables before start of the data mining using I:ZI Miner.[5] [5]

The problem is that we usually have one BKEF file for each data table (sometimes for each analytical question). The user can map the data table to an existing BKEF file, but it is considerably simpler to input preprocessing instructions via the web interface only for the one task. We would like to complete the way of working with knowledge base for data mining. In connection with this it would be appropriate to use an approach which could be useable for unified identification of entity types and their values in case of business rules.

We could think that the better way could be using ontology for knowledge base for data mining (including information of formats and their values) [13]. We have to extend the original concept of necessary information range.

---

[4] Background knowledge exchange format
[5] Web data mining solution based on LISp-Miner.

It should be possible to define relations between categories of values. In reference to the example given in 4.1, there should be possibilities to define relations like:

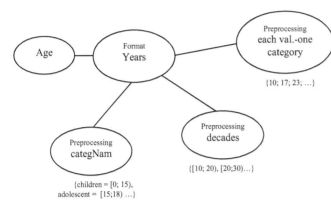

Fig. 1. Example: part of knowledge base for data mining saved in ontology

It would be very usable to define relations between values of the given formats and their categories. Some relation types under consideration (for categories of values): overlap, partial overlap, inclusion. These relations should be completed automatically by user direction. The automatically completion can work within one format and probably could be suggested in mapping between numerical formats. In case of enumeration formats the system could suggest mappings between some values but it have to be confirmed by the domain expert.

In extension to previous paragraph and Fig. 1 we could think of ontology like:

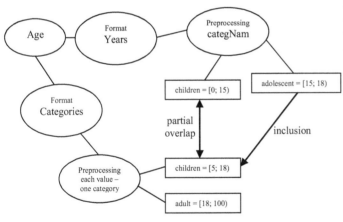

Fig. 2. Example: part of knowledge base for data mining saved in ontology – with relations between data categories

The relations between categories of data values should be used in the user interface of application for administration of data mining results and business rules. When the user selects an entity in a business rule, the system shows to the user details about relations to other entity values, which are used in other rules in the same dataset.

4.2.4 Techniques for "values categories matching"

For properly useable implementation of management of relations between data mining categories (like described before), it is necessary to use a semi-automatic mapping system. This system should suggest to the user all relations between values and their categories, which are saved in different formats of one "meta-attribute". And of course it should auto-complete relations between categories in one format (for example between different preprocessing in Fig. 1).

For this suggestion and mapping, it is necessary select the best similar category (between each two preprocessing within one "meta-attribute"). For the similarity rating we use [14]:

- string similarity functions (trigrams matching, edit distance) for categories defined like enumerations of strings
- overlap rating for categories defined like enumerations of numerical intervals
- inclusion rating for categories defined like enumerations of numbers

A problem for future research is how to compare relations rated as "partial overlap", because in some cases it could mean nearly "overlap" and in some cases "almost different". And it will be necessary to explain it to the user.

5 Problem of conflicting rules

If we have resolved the problem with uncertainty in comparing entities and their values, the business rules system may not give unambiguous results. As mentioned in section 3, the system JBoss Drools does not support conflict resolution. So if we have in the rule base saved rules with different actions, all this actions could be fired in one resolution run. This will be a problem when we want to use these business rules for "recommendations" of consequents from association rules.

It might be possible to move the final choice to the user – for example in case of dealing with one customer. But when we want for example recommendation of preferences of all customers saved in the database, or preferences for the user, which is currently using the company's web site, the system must select one "the best" result.

5.1 Choosing the best rules based on quantifier and interest measure

We want to generate business rules from GUHA Association rules. These rules are characterized with different 4ft-quantifiers (founded implication, double founded implication etc. – LISp-Miner supports 16 different quantifiers) [3]. These quantifiers could be sorted by their "strength" and we could compare them together with confidence, support etc.

Easily said we could sort fired rules by "strength of quantifier" and then compare rules on the same "level" by using their values of interest measures. This approach is the first one which we try to use in implementation of "business rules recommendation" in the LinkedTV EU Project. [16]

If we would like to have a more complex scoring of rules, it could be possible to take into account the length of antecedent of association rule. We can say that the longer condition should be more precise than the shorter one, but it is necessary to compare it together with interest measures. And the answer to the question: "Which rule is better?" is really not easy. We would like to deal with it in the future work.

5.2 Rules rating

Other approach for selection of best result recommendation could be rating of individual business rules. This way is usually used in user-filled business rules system. The user can set up order of saved rules and the system results the first founded result.

Maybe it could be also possible to join this approach to our system. In the future the user should be able to edit and manage the set of saved association rules and so it could be possible to give to the user a possibility to sort them.

Other way for completion of rating for individual rules could be collecting of feedback. When we run the system automatically on the web we should be able to check if the recommendation of user preferences are good or bad. For example in LinkedTV project we could check if the user plays the recommended video. So the business rules component could be followed by a simple machine learning system for correction of conflicting rules.

5.3 LinkedTV implementation

The closest target is a connection of the first implementation into LinkedTV Gain project, where the business rule module should be used for recommendation of user preferences to selected videos and web pages. LinkedTV is an EU project, which is targeted on recommendation rich contextual content for videos, TV stream and web pages. Each part of video stream is annotated with entities like "sport", "city", "person" etc. and the application collects information about reactions of the watcher (skipping parts of the video stream, going out…). On the base of this dataset we can mine association rules about preferences of the user. Finally, after the conversion into business rules, these rules will be used for recommendation, if a concrete annotated video is suitable for the current user. It means, that when a user usually watches sport programs and skips programs about "news", the recommendation system should suggest to him some videos with similar sport context.

6 Conclusion and future work

The author would like to describe a model of transformation from GUHA association rules into business rules and develop a sample implementation of the decision system using generated business rules. The work is currently in progress.

For the using in LinkedTV Project, it will be suitable to implement a hybrid system, which combines recommendations on the base of the preferences of the current user, base of shared user preferences and a machine learning algorithm.

References

[1] OMG (Object management group), "Semantics of Business Vocabulary and Business Rules (SBVR), v1.0.," *SBVR 1.0.* [Online] 2. 1. 2008 [Cited: 13. 1. 2012] http://www.omg.org/spec/SBVR/1.0/PDF

[2] M. Šimůnek, "Academic KDD Project LISp-Miner," *Intelligent Systems Design and Applications.* 2003, vol. 23, pages 263-272.

[3] "The official site of the LISp-Miner project" [Online] [Cited: 1. 6. 2013] http://lispminer.vse.cz/

[4] J. Rauch, M. Šimůnek, "An Alternative Approach to Mining Association Rules," *Foundations of Data Mining and knowledge Discovery.* 2005, Sv. 6, stránky 211-231.

[5] R. Škrabal, M. Šimůnek, S. Vojíř, A. Hazucha, T. Marek, D. Chudán, T. Kliegr, "Association Rule Mining Following the Web Search Paradigm," *ECML-PKDD 2012*, Berlin: Springer, 2012, p. 808--811. ISBN 978-3-642-33486-3

[6] Business rules group, "Defining Business Rules ~ What Are They Really?" [Online] [Cited: 20. 5. 2013] http://www.businessrulesgroup.org/first_paper/br01c3.htm

[7] "Drools," *JBoss Community* [Online] [Cited: 1. 5. 2013] http://www.jboss.org/drools/

[8] "JBoss Drools Tutorial – drools," *JBoss application server tutorials.* [Online] [Cited: 1. 4. 2013] http://www.mastertheboss.com/drools/jboss-drools-tutorial

[9] B-TU Cottbus, "Using Drools: UServ Product derby 2005," [Online] 18. 9. 2008 [Cited: 17. 12. 2011] http://hydrogen.informatik.tu-cottbus.de/wiki/index.php/Userv

[10] W3C, „SWRL: A Semantic Web Rule Language" [Online] http://www.w3.org/Submission/SWRL/

[11] I. Horrocks, et al. "SWRL: A Semantic Web Rule Language Combining OWL and RuleML" [Online] 19. 11. 2003 [Citace: 15. 11. 2011] http://www.daml.org/2003/11/swrl/

[12] N. Abadie, "Schema Matching Based on Attribute Values and Background Ontology,". Leibniz Universität Hannover, Germany : 2009, *12th AGILE International Conference on Geographic Information Science 2009*

[13] T. Kliegr, S. Vojíř, J. Rauch, "Background knowledge and PMML: first considerations," San Diego, California, USA : ACM, 2011. *Proceedings of the 2011 workshop on Predictive markup language modeling.* 978-1-4503-0837-3.

[14] S. Vojíř, T. Kliegr, V. Svátek, O. Zamazal, "Automated matching of data mining dataset schemata to background knowledge," Bonn: 2011, *ISWC 2011*, ISSN 1613-0073

[15] J. Rauch, J., M. Šimůnek, "Dealing with Background Knowledge in the SEWEBAR Project," *Knowledge Discovery Enhanced with Semantic and Social Information. Studies in Computational Intelligence, 2009*, Vol. 220, pp. 89-106.

[16] LinkedTV, "Television linked to the web," [Online] [Cited: 1. 6. 2013] http://www.linkedtv.eu

ITAT 2013: Workshops, Posters, and Tutorials, pp. 15–20
ISBN 978-1490952086, © 2013 Š. Pero

Educational Data Mining: Survey

Štefan Pero

Institute of Computer Science
Faculty of Science, University of Pavol Jozef Šafárik, Košice, Slovakia
Stefan.Pero@student.upjs.sk

Abstract: Educational Data Mining (EDM) has emerged in recent years as a research discipline with a package of computional and psychological methods and research approaches for understanding how students learn. EDM develops methods and applies techniques from different research areas, e.g. statistics, machine learning, and data mining, to analyze data collected during teaching and learning. The main aim of researchers in EDM community is to focus approaches for analyzing educational data to address important educational questions and to discover patterns and trends in those data. EDM researchers help to improve a learning, a cognition and a assessment in the educational process.

This paper surveys the history of EDM community and main applications of data mining techniques in the educational area.

1 Introduction

Educational Data Mining (EDM) has emerged in recent years as a research discipline with a package of computional and psychological methods and research approaches for understanding how students learn. EDM develops methods and applies techniques from different research areas, e.g. statistics, machine learning, and data mining, to analyze data collected during teaching and learning. Computer supported education methods and tools (e.g. intelligent tutoring systems, simulations) allow for collecting and an analysing data from student learning process, to discover patterns and trends in those data, and to make and test new hypotheses about how students learn ([10], [4]).

One of the first cause of expansion of EDM was the pressure in higher education to provide up-to-date information on institutional effectivness ([43]). Student success is important for students as well as for institutions, they are also increasingly held accountable ([13]).

One response to this pressure in education is finding new approaches to apply data mining methods to educationally related data. First outlook was that data mining (DM) is widely used in all sectors of business, like retail, banking, telecommunications, marketing, web mining, medicines etc. ([35, 1, 23, 52]) but its applications in academics is quite limited. However, researchers have found approaches data mining techniques can be applied on educational data collected by management systems[1].

The aim of EDM research is to help the faculty to manage classes, understand students' learning and reflect on teaching and to support learner's reflection and provide proactive feedback to learners ([26]).

EDM consists of appoaches and methods to explore unique types of data in educational settings. From a practical view point, EDM allows to discover new knowledge based on students' usage data, to help validate/evaluate educational systems and models, potentially improve some aspects of the quality of education ([45]).

According to Romero & Ventura in ([44]) EDM is an interdisciplinary research area including but not limited to information retrieval, recommender systems, visual data analytics, domain-driven DM, social network analysis (SNA), psychopedagogy, cognitive psychology, psychometrics, and so on. In fact, EDM can be drawn as the combination of three main areas (see Figure 1): computer science, education, and statistics. The intersection of these three areas also forms other subareas closely related to EDM such as computer-based education, DM and machine learning, and learning analytics.

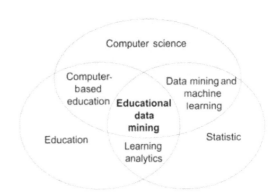

Figure 1: Main areas related to educational data mining ([44])

2 History of Community

The first workshop on EDM was held in 2005, in Pittsburgh, Pennsylvania and was followed by annual workshops. The year 2008 finds the nascent research community of EDM growing and continuing to develop ([6]). The 1st International Conference on EDM held in Montreal,

---

[1] Angel, WebCT, Moodle and Blackboard

Title	Acronym	Type	Since
International Conference on Educational Data Mining	EDM	Annual	2008
Inter. Conference on User Modeling, Adaptation, and Personalization	UMAP	Annual	2009
International Conference on Computer Supported Education	CSEDU	Annual	2009
International Conference on Learning Analytics and Knowledge	LAK	Annual	2011
International Conference on Artificial Intelligence in Education	AIED	Biannual	1982
International Conference on Intelligent Tutoring Systems	ITS	Biannual	1988
International Conference on Advanced Learning Technologies	ICALT	Annual	2000

Table 1: Related conferences about EDM

Quebec (other related conferences are described in Table 1). Annual conferences on EDM were joined by the Journal of EDM, which published its first issue in 2009, with Kalina Yacef as Editor. Two specific books on EDM edited by Romero & Ventura entitled: Data Mining in E-learning ([41]) and the first Handbook of Educational Data Mining ([46]) co-edited by Baker & Pechenizkiy. The survey according to types of data used in ([43]) says that the number of publications about EDM has grown exponentially in the last few years.

In the summer of 2011, the International Educational Data Mining Society [2] (IEDMS) was formed to "promote scientific research in the interdisciplinary field of educational data mining", organizing the conferences and journal, and free open-access publication of conference and journal articles. The EDM community brings together an inter-disciplinary community of computer scientists, learning scientists, psychometricians, and researchers from other traditions ([51]).

A first review on EDM research was presented by Romero & Ventura ([42]), followed by Baker & Yacef ([6]) and very comprehensive review also by Romero & Ventura ([43]).

3 Methods and Techniques

EDM methods consist of a variety of techniques and approaches, including data mining and machine learning, statistics, information visualization, computional modeling, etc.

First, in 2007 Romero & Ventura have categorized EDM methods into the following categories:

- statistics and visualization
- web mining
    - clustering, classification and outlier detection
    - association rule mining and sequential pattern mining
    - text mining

This viewpoint is focused on applications to web data and mostly, analysis of logs of student-computer interaction are provided.

A second viewpoint provided by Ryan Baker in ([4]) categorizes EDM methods as follows:

- prediction
    - classification
    - regression
    - density estimation
- clustering
- relationship mining
    - association rule mining
    - correlation mining
    - sequential pattern mining
    - casual data mining
- distillation of data for human judgement
- discorevy with models

The first three categories of this taxonomy look very similar to common data mining models. The fourth category is not necessarily seen as data mining methods, but is very important for EDM as well as Romero & Ventura's category of statistics and visualization. The fifth category is the most unusual category from a clasiccal data mining perspective. Discovery with models means that a model is developed through any proces and this model is then used as a component in another analysis, such as prediction and relationship mining, e.g. how student behaviour impact students' learning in different ways ([15]), how variations in intelligent tutor design impact students' behaviour over time ([28]).

4 Main Applications

The vast amount of data produced by courses provides a rich source for DM that is relevant to a range of target groups, including educators and instructional designers, and different levels of use, that can be related to pedagogical approaches and decisions, and to organisational needs ([32]).

There are many applications in educational area that have been resolved using DM techniques, for example, Félix Castro in ([14]) proposed the following application of EDM: assessment of the student and the learning performance task, course adaptation and learning recommendation based on the student's behaviour, applications dealing

---

[2]http://www.educationaldatamining.org/

	Application	Users	Educational task
A	Analysis and visualization of data	Educators, Course administrators, Teachers, Tutors	To highlight useful information and support decision making; to analyse the student's course activities and usage information to get a general view of a student's learning
B	Providing feedback for supporting instructors	Authors, Teachers, Administrators	To provide feedback about how to improve student's learning, organise instructional resources, To enable the target group to take appropriate proactive and/or remedial action
C	Recommendation for students	Students	To make recommendations to the students with respect to their personalised activities
D	Predicting student's performance	Teachers, Tutors	To estimate the unknown value that describes the student (performance, knowledge, score, or mark)
E	Student modelling	Teachers, Tutors, Instructors	To develop cognitive models of human users/students including modelling of their skills and declarative knowledge
F	Detecting undesirable students behaviours	Teachers, Tutors, Counsellours	To discover/detect those students who have some problems or unusual behaviours (erroneous actions, low motivation, playing games, misuse, cheating, dropping out, academic failure)
G	Grouping students	Instructors, Developers	To create groups of students according to their customized features, personal characteristics
H	Social network analysis	Students, Teachers, Tutors	To study relationships between individuals, instead of individual attributes or properties
I	Developing concept maps	Instructors, Educators	To help instructors/educators in the automatic process of developing and constructing concept maps
J	Constructing courseware	Instructors, Developers	To carry out the construction and development process of courseware and learning contents automatically, To promote the reuse/exchange of existing learning resources
K	Planning and scheduling	Teachers, Tutors, Students	To enhance the traditional education process by planning future courses, helping with student course scheduling, planning resources allocation, helping the admission and counselling processes

Table 2: Categories proposed by Romero and Ventura ([43])

with the evaluation of learning materials and applications which provide feedback to teacher and students. Later, Ryan Baker in ([6, 4]) gives the proposal of application for EDM, following: improving student models, improving domain models, studying the pedagogical support provided by learning software, scientific research into learning and learners.

Improving student models which represent information about students, described their characteristics and state, e.g. students' current state, attitude and motivation, metacognition. For example, in ([16]) the model of student individual differences is described which improves student learning; in ([5]) a model of student communication with the system is proposed; model of student's experience in ([31]) and student's frustrating in ([18]) are described.

Improving domain models developed through the combination of various domains. For example, in ([8]) a model is developed which automatically discover Q-Matrix from data; in ([17, 33, 34]) models for finding partial order

knowledge structure are developed which explain interrelationships in a domain.

Studying the pedagogical support in the domain of learning software, collaborative learning, etc. The aim is to analyze the types of pedagogical support and discover their effectivity ([37]). One used method is learning decomposition ([9]), an real-world application is the Roundrobin's method ([56]) and Jigsaw's classroom ([3]).

Scientific research into learning and learners provided by extension of educational theories, e.g. the impact of self-discipline on learning ([22]) and searching for successful patterns of interaction within student teams ([38]), etc. ories for the main educational tasks which have used data mining techniques.

4.1 Romero and Ventura's categorization

EDM aims at improving student's learning and performance. EDM research area has emerged in recent years with related research issues as are described in ([43]), shortly: *1) Analysis and visualization of data* to help educators to analyze students' behaviour and learning ([57]), *2) feedback for teachers*, to help teachers in decision making ([27]), *3) recommendations for students* the objective of what is to make pesonalized recommendations on learning materials ([21]), *4) predicting student performance*, to predict the likely performance of a student for given tasks ([54]), and, *5) student modeling* with the objective to develop cognitive models of a student, including skills and knowledges considering his characteristics (learning style, motivation, affective status and etc.) ([20, 2, 19]).

In ([32]) EDM applications are categorized into eleven areas according to Romero and Ventura ([43]), see the Table 2.

All these applications support learning process but from the perspective of the user (D), (G), (L), (M) are related to the organisation of learning, resources, grouping of students and organizing their schedule; (A), (B), (D), (E), (F), (H), (I) are focused especially on tutors, teachers and educators, even (H) focuses social network analysis. (C) is aimed only on students.

This categorization can be seen as the latest comprehensive classification of EDM applications, latest categorizations are mostly derived, for instance in the Handbook of EDM ([46]).

5 Educational Recommender Systems

Recommender systems (RSs) attempt to predict items for a user in which he might be interested. According to Ricci in ([40]) RSs are software tools and techniques providing suggestions for items to be of use to a user. The recommendations relate to various decision-making processes, such as what products to buy, what music to listen, what news to read or what destination to choose for a trip, etc.

Specific and general terms of RSs are "item" and "user". The "item " is denoted what the system recommends to the "user". Items are selected from the specific domain (e.g. films, music, news or hotels) which determine the core recommendation technique, graphical user interface for presentation of suggestions, etc.

RSs are very interesting for a company, e.g. to sell more and diverse items, to increase users' satisfaction and fidelity, to better understand users' needs. However, users have also their own requirements on RSs, for example, to find some good items with a relatively small effort, to express herself by providing ratings or opinions, to help other by contributing with information to the community ([25]).

RSs collect and exploit various types of information about users, items (products), and interactions between users and items. The output of RSs is a personalized list of items which meets user's needs (preferences). This information may be gathered while the user is interacting with the system, for instance, many times using the set of subjective ratings assigned by the users to previously experienced items. These information serves the system for predicting the rating for items not yet experienced. Finally, the products with the highest ratings are then recommended to a user ([7]).

According to Burke, RSs techniques are classified into four main categories: collaborative filtering, content based filtering, knowledge based filtering and hybrid systems ([12]).

Collaborative filtering (CF) is a recommendation technique which uses a simple social strategy called "word-of-mouth" ([24]). Personalized recommendations for the target user are sugessted using opinions of users having similar tastes to those of the target user ([39]). CF techniques recognize similarities between users according to their feedbacks and recommend items preferred by the like-minded users ([25]). This is a domain independent approach computed by leveraging historical log data of users' online behaviour.

Content based filtering (CBF) is a recommendation technique which suggests recommendations for a user by analyzing only the rating of the target user. CBF techniques analyze items' descriptions to identify interesting items to the target user ([36]). CBF techniques learn user's interests based on the features of items previously rated by the user using supervised machine learning techniques ([25]).

Knowledge based filtering (KBF) techniques use a decision model to make inferences about to the user needs. Usually KBF techniques compute some recommendation rules designed by the domain expert ([49]). KBF recommendations are based on knowledge about users' needs and preferences ([25]).

Hybrid systems (HSs) combines several RSs techniques to overcome limitations of pure techniques with better accuracy ([12, 50]). HSs are useful to integrate some additional information to the system, for instance, provide a way to integrate context into the prediction model ([7]).

Recently, RSs have shown to be sucessful in many domains where information overload exists. This success is also a motivation for researchers to deploy RSs in educational scenarious. The amount of data generated by students, teachers and educators during the learning process is so large that it is very difficult to understand to data.

Educational recommender systems (ERS) share the same key objectives as RSs for e-commerce applications, for instance, to help users to select the best item from a large information pool. However, there are some particularities for which applying existing solutions from RSs applications is not so straighforward, for instance, recommendations in the educational domain should not be sugessted only by the learners' preferences but also by educational criteria. However, most ERS appoaches have focused on applying traditional RSs techniques to find suggestions for students and teachers in the learning process ([48]).

According to Santos & Boticario, favorite topics of ERS are the following: knowledge modeling for the recommendation process ([55]); techniques and algorithms to produce recommendations in e-learning settings ([53]); methodologies to develop ERS ([47]); architectures to support the recommendation process ([11]); evaluation methods to measure the recommendations' impact on users ([30]); and application of ERS in real world scenarious ([29]).

6   Conclusion

EDM is a multidisciplinary research area consisting of computer science, education, psychology, psychometrics and statistics to analyse, understand and answer educational research questions. Increase in the usage of educational software and monitoring tools of learning processes enabled to create large repositories of data reflecting how students learn. The main aim of community of EDM is to focus approaches for analyzing those data to address important educational questions and to discover patterns and trends in those data. The same aim of researchers from various research fields is to support the education, to better understand and improve learning, and to provide information about the learning process.

References

[1] P. Adriaans and D. Zantinge. *Data mining.* Addison-Wesley, Boston, MA, 2005.

[2] S. Amershi and C. Conati. Combining unsupervised and supervised classification to build user models for exploratory learning environments. *Journal of Education Data Mining,* pages 18–71, 2009.

[3] E. Aronson and S. Patnoe. *Cooperation in the classroom: The jigsaw method.* Pinter and Martin, Ltd, London, 2011.

[4] R. S. J. D. Baker. *Data mining for education.* International Encyclopedia of Education, B. McGaw, P. Peterson, and E. Baker, Eds., 3rd ed., U.K.: Elsevier, Oxford, 2010.

[5] R. S. J. D. Baker, A. T. Corbett, and K. R. Koedinger. Detecting student misuse of intelligent tutoring systems. *Proceedings of the 7th International Conference on Intelligent Tutoring Systems,* pages 531–540, 2004.

[6] R. S. J. D. Baker and K. Yacef. The state of educational data mining in 2009: A review and future visions. *JEDM - Journal of Educational Data Mining,* 1:3–17, 2009.

[7] L. Baltrunas. Context-aware collaborative filtering recommender systems. *PhD Thesis in Computer Science at Free University of Bolzano, Italy. Department of Database Information Systems,* 2011.

[8] T. Barnes. The q-matrix method: Mining student response data for knowledge. *Proceedings of the AAAI-2005 Workshop on Educational Data Mining,* 2005.

[9] J. E. Beck and J. Mostow. How who should practice: Using learning decomposition to evaluate the efficacy of different types of practice for different types of students. *Proceedings of the 9th International Conference on Intelligent Tutoring Systems,* pages 353–362, 2008.

[10] M. Bienkowski, M. Feng, and B. Means. *Enhancing Teaching and Learning Through Educational Data Mining and Learning Analytics: An Issue Brief.* U.S. Department of Education, Washington, D.C, 2012.

[11] P. H. S. Brito, I. I. Bittencourt, A. P. Machado, E. Costa, O. Holanda, R. Ferreira, and T. Ribeiro. A systematic approach for designing educational recommender systems. *Educational Recommender Systems and Technologies: Practices and Challenges,* pages 232–256, 2012.

[12] R. Burke. Hybrid recommender systems: Survey and experiments. *User Modeling and User-Adapted Interaction, 12,* pages 331–370, 2002.

[13] J. P. Campbell and D. G. Oblinger. *Academic Analytics.* EDUCAUSE Center for Applied Research, 2007.

[14] F. Castro, A. Vellido, A. Nebot, and F. Mugica. Applying data mining techniques to e-learning problems. *Evolution of Teaching and Learning Paradigms in Intelligent Environment (Studies in Computational Intelligence),* 62:183–221, 2007.

[15] M. Cocea, A. Hershkovitz, and R. S. J. D. Baker. The impact of off-task and gaming behaviors on learning: Immediate or aggregate? pages 507–514, 2009.

[16] A.T. Corbett. Cognitive computer tutors: Solving the two-sigma problem. *Proceedings of the International Conference on User Modeling,* pages 137–147, 2001.

[17] M. C. Desmarais and X. Pu. A bayesian student model without hidden nodes and its comparison with item response theory. *International Journal of Artificial Intelligence in Education 15,* pages 291–323, 2005.

[18] S. K. D'Mello, S. D. Graig, A. Witherspoon, B. McDaniel, and A. Grasser. Automatic detection of learner's affect from conversational cues. *User Modeling and User-Adapted Interaction 18,* pages 45–80, 2008.

[19] M. Feng, N. Heffernan, and K. Koedinger. Addressing the assessment challenge with an online system that tutors as it assesses. *User Modeling and User-Adapted Interaction 19,* pages 243–266, 2011.

[20] E. Frias-Martinez, S. Chen, and X. Liu. Survey of data mining approaches to user modeling for adaptive hypermedia. *IEEE Transactions on Systems, Man, Cybernetics-Part C,* page 734749, 2009.

[21] M. Girones and T. A. Fernandez. Ariadne, a guiding thread in the learning process's labyrinth. *Proceedings of Intrnational Conference on Current Developments in Technology-Assist. Educucation,* pages 287–290, 2006.

[22] Y. Gong, D. Rai, J. Beck, and N. Heffernan. Does self-discipline impact students' knowledge and learning? *In Proceedings of the 2nd International Conference on Educational Data Mining,* pages 61–70, 2009.

[23] J. Han. *Data Mining: Concepts and Techniques.* Morgan Kaufmann Publishers Inc., San Francisco, CA, USA, 2005.

[24] W. Hill, L. Stead, M. Rosenstein, and G. Furnas. Recommending and evaluating choices in a virtual community of use. *CHI 95: Proceedings of the SIGCHI conference on Human factors in computing systems,* pages 194–201, 1995.

[25] T. Horváth. Recommender systems. *Tutorial at the 11th conference Znalosti,* 2012.

[26] R. A. Huebner. A survey of educational data-mining re-

search. *Research in Higher Education Journal*, 19, 2013.

[27] T. Hurley and S. Weibelzahl. Using motsart to support online teachers in student motivation. *Proceedings of European Conference on Technology Enhanced Learning*, pages 101–111, 2007.

[28] H. Jeong and G. Biswas. Mining student behavior models in learning-by-teaching environments. *The First International Conference on Educational Data Mining*, pages 127–136, 2008.

[29] J. Leino. Material additions, ratings, and comments in a course settings. *Educational Recommender Systems and Technologies: Practices and Challenges*, pages 258–280, 2012.

[30] N. Manouselis, H. Drachsler, R. Vuorikari, H. Hummel, and R. Koper. Recommender systems in technology enhanced learning. *Recommender Systems Handbook*, 2011.

[31] S. McQuiggan, B. W. Mott, and J. C. Lester. Modeling self-efficacy in intelligent tutoring systems: An inductive approach. *User Modeling and User-Adapted Interaction 18*, pages 81–123, 2008.

[32] G. Paviotti, P. G. Rossi, and D. Zarka. *I-TUTOR: Intelligent Tutoring Systems: an Overview*. Pensa MultiMedia Editore s.r.l., 2012.

[33] P. Pavlik, H. Cen, and K. R. Koedinger. Learning factors transfer analysis: Using learning curve analysis to automatically generate domain models. *Proceedings of the 2nd International Conference on Educational Data Mining*, pages 121–130, 2009.

[34] P. Pavlik, H. Cen, L. Wu, and K. R. Koedinger. Using item-type performance covariance to improve the skill model of an existing tutor. *Proceedings of the 1st International Conference on Educational Data Mining*, pages 77–86, 2008.

[35] F. C. Payton. Data mining in health care applications. *Data mining: opportunities and challenges*, pages 350–365, 2003.

[36] M. J. Pazzani and D. Billsus. Content-based recommendation systems. *The Adaptive Web, Methods and Strategies of Web Personalization, volume 4321*, pages 325–341, 2007.

[37] M. Pechenizkiy, T. Calders, E. Vasilyeva, and P. De Bra. Mining the student assessment data: Lessons drawn from a small scale case study. *Proceedings of the 1st International Conference on Educational Data Mining*, pages 187–191, 2008.

[38] D. Perera, J. Kay, I. Koprinska, K. Yacef, and O. Zaiane. Clustering and sequential pattern mining to support team learning. *IEEE Transactions on Knowledge and Data Engineering 21*, pages 759–772, 2009.

[39] P. Resnick, N. Iacovou, M. Suchak, P. Bergstrom, and J. Riedl. Grouplens: an open architecture for collaborative filtering of netnews. *CSCW '94: Proceedings of the 1994 ACM conference on Computer Supported Cooperative Work*, pages 175–186, 1994.

[40] F. Ricci, L. Rokach, B. Shapira, and P. B. Kantor. *Recommender Systems Handbook*. Springer, 2011.

[41] C. Romero and S. Ventura. *Data Mining in E-Learning*. Wit Press, shurst,Southampton, 2006.

[42] C. Romero and S. Ventura. Educational data mining: A survey from 1995 to 2005. *Expert Systems with Applications*, 33(1):135–146, 2007.

[43] C. Romero and S. Ventura. Educational data mining: a review of the state of the art. *Trans. Sys. Man Cyber Part C*, 40:601–618, November 2010.

[44] C. Romero and S. Ventura. Data mining in education. *Wiley Interdisciplinary Reviews: Data Mining and Knowledge Discovery*, 3:12–27, 2012.

[45] C. Romero, S. Ventura, and P. De Bra. Knowledge discovery with genetic programming for providing feedback to courseware authors. *User Modeling and User-Adapted Interaction*, 14(5):425–464, 2005.

[46] C. Romero, S. Ventura, M. Pechenizky, and R. S. J. D. Baker. *Handbook of Educational Data Mining*. Editorial Chapman and Hall/CRC Press, Taylor and Francis Group. Data Mining and Knowledge Discovery Series, 2011.

[47] O. C. Santos and J. Boticario. Requirements for semantic educational recommender systems in formal e-learning scenarios. *Algorithms*, 4(2):131–154, 2011.

[48] O. C. Santos and J. G. Boticario. *Educational Recommender Systems and Technologies: Practices and Challenges*. IGI Global, 2012.

[49] J.B. Schafer, J. Konstan, and J. Riedi. Recommender systems in e-commerce. *EC '99: Proceedings of the 1st ACM conference on Electronic Commerce*, pages 158–166, 1999.

[50] A. Schelar, A. Tsikinovsky, L. Rokach, and L. Antwarg. Ensemble methods for improving the performance of neighborhood-based collaborative filtering. *Proceedings of the third ACM conference on Recommender Systems (RecSys '09)*, pages 261–264, 2009.

[51] G. Siemens and R. S. J. D. Baker. Learning analytics and educational data mining: towards communication and collaboration. *Proceedings of the 2nd International Conference on Learning Analytics and Knowledge*, pages 252–254, 2012.

[52] S. Sumathi and S.N. Sivanandam. *Introduction to Data Mining and its Applications*, volume 29. Springer-Verlag, 2006.

[53] N. Thai-Nghe, L. Drumond, T. Horváth, A. Nanopoulos, and L. Schmidt-Thieme. Matrix and tensor factorization for predicting student performance. *Proceedings of 3rd Internaitonal Conference on Computer Supported Education*, 2011.

[54] N. Thai-Nghe, L. Drumond, A. Krohn-Grimberghe, T. Horváth, A. Nanopoulos, and L. Schmidt-Thieme. Factorization techniques for predicting student performance. *Educational Recommender Systems and Technologies: Practices and Challenges*, pages 129–153, 2011.

[55] J. S. Underwood. Metis: A content map-based recommender system for digital learning activities. *Educational Recommender Systems and Technologies: Practices and Challenges*, pages 24–42, 2012.

[56] P. Vermette. *Making cooperative learning work: Student teams in K12 classrooms*. Prentice Hall Career & Technology, 1998.

[57] A. Wu and C. Leung. Evaluating learning behavior of web-based training (wbt) using web log. *Proceedings of International Conference on Computers in Educucation*, pages 736–737, 2002.

Opinion-Driven Matrix Factorization for Rating Prediction

The UMAP'13 talk and the received feedbacks

Štefan Pero and Tomáš Horváth

Institute of Computer Science,
Pavol Jozef Šafárik University, Košice, Slovakia
stefan.pero@student.upjs.sk,tomas.horvath@upjs.sk

Abstract. Rating prediction is a well-known recommendation task aiming to predict a user's rating for those items which were not rated yet by her. Predictions are computed from users' explicit feedback, i.e. their ratings provided on some items in the past. Another type of feedback are user reviews provided on items which implicitly express users' opinions on items. Recent studies indicate that opinions inferred from users' reviews on items are strong predictors of user's implicit feedback or even ratings and thus, should be utilized in computation. As far as we know, all the recent works on recommendation techniques utilizing opinions inferred from users' reviews are either focused on the item recommendation task or use only the opinion information, completely leaving users' ratings out of consideration. The approach proposed in this paper is filling this gap, providing a simple, personalized and scalable rating prediction framework utilizing both ratings provided by users and opinions inferred from their reviews. Experimental results provided on a dataset containing user ratings and reviews from the real-world Amazon Product Review Data show the effectiveness of the proposed framework.

The proposed method was accepted for presentation to the 21st Conference on User Modeling, Adaptation and Personalization (UMAP 2013) being held in Rome, Italy June 10-14, 2013 [1]. The presentation at the ITAT'13 workshop will contain and discuss also the feedbacks received from the UMAP community.

Acknowledgements: This work was partially supported by the research grants *VEGA 1/0832/12* and *VVGS-PF-2012-22*. We would like to thank to anonymous reviewers of the UMAP'13 conference for their helpful and motivating comments and suggestions.

References

1. Š. Pero and T. Horváth. Opinion-Driven Matrix Factorization for Rating Prediction. Carberry, S.; Weibelzahl, S.; Micarelli, A.; Semeraro, G. (Eds.) Proceedings of the 21th International Conference, UMAP 2013, Rome, Italy: Lecture Notes in Computer Science, Vol. 7899, Springer-Verlag, 2013.

ITAT 2013: Workshops, Posters, and Tutorials, pp. 22–26
ISBN 978-1490952086, © 2013 L. Peška

How Far Ahead Can Recommender Systems Predict?

Ladislav Peška

Faculty of Mathematics and Physics
Charles University in Prague
Malostranske namesti 25, 11800, Prague, Czech Republic
peska@ksi.mff.cuni.cz

Abstract. *The following paper presents our work in progress to deal with time dependence on e-commerce recommending system. We are particulary interested in rather specific e-commerce sub-domain with low consumption rate and not very loyal customers. Time dependence in such domains is rather lower than e.g. in multimedia portals, however our experiments corroborated that it still plays an important role in quality of recommendations.*

Experimented methods shown decreasing recommendation quality (according to nDCG) with increased time distance, however the overally best method, content boosted matrix factorization suffers from more significant decline. In conclusion, we point out several approaches how to further improve recommendations by incorporating time-awareness.

1 Introduction

Recommending on the web is both an important commercial application and popular research topic. The amount of data on the web grows continuously and it is nearly impossible to process it directly by a human. Also the number of trading activities on the web steadily increases for several years. The keyword search engines were adopted to fight information overload but despite their undoubted successes, they have certain limitations. Recommender systems can complement onsite search engines especially when user does not know exactly what he/she wants.

1.1 Recommending on E-Commerce Domain

Recently, a lot of attention was attracted by the Netflix prize aiming to predict future user rating based on previously rated objects (optimizing RMSE). Netflix is a multimedia portal, where users are properly identified, user ratings can be collected quite easily and average consumption rate per customer is rather high. However these preconditions need not to be true in other domains.

The E-Commerce domain may serve as an example of completely different situation. Throughout the e-commerce domain, users are less willing to provide explicit feedback. Furthermore in the most cases, user can relevantly rate only those objects, they already obtained and tested. Given the much lower consumption rate particulary on some domains (e.g. typical user buys at most one holiday tour per year) we cannot obtain enough explicit feedback to employ personalized recommendations.

Another problem is user identification. The vast majority of e-shops do not force users to register at all or only during the purchase. In order not to lose too much data, we need to track also unlogged users. They are usually tracked by cookies stored within the browser. The cookie is however removed automatically after a few months at best, so it might not be possible to track user between his/her consecutive purchases.

Given the described preconditions, the vast majority of users appear to be new users exacerbating the cold start problem. We cannot hope for tens of ratings as in multimedia portals, but rather need to cope with a few visited pages.

On the other hand, we can monitor additional data to improve our prospects. It is possible to record various types of implicit feedback (page-views, time on page, mouse usage, scrolling etc.) or track user behavior on category pages. Objects of the e-shops also contain vast number of content-based attributes. We described problematic of recommending on e-commerce more detailed in our previous work [8]. According to our experiment, hybrid approach *"Content boosted matrix factorization"* [2] combining matrix factorization with content-based object attributes was able to best adapt to the e-commerce specifics.

1.2 Temporal Dependence and Preference Shift

One of the substantial problem of long-deployed recommender systems is the change of user preferences over time. This phenomenon is usually refered as concept drift or preference shift. Common approachs to deal with preference shift is either to ommit older data (time window) or to decrease their weight (instance weighting), but again we might be losing too much data.

One of the principal work on the field of time-aware recommending is Koren[5]. The proposed method (refered as *"timeSVD++"*) adjusts baseline predictors and user factors and take them as a function of time. Their approach distinguish between gradual and sudden concept drift (only present for users). According to the using time-aware matrix factorization on Netflix dataset can significantly improve prediction accuracy.

Again the situation on E-Commerce is slightly different. On on hand problems with user identification may lead to decrease of observed user preference shift. Discarding cookies after a period of inactivity will cause a loss of historical data with too large gap from the more recent ones. We refer to this problem as the "implicit time window", but - at least with state of the art technologies - we believe it is unavoidable.

The content based attributes might be helpful in capturing long-term preferences and e.g. better separate drifting and stable components of user preference.

1.3 Our Motivation

Although preference shift is well known problem in many data mining applications, its impact on e-commerce recommending is yet to be shown. The implicit time window problem caused by low consumption rate and imperfect user identification could seriously decrease impact of the preference shift. Our first research question is then whether it is possible to identify this phenomenon in our data.

If so, our key research question is how to model and incorporate it into the personalized recommendations. Time-aware recommending methods should be able not only to better employ historical user feedback, but also to derive reasonable recommendations further ahead from the time-point, they were trained. This might be useful if the training algorithm is time-consuming and cannot be repeated too often.

1.4 Main Contribution

The main contributions of this paper are:

- Identifying key constraints affecting time-aware recommendation on e-commerce.
- Corroborate impact of preference shift on recommendation quality.
- Proposed methods how to deal with preference shift and to derive time-aware recommendations.

The rest of the paper is organized as follows: We conclude section 1 with review of some related work. In section 2 we describe travel agency dataset used during our experiments and in section 3 several methods suitable to recommend under e-commerce preconditions (see 1.1) Section 4 contains results of off-line experiment on how well the methods predict for further future. Finally section 5 points out possibilities how to derive time-aware recommendations on e-commerce and section 6 concludes our paper and points to our future work.

1.5 Related Work

The area of recommender systems has been extensively studied recently and it is out of scope of this paper to provide more elaborated overview. We suggest Konstan and Riedl [4] paper as a good starting point.

Matrix factorization techniques [6] are currently mainstream algorithm to learn user preferences gaining their popularity during NetFlix prize. We use content-boosted matrix factorization as proposed in Forbes and Zhu [2] as one of the preference learning methods. Other approach to incorporate content-based attributes into the collaborative filtering proposed Eckhardt[1].

One of the key papers on time-aware recommending methods is Koren[5], we describe its findings in section 5. We would like to mention also Takahashi et al. [9] analyzing drifting preferences of supermarket customers and Ito et al. [3] aiming to identify preference shift by using time-series clustering.

2 Dataset

We have collected usage data from one of the major Czech travel agencies. Data were collected from December 2012 to April 2013. Travel agency is typical e-commerce enterprise, where customers buy products only once in a while (most typically once a year). The site does not force users to register and so we can track unique users only with

cookies stored in the browser. User typically browses or search through several categories, compares few objects (possibly on more websites) and eventually buys a single object. Buying more than one object at the time is very rare.

2.1 Implicit Feedback Data

In our previous work [7], only the user behavior on objects was monitored. Certain actions user committed was stored into database table to serve as implicit feedback. The table is in form of:

ImpFeedback(*UID, OID, PageView, Mouse, Scroll, Time*)

UID and *OID* are unique user and object identifiers and Table 1 contains full description of implicit feedbacks. Note that *UID* is based on cookie stored by browser, so we cannot e.g. distinguish between two persons using the same computer. Table contains approx. 39 000 records with 0.09% density of *UID x OID* matrix.

Table 1. Description of the considered implicit feedbacks for user visiting an object.

Factor	Description
PageView	Count(*OnLoad()* event on object page)
Mouse	Count(*OnMouseOver()* events on object page)
Scroll	Count(OnScroll() events on object page)
Time	Sum(time spent on object page)

Click Stream Data

Pages showing detail of an object represents less than 50% of visited pages. The rest consists mostly from various category pages accessed either via site menu or attributes search. In order to determine importance of category pages for computing user preference, we have collected dataset containing user's click-stream throughout the website. The table is in form of:

ClickStream(*UID, PageID, SessionNo, Timestamp*)

PageID serves as unique identifier of visited page. There is unique mapping from *OID* to *PageID*. **ClickStream** table contains approx. 121900 records and matrix *UID x PageID* has density of 0.17%.

Table 2. Description of content-based attributes and their cardinality per tour.

Attribute	Description
TourType	Type of the tour (e.g. sightseeing) [1]
Country	Destination country of the tour (e.g. Spain) [1..n]
Destination	More specific destination (e.g. Costa Brava) [0..n]
AccType	Quality of the accommodation (e.g. 3*); [1]
Accommodation	Specific accommodation for the tour [0..n]
Board	Type of board (e.g. breakfast, half-board) [1]
Transport	Type of transport (coach, air…) [1]
Price	Base price per person; integer [1]
AdditionalInfo	IDs of information linked to the tour (e.g. about visited places, destination country etc.) [0..n]

2.2 Content Based Attributes

Finally each object and category page can be assigned with several content-based attributes. Table 2 contains description of attributes available for travel agency domain. In order to handle attributes properly in the experiments, they were transferred into the Boolean vector (Integer values e.g price was discretized equipotently into 10 intervals). The resulting **Attributes** matrix contains 2300 objects (and categories) with 925 features each.

3 Recommending Methods

Matrix factorization techniques are currently leading methods for learning user preferences, so we decided to adopt and slightly adjust them to suit our needs. For space reasons we skip more elaborated introduction on matrix factorization. We suggest consulting Koren et al. [6] instead.

Given the list of users $U = \{u_1,...,u_n\}$ and objects $O = \{o_1,...,o_m\}$, we can form the user-object rating matrix $\mathbf{R} = [r_{uo}]_{n \times m}$. With lack of explicit feedback, user-object rating r_{uo} in our case carries only Boolean information whether user u visited object o. For a given number of latent factors f, matrix factorization aims to decompose original $\mathbf{R}$ matrix into $\mathbf{UO}^T$, where $\mathbf{U}$ is $n \times f$ matrix of user latent factors and $\mathbf{O}^T$ is $f \times m$ matrix of object latent factors.

$$\mathbf{R} \approx \mathbf{UO}^T = \begin{bmatrix} \mu_1^T \\ \mu_2^T \\ \vdots \end{bmatrix}_{n \times f} \times \underbrace{[\sigma_1 \quad \sigma_2 \quad ...]}_{f \times m} \quad (1)$$

Unknown rating for user i and object j is predicted as $\hat{r}_{ij} = \mu_i^T \sigma_j$. Matrixes $\mathbf{U}$ and $\mathbf{O}$ can be learned e.g. by Stochastic Gradient Descent (SGD) technique iterating for each object and user vectors

$$\mu_i = \mu_i + \eta \left(\sum_{j \in K_{ui}} (r_{ij} - \mu_i^T \sigma_j) \sigma_j - \lambda \mu_i \right)$$

$$\sigma_j = \sigma_j + \eta \left(\sum_{i \in K_{oj}} (r_{ij} - \mu_i^T \sigma_j) \mu_i - \lambda \sigma_j \right) \quad (2)$$

Where η is learning rate, K_{ui} set of all objects rated by user u_i and K_{oj} set of all users, who rates object o_j. Described method represents the **baseline** algorithm. We now present three possible extensions to this method. The extensions are independent of each other and can be combined freely.

Category extension expands list of objects to include also category pages covered in **ClickStream** dataset (see section 2.2). The rest of the algorithm remains the same. Note that both objects and categories may share some content attributes and thus we can infer their similarity.

Implicit feedback extension involves deeper studying of user activity within the object and thus better estimating how much it is preferred. User activity is stored in **ImpFeedback** dataset (currently page views, time on page, mouse moves and scrolling events are captured). The improved user-to-object rating r_{uo}^+ replaces original

Boolean r_{uo} where possible. The algorithm for computing r_{uo}^+ was presented in our previous work [7]. It is based on how well each feedback type explains purchasing behavior. Higher ratings receive those user-object pairs, where there are other users with similar feedback on an object, who actually bought it.

Attributes extension involves using content-based attributes of objects (and categories). We adopt approach of *Forbes and Zhu* [2] to deal with object attributes and implement their algorithm as PHP library. Their *"content boosted matrix factorization method"* is based on the assumption that each object's latent factors vector is a function of its attributes. Having $\mathbf{A}_{m \times a}$ matrix of object attributes and $\mathbf{B}_{a \times f}$ matrix of latent factors for each attribute, the constraint can be formulated as:

$$\mathbf{O} = \mathbf{AB} \qquad (3), (6\,[2])$$

Under the constraint (3), we can reformulate both matrix factorization problem (1) and gradient descend equations (2):

$$\mathbf{R} \approx \mathbf{UO}^T = \mathbf{UB}^T\mathbf{A}^T = \begin{bmatrix} \mu_1^T \\ \mu_2^T \\ \vdots \end{bmatrix}_{n \times f} \times \underbrace{\mathbf{B}^T}_{f \times a} \times \underbrace{[a_1 \quad a_2 \quad ...]}_{a \times m} \quad (1a)$$

$$\mu_i = \mu_i + \eta \left(\sum_{j \in K_{ui}} (r_{ij} - \mu_i^T \mathbf{B}^T a_j)\mathbf{B}^T a_j - \lambda \mu_i \right) \quad (2a)$$

$$\sigma_j = \sigma_j + \eta \left(\sum_{(i,j) \in K} (r_{ij} - \mu_i^T \mathbf{B}^T a_j) a_j \mu_i^T - \lambda \mathbf{B} \right) \quad (8,9\,[2])$$

Figure 1 shows informaitve results of recommending methods in an off-line testing. The train/test split was performed on per-user basis according to the his/her clickstream. Methods were evaluated over **nDCG**. Please see our previous work [8] for more details.

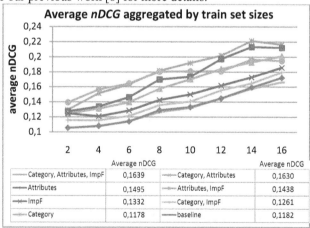

Figure 1: Average nDCG aggregated by train set sizes per user. Legend shows average nDCG per all users and train set sizes.

4 Distant Predictions Experiment

Our first research question is to determine, whether preference shift phenomenon is presented in our dataset. This might be a bit problematical, because we do not have any explicit user feedback, so we cannot measure user preference directly. Infering user preference from implicit feedback is possible, but there isn't a general conclusion yet about how exactly should such method work. So we chose an indirect approach stating that if user preference changes, it will result in decrease of recommending accuracy if based on the data before the change.

Idea of the experiment is following: for each user, we use only a small portion of his/her feedback as the train set (currently data from his/her first session). Then we let the methods to recommend and check how well they can predict future user behavior as a function of time.

4.1 Experiment Settings

We first needed to set experiment goals and success metrics. As the datasets contains only implicit feedback, we cannot rely on user rating and related error metrics e.g. RMSE or MAE (no need to mention, that those metrics do not reflect well real-world success metrics anyway). Typical usage of recommender systems in e-commerce is to present list of top-k objects to the user. We let recommending methods to rank objects and denote as success if the algorithm manages to rank well enough those objects, we have some evidence of their positive preference. The *nDCG* metrics is suitable for this kind of tasks.

As we lack any explicit feedback, we need to infer positive preference from the implicit data. For the purpose of this rather early work we consider that every object the user has visited is positively preferred by him/her. It is possible to use more selective meanings of positive preference e.g. to consider only purchased objects as positively preferred. However this will lead to insufficient amount of data in the test set so we leave the problem of finer grained preference to the future work.

Another question was how to model time: we chose taking sessions as unit of time instead of real-time. We believe that continuous user actions as captured in single session better reflects single user interest and thus stable preference. Sessions also fits better to different user customs and behavioral patterns.

Recommending method evaluation was carried out as follows: For each user, data from his/her first session was added into the *train set* and the rest into the *test set*. We filtered users to only those with at least three sessions. The resulting train set contains 7650 records from 830 users. The test set contains 23400 records (objects only, as we intent to recommend only objects to the user).

All learning methods were initialized and trained with the same *train set*, 10 latent factors and maximal 50 iterations.

Then for each user, each method rate all objects, sort them according to the rating, look up positions of objects from the *test set* and aggregate results according to the session number.

4.2 Experiment Results

Figure 2 displays results of recommending methods in *nDCG* aggregated by the number of session to which each object belongs. Table 3 shows Pearsons correlation between nDCG and session number.

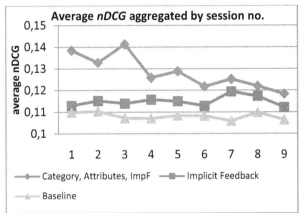

Figure 2: Average nDCG aggregated by session number. Decrease of nDCG should be caused by users preference shift.

The results seems to corroborate decrease of recommendation quality – at least for attribute based recommending methods. For others there might be too much noise as they predicted poorly in general, so we accept the existence of preference shift in our dataset.

Table 3. Pearsons correlation between nDCG and session number.

Method	Correlation	p-value
Baseline	-0.04	0.015
Implicit Feedback	0.02	0.313
Attributes	-0.04	0.015
Category, Attributes, ImpF	-0.05	0.002

5   Time-aware Recommending

This section describes several possible extensions to the current time-aware recommending methods to better reflect e-commerce reality. We chose two papers as our starting point: *Collaborative filtering with temporal dynamics* by Koren [5] and *Similarity of content-based preference models for Collaborative filtering* by Eckhardt [1].

Koren [5] describes several variants of concept drift and how to incorporate them into collaborative filtering.

- Time changing baseline predictors including gradual (linear or splines) drift of user preferences, short-term change in user preferences and interval-based changes of preference on items. Time changing baseline predictors captures overall changes per user (e.g. user tends to rate objects higher over time) and per objects (e.g. as object grew older, it receives poorer ratings).

- Time changing user factors (μ_i^T from equation (1)) reflecting change of user to object preferences. (e.g. a fan of crimi movies starts to like comedies after some time).

Using of both time changing baseline predictors and user factors led to the improvement of RMSE over Netflix dataset.

Eckhardt [1] presents two-step user preference learning method. It first decompose user preferences on objects into the preference on object attributes and then learns aggregating function combining attribute preferences together. The benefits of this method is simple and direct way how to compute user preference for new or changed objects and compare users without common objects.

In the paper, standard collaborative filtering was applied with user similarity based on the two-step method and successfully tested on the Netflix dataset with RMSE measure.

There are several important differences between Netflix and E-Commerce use-cases: possibility of extracting object attributes can significantly improve our prospect in capturing long-term user preferences. Also recording user actions might be usefull.

1. Some of the object attributes, let us call them the "soft attributes" are changeable over time. The most important one are probably prices and discounts, but there are also others depending on the domain (e.g. warranty, stock availability, range of services, promotions etc.).
2. Ordered attributes should be considered according to the context of available objects at the time being, especially at fast evolving domains e.g. computers, cellphones, cars etc. This might help us in capturing long-term preferences: attributes of high-end computer became average within a year, but the user will probably still prefer high-end computers.
3. Last but not least, due to rather complex monitoring of user behavior, we might be able to infer user actions leading to preference shift (purchase action is a good candidate) and/or periodical behavior.

We plan to adjust Koren's model to incorporate attributes and treat them relatively with respect to their current range. The changes of the object's attributes can be recorded, so we can restore their values at any time-point, however the question is how to model the same object with different attributes at different time-points.

Eckhards method provides simple way how to compute user preference for any set of attribute values, so we plan to experiment with changing users previous ratings as results of users or objects actions.

6   Conclusions

In this paper we focused on recommending for e-commerce portals. We were particularly interested in time-aware recommending. We described problems and constraints of e-commerce domain and presented methods capable to deal with them.

An off-line experiment corroborated negative dependence of increasing time-distance between training and recommending on the quality of recommendations (measured by nDCG) and thus need of time-aware methods. We concluded the paper with several proposals on adjusting contemporary recommending methods to better reflect time-drifting nature of e-commerce datasets.

Acknowledgment

The work on this paper was supported by the grant SVV-2013-267312, GAUK-126313 and P46.

References

[1] Eckhardt, A. Similarity of users (content-based) preference models for Collaborative filtering in few ratings scenário. *EXPERT SYST APPL,* **2012**, *39,* 11511 - 11516

[2] Forbes, P. & Zhu, M. Content-boosted matrix factorization for recommender systems: experiments with recipe recommendation. *In RecSys 2011, ACM,* **2011**, 261-264

[3] Ito, F.; Hiroyasu, T.; Miki, M.; Yokouchi, H.; Detection of preference shift timing using time-series clustering, *In FUZZ-IEEE 2009, IEEE,* **2009**, 1585 - 1590

[4] Konstan, J. & Riedl, J. Recommender systems: from algorithms to user experience. *UMUAI,* **2012**, *22,* 101-123.

[5] Koren, Y. Collaborative filtering with temporal dynamics. *In ACM SIGKDD 2009, ACM,* **2009**, 447-456.

[6] Koren, Y.; Bell, R. & Volinsky, C. Matrix Factorization Techniques for Recommender Systems. *Computer, IEEE,* **2009**, *42,* 30-37.

[7] Peska, L.; Vojtas, P.: Negative Implicit feedback in E-commerce Recommender Systems. I*n WIMS 2013, ACM, 2013,* 45:1 – 45:4

[8] Peska, L.; Vojtas, P Recommending for Disloyal Customers with Low Consumption Rate. *In review for RecSys 2013,* *http://www.ksi.mff.cuni.cz/~peska/recsys2013.pdf*

[9] Takahashi M., Nakao T., Tsuda K. and Terano T. Generating Dual-Directed Recommendation Information from Point-of-Sales Data of a Supermarket, *In KES 2008, Springer,* **2008**, 1010 - 1017

ITAT 2013: Workshops, Posters, and Tutorials, pp. 27–32
ISBN 978-1490952086, © 2013 T. Nguyen, Š. Pero

Extrakcia vlastností produktu z komentárov užívateľov

Tomáš Nguyen a Štefan Pero
Ústav informatiky
Prírodovedecká fakulta, Univerzita Pavla Jozefa Šafárika v Košiciach
Jesenná 5, 040 01 Košice
{Tomas.Nguyen, Stefan.Pero}@student.upjs.sk

Abstrakt. *Neoddeliteľnou súčasťou odporúčacieho systému na internete je nielen možnosť hodnotiť daný produkt formou číselného hodnotenia (rating), ale aj možnosť zhodnotiť daný produkt formou textového komentára a tak popísať detailnejšie jeho kvality, resp. negatíva. Takýto textový komentár môže užívateľovi viac pomôcť správne si vybrať správny a jemu najviac vyhovujúci produkt (počítač, auto, dovolenku). Avšak, práca s textom má svoje špecifiká a vyžaduje si oveľa väčšie nároky v procese odporúčania ako rating. Našim cieľom je analyzovať textové komentáre a extrahovať z nich relevantné vlastnosti produktu, ktoré použijeme v procese odporúčania. Experimenty sme realizovali na voľne dostupných dátach z Amazonu.*

1 Úvod

Jedným z hlavných problémov pri procese extrahovania vlastností z textových komentárov je fakt, že komentáre sú zväčša písane vo forme voľného/neštruktúrovaného textu, ktorý ešte využíva rôzne vlastnosti a prvky jazyka. V taomto texte je pomerne zložité zistiť, ktoré slová sú dôležité vzhľadom na hodnotenie a ktoré slová sú úplne nepodstatné pri hodnotení. Ďalšou prekážkou je fakt, že ľudia v komentároch píšu aj veci, ktoré nemajú s hodnotením nič spoločné. To v podstate znamená, že sa v komentároch nachádzajú aj slovné spojenia, ktoré by sme mohli pri extrahovaní, ale aj pri hodnotení úplne ignorovať. Ako príklad si môžeme zobrať nasledujúci komentár:

„*This **book** is totally awesome. **Story** was well written and **characters** were cool and memorable. I just couldn't get away from it. I literally spend whole night reading. But I finished it in just 3 days so it could have been longer. Very good **book**. You should definitely buy it.*"

Hrubo zvýraznené slová sú vlastnosti, ktoré sa snažíme extrahovať, lebo sú dôležité pri hodnotení. Však modely na extrahovanie si teda musia vedieť poradiť s veľkým množstvom nepodstatných informácií. Vlastnosti však nemusia byť vždy vyjadrené explicitne ako je tomu v prvej alebo druhej vete, ale môžu byť vyjadrené aj implicitne, ako vo vete „*But I finished it in just 3 days so it could have been longer.*" ktorá nepriamo opisuje dĺžku knihy.

Problematike extrakcie vlastností sa v dnešnej dobe venuje veľa pozornosti, hlavne kvôli zväčšujúcemu sa množstvu internetových obchodov, ktoré využívajú hodnotenie produktov formou užívateľských komentárov. Systémy OPINE [9] alebo Opinion Observer [7] sú jednoduché modely na extrakciu vlastností, ktoré sa viac venujú hodnoteniu komentárov.

1.1 Liu a Hu model

Bing Liu a Minqing Hu [4] navrhli spôsob generovania sumarizácie komentárov užívateľov na základe vlastností produktu, snažili sa zistiť mieru ako pozitívne alebo negatívne bol produkt ohodnotený. Ako vstup sa vyžaduje množina komentárov jedného produktu. Generovanie tejto sumarizácie pozostáva z troch krokov:

- Extrakcia relevantných vlastností
- Identifikácia slov, ktoré vyjadrujú pozitívny alebo negatívny názor na produkt
- Vytvorenie sumarizácie

Liu a Hu model je zobrazený na Obr.1 a pozostáva z nasledujúcich troch krokov: Part-of-Speech Tagging, určovanie častých vlastnotí a orezávanie vlastnotí.

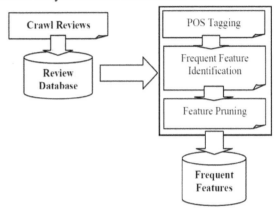

Obr. 1. Model extrahovania vlastností (Liu a Hu, [4])

1.1.1 Part-of-Speech Tagging

Pomocou Part-of-Speech Tagging [8] (skrátene POS tagging), čo je označovanie slovných druhov v texte, je každá veta uložená do databázy komentárov aj s jej slovným druhom a zároveň sa vytvorí aj transakčný súbor na generovanie vlastností s vysokým výskytom. V každom riadku tohto súboru sa nachádza slovo z jednej vety, ktoré bolo identifikované ako podstatné meno alebo slovná fráza. Iné časti vety, ako napríklad spojky a číslovky, zrejme nebudú vlastnosťami produktu. Taktiež sú vykonané aj základné predspracovanie slov, ktoré zahŕňa odstránenie stopových slov (is, want, have, I, ...) a orezávanie slov do pôvodného tvaru.

1.1.2 Určovanie častých vlastností

Pri vyhľadávaní vlastností na nájdenie množiny častých položiek sa využívajú asociačné pravidlá [2]. Použije sa asociačný dolovací modul CBA [6] (založený na Aprioriho algoritme) na transakčný súbor z predchádzajúceho kroku. Výstupom je množina častých položiek. Položka sa považuje za častú ak sa vyskytuje vo viac ako 1% viet komentára. Výsledná množina častých položiek obsahuje slová alebo slovné frázy, ktoré nazveme potenciálne vlastnosti. Avšak nie všetky potenciálne vlastnosti sú skutočnými vlastnosťami produktu, tie sa získajú orezávaním potenciálnych vlastností.

1.1.3 Orezávanie vlastností

Orezávanie vlastností pozostáva z dvoch krokov. Najprv sa orezávajú vlastnosti, ktoré obsahujú dve alebo viac slov. Algoritmus použitý na ich získanie neberie do úvahy poradie slov vo vete. Avšak slová vyskytujúce sa spolu v určitom poradí majú väčšiu šancu, že sú relevantné. Preto niektoré potenciálne vlastnosti vygenerované asociačnými pravidlami nemusia byť korektné. Cieľom tohto orezávania je teda odstrániť tie potenciálne viacslovné vlastnosti, ktorých slová nie sú v špecifickom poradí.

Druhé orezávanie odstraňuje jednoslovné potenciálne vlastnosti, ktoré sú označené ako nepodstatné. Na označenie nepodstatných vlastností sa používa koncept p-support *(pure support)* [5]. P-support vlastnosti sa označuje ftr a vyjadruje počet viet v ktorých sa vlastnosť nachádza ako podstatné meno. Zároveň tieto vety nesmú obsahovať žiadne slovné frázy, ktoré sú nadmnožinou danej vlastnosti. Ak je p-support hodnota vlastnosti menšia ako minimum p-support *(vopred zvolené číslo)* a zároveň vlastnosť nie je podmnožinou inej slovnej frázy, tak sa vlastnosť odstráni ako nepodstatná. Napríklad slovo *life* je samo o sebe bezvýznamné vzhľadom na doménu *fotoaparát*, ale jeho nadmnožina *battery life* už predstavuje vlastnosť pomocou ktorej sa môže produkt hodnotiť.

1.2 Garenini a kol. model

Tento model využíva vopred, užívateľom definované vlastnosti (UDF) [3] a extrakcia pozostáva z kombinácie nekontrolovaného *(crude features)* a kontrolovaného učenia *(pomocou UDF)*.

1.2.1 Crude features model

Veľkou výhodou tohto prístupu je jednoduchosť, keďže potrebuje len množinu vstupných komentárov, ale jeho výstup je problematický keďže obsahuje priveľa zbytočných vlastností aj napriek vykonaným orezávaniam. Jendou z nevýhod tohto riešenia je aj fakt, že neberie do úvahy lexikálnu zhodu medzi dvoma rôznymi získanými vlastnosťami. Ako príklad môžeme uviesť vlastnosti *obrázok* a *fotografia*, ktoré sú v doméne fotoaparát významovo zhodné, ale v tomto prístupe sú brané ako dve rozdielne vlastnosti. Extrakcia v tejto práci využíva výstup z modelu A nazvaný tiež ako „surové vlastnosti" (crude features - CF).

1.2.2 UDF model

Pomocou užívateľom definovaných vlastností sa vytvorí tréningová množina komentárov. Následne sa z nej pomocou kontrolovaného učenia získa klasifikátor, ktorý sa použije na vstupnú množinu komentárov. Tento prístup funguje celkom dobre na špecifickej doméne no je v celku nepraktický, keďže pri každej zmene domény sa musí vytvoriť nová tréningová množina a opätovne sa v nej musia označiť UDF.

1.2.3 Kombinácia Crude features a UDF modelov

Kombináciou týchto dvoch modelov sa snažíme odstrániť zbytočné vlastnosti, ktoré sú obsiahnuté v modeli *crude features*, no bez nutnosti vytvárania tréningovej množiny. To zaistí jednoduchší a hlavne rýchlejší prechod na inú doménu, keďže bude potrebné zmeniť len množinu UDF. Najdôležitejšiu úlohu v tomto prístupe zohráva proces nazvaný *similarity matching*, ktorý vlastnosti z výstupu *crude features* modelu pridelí k *UDF*, s ktorým je podobný alebo zhodný. Určovanie podobnosti medzi vlastnosťou r (patrí do výstupu modelu crude features) a w (patrí do výstupu UDF modelu) prebieha v dvoch krokoch:

- Jednoduché porovnávanie zhody reťazcov. Ak sa reťazec $r=w$ tak sa vlastnosť r priradí k w.
- Tu sa overuje významová zhoda vlastností pomocou synoným. Na to sa použije WordNet. Ak sa vlastnosť r nachádza v nejakej množine synoným w, tak sa r priradí k w.

Takýmto pridelením sa odstránia zbytočné vlastnosti, ktoré boli prítomné vo výstupe prvého modelu. Pridelené vlastnosti k UDF sú znázornené na Obr. 22.

Camera	Image
Lens	Image Type
Aperture Modes	TIFF
Optical Zoom	JPEG
...	...
Editing/Viewing	Resolution
Viewfinder	Effective Pixels
...	Aspect Ratio
Flash	...
...	

Obr. 2 Spôsob priradenia vlastností k UDF

Výsledkom tohto procesu je množina zlúčených vlastností (merged features - *MF*). Vlastnosti v *MF* môžu byť ešte upravené užívateľom aby sa odstránili prípadné chyby. Ak užívateľ pri revízii zistí, že v množine UDF nejaká vlastnosť chýba, alebo je nadbytočná, tak stačí UDF upraviť a spustiť similarity matching znova.

2 Náš prístup

Využívame princíp vysokého výskytu slov a princíp užívateľom definovaných vlastností. Zároveň využívame aj TF-IDF na určenie dôležitosti slov. Naše riešenie sa zaoberá len extrakciou explicitných jednoslovných vlastností. Na rozdiel od predchádzajúcich riešení v našej práci sme sa rozhodli vykonávať extrakciu z celej domény a nie len jedného produktu.

2.1 Využitie vysokého výskytu slov

Naše využite slov s vysokým výskytom je oveľa jednoduchšie ako v práci [4]. V našej práci určujeme len jednoslovné vlastnosti a nehodnotíme prídavnými menami. Z toho dôvodu by bolo zbytočné používať zložitý POS tagging. Stačí nám využiť už uvedený WordNet. Postup akým získavame najčastejšie slová je veľmi jednoduchý a prebieha nasledovne:

```
Procedura casteSlova mnozinaKomentarov){
   množinaSlov je prázdna
   pre každé slovo w v mnozKomentarov{
      keď (je slovo w podstatné meno a
      nenachádza sa v mnozinaSlov){
         pridaj w do mnozinaSlov a nastav
         počet na 1
      }
      keď (je slovo w podstatné meno a
      nachádza sa v mnozinaSlov)
         zvýš počet w o 1
   }
}
```

Na to aby sme overili či je slovo *w* podstatné meno použijeme *WordNet*, ktorý vráti množinu synoným slova w obsahujúce len podstatné mená. Ak vráti ľubovoľnú neprázdnu množinu, tak vieme povedať, že v nejakom kontexte je slovo w podstatné meno. V opačnom prípade vieme povedať, že slovo w nie je podstatné meno. Následne po spočítaní výskytu všetkých slov sa slová zoradia od najčastejšieho až po najzriedkavejšie a získame tak usporiadanú množinu najčastejších slov (ďalej označovanú ako M1). Na rozdiel od práce [4] nevykonávame orezávania až na výber podstatných mien. Ďalšie potrebné orezávania sa vykonajú v neskorších krokoch. Problém s takýmto výstupom by bol v tom, že by tam bolo príliš veľa zbytočností. Tento problém sme sa rozhodli čiastočne vyriešiť zahrnutím TF-IDF do nášho riešenia.

2.2 Využitie TF-IDF

TF-IDF *(term frequency–inverse document frequency)* je číselná štatistika, ktorá sa zaoberá dôležitosťou slov v dokumente vzhľadom na dátovú sadu dokumentov. V našom prípade určujeme dôležitosť slov v komentári z celej množiny komentárov. Hodnota TF-IDF sa vypočíta nasledovne:

$$tfidf(w,k,D) = tf(w,k) \times idf(w,D) \qquad (1)$$

$$tf(w,k) = \frac{f(w,k)}{\max\{f(w',k):w' \epsilon k\}} \qquad (2)$$

$$idf(w,D) = log \frac{|D|}{|\{k \in D : w \in k\}|} \qquad (3)$$

$$f(w,k) \qquad (4)$$

Rovnica (2) určuje normalizovanú frekvenciu slova *s* v komentári *k*, pričom rovnica (4) určuje počet výskytu slova *w* v *k*. Hodnota *tf* sa získa jednoduchým delením počtu výskytu s najčastejším slovom v komentári.

Rovnica (3) určuje, či je slovo *s* časté alebo zriedkavé v množine komentárov *D*. *Idf* sa získa delením celkového počtu komentárov v množine komentárov *D* s počtom komentárov obsahujúcich slovo *s* a logaritmovaním tohto výsledku. Základ logaritmu je v tomto prípade nepodstatný, nakoľko nás zaujíma skôr porovnávanie hodnôt než ich presnosť.

Hodnota TF-IDF sa získa už jednoduchým vynásobením hodnôt z (2) a (3). Veľmi dobrou vlastnosťou TF-IDF je to, že ak je slovo príliš časté, alebo príliš zriedkavé tak jeho hodnota bude horšia. V našej práci nevyužívame jednotlivé hodnoty TF-IDF ale ich priemer, ktorý nám ukáže priemernú dôležitosť slova. Čím je priemerná hodnota menšia tým je slovo dôležitejšie. Príklad výpočtu a priemeru je znázornený na Obr.3.

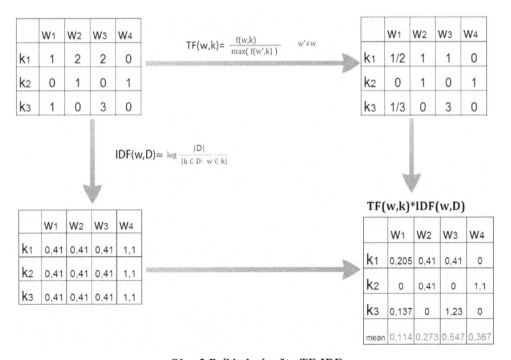

Obr. 3 Príklad výpočtu TF-IDF

V pravom hornom rohu je tabuľka výskytu slov *w1*, *w2*, *w3*, *w4* v komentároch *k1*, *k2*, *k3*. Pomocou rovníc (2) a (3) vytvoríme dve rôzne tabuľky uchovávajúce hodnoty *tf* a *idf*. Následne hodnoty v tabuľke vynásobíme z čoho nám vznikne tabuľka obsahujúca hodnoty TF-IDF. Nakoniec z hodnôt všetkých slov vypočítame priemer, ktorý je na Obr. v štvrtom riadku. Slovo w3 ktoré je veľmi bežné a slovo w4, ktoré je veľmi zriedkavé majú najväčšiu priemernú hodnotu a tým pádom ich nebudeme považovať za dôležité. Keďže slová w1 a w2 majú priemernú najmenšiu hodnotu, tak ich považujeme za dôležité. Je dôležité dodať, že nás nezaujíma konkrétna hodnota priemerov, ale skôr len niekoľko najmenších hodnôt, ktoré budeme považovať za potenciálne vlastnosti. Tak ako aj v predchádzajúcom kroku aj tu využívame WordNet na výber len podstatných mien. Tento výber sa však deje až po vyrátaní TF-IDF priemerov.

Z tohto kroku dostaneme zoznam podstatných mien s ich priemernou TF-IDF hodnotou, ktorý následne usporiadame od slov s najmenšou hodnotou až po tie s najväčšou. Výsledkom bude usporiadaná množina najdôležitejších slov (ďalej označovanú ako M2). V ďalšom kroku budeme využívať nielen tento, ale predošlý usporiadaný zoznam.

2.3   Určovanie relevantných vlastností

Pri určovaní relevantných vlastností využívame aj užívateľom definované vlastnosti. Naše využitie UDF je podobné prístupu opísanom v podkapitole 1.2.2. Vopred si zadáme množinu slov, ktoré budú predstavovať množinu UDF pre danú doménu, v našom prípade knihy, filmy a hudba.

2.3.1   Similarity matching

Vstupom pre similarity matching sú usporiadané množiny najčastejších a najdôležitejších slov (množiny M1 a M2), ktoré tvoria naše potenciálne vlastnosti.

Priradzovanie slov k UDF prebieha tak, že si všetky slová z usporiadanej množiny najčastejších alebo najdôležitejších slov porovnávame so slovami v UDF. Výsledkom je množina zlúčených vlastností (množina MF). Tento výstup je však oveľa jednoduchší ako predchádzajúci, keďže obsahuje len riadky v ktorých je potenciálna vlastnosť s UDF vlastnosťou.

2.3.2   Zoznam výskytu slov

V tomto kroku využijeme ako vstup množiny *M1*, *M2* a *MF* získané z predošlých krokov. Zvolíme číslo *x*, ktoré bude predstavovať počet prvých slov z celkového počtu slov z množiny *M1* a číslo *y*, ktoré bude predstavovať počet prvých slov z celkového počtu slov z množiny M2 .

Cieľom tohto kroku je vytvorenie zoznamu výskytu jednotlivých slov. Tento zoznam obsahuje slová, ktoré sa nachádzajú medzi najčastejšími slovami *(prvých x % slov)*, medzi najdôležitejšími slovami *(prvých y % slov)* a ďalej či sa slovo nachádza v množine MF, t.j. či je to slovo podobné s nejakým slovom z UDF. Príklad výskytu slova vyzerá nasledovne:

```
book        0        1        1
```

Slovo book sa nevyskytuje v najčastejších slovách (0), nachádza sa v najdôležitejších slovách (1) a vyskytuje sa v množine MF (1).

2.3.3   Hodnotenie slov

Hodnotenie slov prebieha nasledovne:

```
pre každé slovo v zozname výskytov{
  ak je výskyt typu 100 alebo 010 tak
      slovu priradíme index α
  ak je výskyt typu 110 tak slovu
      priradíme index β
  ak je výskyt typu 101 alebo 011 tak
      slovu priradíme index γ
  ak je výskyt typu 111 tak dáme slovu
      priradíme index δ
}
```

Pre každý model vopred nastavíme jeho dôležitosť pri súhrnom vyhľadávaní vlastností, napríklad tieto štyri indexy si môžeme zvoliť nasledovne: α - 0.0; β - 0.5; γ - 1.0; δ - 2.0. Tieto konkrétne hodnotenia sme si zvolili hlavne pre jednoduchšiu vizuálnu a číselnú reprezentáciu. Dôvody jednotlivých ohodnotení sú nasledovné:

Ak sa slovo nachádza len v jednej množín *M1* alebo *M2* a zároveň sa nenachádza ani v množine *MF*, tak slovo má len malú šancu byť relevantnou vlastnosťou. Preto dostáva hodnotenie 0.0.

Ak sa slovo nachádza v oboch množinách *M1* a *M2*, ale sa nenachádza v množine *MF*, tak dostanie hodnotenie 0.5. Dôvodom tohto hodnotenia je to, že slovo sa nenachádza v *MF*, preto ho nebudeme považovať za relevantnú vlastnosť. Zároveň sa však nachádza v *M1* a *M2* a tým pádom tu je možnosť, že slovo je vlastnosťou ale jeho synonymum nie je v množine UDF.

Ak sa slovo nachádza v jednej z množín *M1* alebo *M2* a zároveň v množine *MF*, tak slovo dostane hodnotenie 1.0. V tomto prípade je slovo označené ako najdôležitejšie, alebo najčastejšie a je podobné/zhodné s nejakým slovom z UDF. Preto ho budeme považovať za relevantnú vlastnosť.

Ak sa slovo nachádza v oboch množinách *M1* a *M2* a zároveň sa nachádza v množine *MF*, tak dostane hodnotenie 2.0. Takéto slovo budeme považovať za relevantnú vlastnosť, lebo je označené ako dôležité aj časté a je podobné s nejakým slovom z množiny UDF.

Výstup bude obsahovať vlastnosti ku ktorým je pridelené hodnotenie. Následne vyberieme len tie s hodnotením 1.0 alebo 2.0 ako relevantné. Vlastnosti s hodnotením 0.5 môžeme použiť na overenie korektnosti našej UDF množiny. Ak sa medzi týmito slovami nachádza nejaké slovo pri ktorom sme si istý, že je vlastnosťou, tak ho (alebo jeho synonymum) pridáme do UDF.

3   Experimenty

3.1   Dátová sada

UDF množina z domény knihy, filmy a hudba obsahuje vlastnosti (napr. book, film, story, music, length, character, album, lyrics) získané pomocou doménového expert z IMDB.com.

Naša dátová sada obsahuje vyše päť miliónov komentárov z AMAZON.com. Dáta obsahujú informácie o produkte, jeho hodnotenie a textový komentár. Používali sme túto dátovú sadu v štyroch veľkostiach (Tab. 1).

Tab 1. Veľkosti dátových sád

Sada	Počet komentárov
Sada1	50 000
Sada2	100 000
Sada3	250 000
Sada4	400 000

3.2 Výsledky testovania na celej doméne

V prvom teste sme sa rozhodli zobrať pri hodnotení prvých 5% najčastejších slov (množina $M1$) a prvých 20% najdôležitejších slov (množina $M2$). Pozorovaním dát sme zistili, že relevantné vlastnosti v množine $M2$ sa nachádzajú oveľa „hlbšie" v zozname ako v $M1$ a z toho dôvodu berieme viac slov z $M2$ ako z $M1$. Výsledky sú zobrazené v Tab.2. Ako výsledné vlastnosti sme zobrali tie s hodnotením väčším alebo rovným ako 1.0. Pri dátovej sade 1 môžeme vidieť iba štyri slová s hodnotením 2.0 pričom pri väčších vzorkách je ich viac. To je spôsobené hlavne veľkosťou prvej vzorky. Ďalej sme si všimli, že so zväčšujúcou sa vzorkou sa nezväčšuje počet nových slov s priaznivým hodnotením. Tento fakt nám ukazuje to, že keď sa zväčšuje vzorka tak sa pozícia najčastejších a najdôležitejších slov výrazne nezhoršuje a tým pádom sú tieto slová pravdepodobnejšími vlastnosťami. Keď sa ale pozrieme bližšie na niektoré slová, tak nájdeme také, ktoré nám nepripadajú ako relevantné vlastnosti v našej doméne. Sú to slová ako napríklad: account alebo history. Hlavne

slovo history sa objavuje vo väčších vzorkách s hodnotením 2.0 čo znamená že je medzi prvou tisíckou najčastejších ale aj najdôležitejších slov. No táto vlastnosť nie je relevantná v našej doméne. Dôvodov môže byť hneď niekoľko.

Prvým z možných dôvodov je rozmanitosť našej vzorky, nakoľko pracujeme až na troch doménach súčasne, pričom modely na ktoré sme nadväzovali sa zaoberali extrakciou len z množiny komentárov jedného produktu.

Ďalším z možných dôvodov môže byť veľké striedanie rôznych produktov v našich vzorkách. Opätovne problém s viacerými produktmi spracovanými zároveň. Aby sme si naše predpoklady overili vykonali sme testovanie na vzorke obsahujúcej len komentáre pre jeden produkt.

3.3 Výsledky testovania pre jeden produkt

Pre tento test sme vytvorili testovacie vzorky, ktoré obsahovali komentáre o jednom filme (príklad Sada5 a Sada6). Keďže sme testovaciu doménu zúžili na filmy, tak sme tomu museli prispôsobiť našu množinu UDF.

V tomto prípade sme takisto zobrali prvých 5% slov z množiny $M1$ a prvých 20% slov z množiny $M2$ v oboch dátových sadách. Ohodnotené vlastnosti sú zobrazené v Tab.3.

Tab. 3 Ohodnotené vlastnosti pre jeden produkt

Sada 5		Sada 6	
1.0	**2.0**	**1.0**	**2.0**
movie	film	part	film
story		length	movie
part		cinema	story
length			
cinema			
case			

Tab. 2 Ohodnotené vlastnosti testovacích vzoriek

Sada1		Sada2		Sada3		Sada4	
1.0	**2.0**	**1.0**	**2.0**	**1.0**	**2.0**	**1.0**	**2.0**
album	book	album	book	album	book	album	book
movie	story	movie	story	movie	story	movie	story
film	part	film	part	film	part	film	part
music	charact	music	charact	music	charact	music	charact
history		quality	history	quality	history	quality	history
quality		role	case	words	case	role	case
case		words		picture	role	words	
role		picture		record		picture	
words		record		level		record	
picture		level		tale		level	
record		tale		type		tale	
level		type		volume		type	
tale		volume		langua		volume	

Pozorovaním týchto výsledkov sme prišli na to, že väčšina slov s ohodnotením 1.0 aj 2.0 môžu byť považované za relevantné v oboch dátových sadách. Tiež si môžeme všimnúť zlepšenie hodnotenia vlastností *movie* a *story* v dátovej sade 6, v ktorej sa už nevyskytuje vlastnosť *case*, ktorá nebola vzhľadom na našu doménu relevantná.

Oproti testovaniu na celej doméne tu značne poklesol počet diskutabilných vlastností. Zvýšila sa taktiež presnosť extrahovaných vlastností. Tieto výsledky taktiež podporujú naše predchádzajúce predpoklady, že s rozširujúcou sa doménou a rôznorodosťou produktov sa výsledky skresľujú.

Záver

Cieľom tejto práce bolo navrhnúť model na extrakciu vlastností produktov z komentárov užívateľov. Navrhli sme vlastné riešenie, ktoré nadväzovalo na existujúce riešenia v tejto problematike, napr. číselnú štatistiku TF-IDF, ktorá určuje dôležitosť slov v komentári na základe ich výskytu.

Následne sme na našej vzorke komentárov vykonali potrebné testy na overenie funkcionality nášho riešenia. Vzorka bola širšieho charakteru keďže obsahovala komentáre produktov rôznych domén. Tieto testy ukázali, že naše riešenie úspešne extrahuje vlastnosti produktov z väčších domén. Testami sme však zistili aj to, že presnosť extrakcie sa znižuje na dátových sadách, ktoré obsahujú viacero domén a naopak presnosť je veľmi dobrá ak vzorka obsahuje komentáre len z jednej domény.

V našej práci sme sa zaoberali extrakciou vlastností produktov za účelom hodnotenia týchto produktov, ale naše riešenie sa dá použiť aj na iné účely ako sú napríklad odporúčacie systémy produktov. Takéto systémy sa pokúšajú odhadnúť, aké položky by užívateľa zaujímali na základe dostupných informácii o zákazníkovi a produktoch [1].

V budúcich prácach môžeme nadviazať na túto prácu s tým, že by sme aj hodnotili produkty pomocou prídavných mien. Taktiež by sme doplnili extrakciu menej častých vlastností a podobne.

Poďakovanie

Táto práca bola podporená v rámci výskumných projektov *VEGA 1/0832/12* a *VVGS-PF-2013-102*.

Referencie

[1] Aciar, Silvana, Debbie Zhang, Simeon Simoff a John Debenham. Informed Recommender: Basing Recommendations on Consumer Product Reviews. IEEE Intelligent Systems. roč. 22, č. 3, s. 39-47. ISSN 1541-1672. DOI: 10.1109/MIS.2007.55

[2] Agrawal, Rakesh a Ramakrishnan Srikant. 20th VLDB Conference: September 12 -15, 1994, Santiago - Chile : proceedings of the 20th International Conference on Very Large Data Bases. San Francisco: Morgan Kaufmann Publishers, 1994, s. 487-499. ISBN 1558601538.

[3] Carenni, Giuseppe, Raymond T. NG a Ed Zwart. Proceedings of the Third International Conference on Knowledge Capture: K-CAP '05 : October 2-5, 2005, Banff, Alberta, Canada. New York, N.Y.: Association for Computing Machinery, c2005, s. 11-18. ISBN 1-59593-163-5.

[4] Hu, Minqing a Bing Liu. Mining and summarizing customer reviews. Proceedings of the 2004 ACM SIGKDD international conference on Knowledge discovery and data mining - KDD '04. New York, New York, USA: ACM Press, 2004, s. 168-177. DOI: 10.1145/1014052.1014073.

[5] Hu, Minqing a Bing Liu. Proceedings: Nineteenth National Conference on Artificial Intelligence (AAAI-04) : Sixteenth Innovative Applications of Artificial Intelligence Conference (IAAI-04). Cambridge, Mass.: MIT Press, c2004, s. 755-760. ISBN 0-262-51183-5.

[6] Hu, Minqing a Bing Liu. Proceedings. Menlo Park, Calif.: AAAI Press, c1998, s. 80-86. ISBN 1-57735-070-7.

[7] Liu, Bing, Minqing Hu a Junsheng Cheng. Opinion observer. Proceedings of the 14th international conference on World Wide Web - WWW '05. New York, New York, USA: ACM Press, 2005, s. 342-351. DOI: 10.1145/1060745.1060797.

[8] Manning, Christopher D. Foundations of statistical natural language processing. Cambridge: MIT Press, c1999, xxxvii, 680 s. ISBN 02-621-3360-1.

[9] Popescu, Ana-Maria a Oren Etyioni. Extracting product features and opinions from reviews. Proceedings of the conference on Human Language Technology and Empirical Methods in Natural Language Processing - HLT '05. Morristown, NJ, USA: Association for Computational Linguistics, 2005, s. 339-346. DOI: 10.3115/1220575.1220618

Workshop on Bioinformatics in Genomics and Proteomics

At the beginning of the year 2013 I was asked by Tomas Vinar and other organizers of ITAT to help organize a bioinformatics workshop at this year's conference. Organizing such workshop at ITAT was seen as a way to bridge the slowly narrowing gap and ease the relative isolation of the Czech and Slovak IT and molecular biology communities. The arrival of high-throughput techniques of genomics and proteomics to our laboratories in the last few years has increased the pressure on using state of the art bioinformatics to crunch the ever increasing mountain of data. What used to be single-gene or single-protein studies a few years ago is now being studied in a whole-genome or whole-proteome context. I selected the workshop focus and title to specifically attract papers from the the area of big-data studies. However, being a first attempt of this kind, we also tried to keep the workshop open to as many interested participants as possible. We therefore encouraged contributions from systems biology, medical bioinformatics and other closely related disciplines.

The cross-disciplinary workshop setting partly reflects the dual reality of bioinformatics teaching and research at Czech and Slovak universities. On one hand, bioinformatics is firmly rooted in natural science curricula, either independently as is the case of the Faculty of Science of Masaryk University in Brno and the Faculty of Science of the South Bohemian University in Ceske Budejovice, or even hidden in courses, such as "Protein structure and function", "Genome evolution", etc. On the other hand, we also see bachelor and master programs in bioinformatics created as extensions of teaching computer science. This is the case of the bioinformatics programs at the Faculty of Informatics at Masaryk University in Brno and Faculty of Electrical Engineering and Communication at the Brno University of Technology. It is also present in the curricula of the Faculty of Mathematics, Physics and Computer Science of the Comenius University in Bratislava, Faculty of Electrical Engineering of the Czech Technical University in Prague and Faculty of Chemical Technology of the Institute of Chemical Technology in Prague.

Although this workshop is one of the first bioinformatics workshops organized in the context of a computer science conference, there is now quite a history of Czech and Slovak bioinformatics conferences and workshops that shared the same organizers or participants, or both. This includes a series of conferences called Bioinformatics I, II and III organized during the INVEX fair in Brno by Dr. Jiri Damborsky in the years 2004-2006. The most prominent series of meetings is beyond doubt the FOBIA annual or biannual meeting of Czech and Slovak bioinformatics communities taking place at various locations from the year 2004, first organized by Dr. Jan Paces (http://fobia.img.cas.cz/). I had the honor to organize the next meeting in Telč in 2005. The last meeting was the ENBIK conference in Cesky Sternberk in 2012 organized by Dr. Daniel Svozil. A series of summer schools in bioinformatics has been repeatedly organized by Dr. Tomas Vinar and Dr. Brona Brejova in Slovakia since the year 2007.

To underline the planned focus of the workshop on problems in genomics and proteomics, I invited Dr. Eduard Kejnovsky from the Institute of Biophysics of the Czech Academy of Sciences to provide us with an introduction to the area of studying genomes. He kindly accepted the invitiation. His lecture titled "Jumping genes – parasites or helpers?" should bring home the idea that genomes are not static objects, but rather living systems in their own merit and that any observations we make are only snapshots of a highly dynamic system.

This workshop has attracted a modest number of papers from authors from Bratislava, Brno, Košice and Prague, with co-authors also from institutions in Canada and Mexico. The papers cover the areas of RNA structure analysis and prediction (Budis and Brejova, Rampasek et al., Simalova), DNA sequence analysis (Brazdova et al.), genome-wide association studies (Stefanic and Lexa), pathway and expression analysis (Andel et al., Ihnatova), plant genome analysis (Didi et al., Hrdinova et al.) and comparative genomics (Vinar and Brejova). Each paper was refereed by a minimum of two referees who provided valuable feedback to authors and helped to rank the submitted papers. Because the submitted papers only slightly exceeded the capacity of the workshop and all were within the scope of the workshop, we shortened the time allocated to lower-ranking papers, but finally accepted all 10 papers for oral presentation at the workshop. Five authors provided a 1-page abstract, the other five opted for a full-length paper. All of them are published here in their full length.

We sincerely hope the workshop will fulfill the desired goal to become a place of meaningful knowledge sharing for both the computer science and molecular biology communities.

Matej Lexa
Masaryk University, Brno
Workshop Program Chair

Workshop Program Committee

Broňa Brejová, Comenius University in Bratislava
Ľuboš Kľučár, Slovak Academy of Sciences, Bratislava
Matej Lexa, Masaryk University, Brno (PC chair)
Tomáš Martínek, Brno University of Technology
David Šafránek, Masaryk University, Brno

Using Motifs in RNA Secondary Structure Prediction

Jaroslav Budiš, Broňa Brejová

Faculty of Mathematics, Physics and Informatics, Comenius University in Bratislava, Slovakia
budis@dcs.fmph.uniba.sk

Biological function of an RNA molecule is closely related to its three-dimensional structure. Since technologies that determine the shape directly are very expensive and time-consuming, we usually have only information about the primary sequence, that is specific order of basic building blocks, nucleotides, forming the RNA molecule. The overall shape of the molecule can be predicted from the sequence computationally which significantly reduces the expenses. An important step of the prediction process is identification of RNA secondary structure describing bonds between nucleotides, which stabilize the molecule in its final shape.

The standard model of secondary structure represents only canonical Watson-Crick base pairings. In this model, each nucleotide is either unpaired or interacts with one other nucleotide. Base pairs are arranged in the nested manner, forming regular shapes stabilized by regions of stacked canonical base pairs. Optimal secondary structure that satisfies these restrictions can be calculated in polynomial time which makes this model suitable for computational analysis.

The accuracy of secondary structure prediction tools based on the standard model is however still not sufficient, mainly because of overly simplified representation of possible interactions. Although these regular stem areas account for a major portion of a typical molecule, remaining parts generally form irregular conformations stabilized by complex interactions which are not included in the standard model.

A lot of effort has been put into prediction of the non-nested base pairs, *pseudoknots*. General problem of prediction of the optimal non-nested structures is however NP-hard, therefore, in practice, algorithms generally use a restricted model with a limited class of pseudoknots (summarized in [1]).

The growing number of experimentally determined RNA structures revealed a variety of non-canonical interactions which have been classified into 12 families [2]. In contrast with the standard pairing, each nucleotide may create several non-canonical bonds with other nucleotides. Incorporation of these interactions in the prediction process is challenging, mainly because they significantly increase the complexity of the scoring scheme; however the improvement of prediction quality is promising [3].

Non-canonical base pairs are often arranged in a non-nested form which generally leads to highly irregular shapes. Comparison of these units in a database of RNA structures revealed segments with highly similar conformations that are localized repeatedly in unrelated molecules [4]. These recurrent structural units are called *RNA motifs*.

Growing set of known RNA motifs has been incorporated into the prediction process by the RNA-MoIP tool [5] which uses motifs to refine structures predicted by algorithms based on the standard model. It identifies motif instances in certain regions of these structures and assign them non-canonical interaction pattern of the motif. This approach facilitates identification of complicated pairing patterns, such as k-way junctions or distant pseudoknots, which are not satisfactorily predicted by majority of existing algorithms. Considering only motifs extracted from known RNA structures allows to avoid prediction artefacts with unnatural shapes.

We propose an improvement of the scoring scheme of the RNA-MoIP method. The original method scores motifs only based on their lengths, whereas we plan to take into account their contribution to free energy reduction. It is the initial step of the series of suggested modifications that have potential to markedly improve the speed and the accuracy of the RNA-MoIP tool.

Acknowledgments. This research is supported by VEGA grant 1/1085/12.

References

[1] M. E. Nebel and F. Weinberg. Algebraic and combinatorial properties of common RNA pseudoknot classes with applications. *Journal of Computational Biology*, 19(10):1134–1150, 2012.

[2] N. B. Leontis and E. Westhof. Geometric nomenclature and classification of RNA base pairs. *RNA (New York, N.Y.)*, 7(4):499–512, 2001.

[3] Ch. H. zu Siederdissen, S. H. Bernhart, P. F. Stadler, and I. L. Hofacker. A folding algorithm for extended RNA secondary structures. *Bioinformatics*, 27(13):i129–i136, 2011.

[4] D. K. Hendrix, S. E. Brenner, S. R. Holbrook, et al. RNA structural motifs: building blocks of a modular biomolecule. *Quarterly reviews of biophysics*, 38(3):221–244, 2005.

[5] V. Reinharz, F. Major, and J. Waldispühl. Towards 3D structure prediction of large RNA molecules: an integer programming framework to insert local 3D motifs in RNA secondary structure. *Bioinformatics*, 28(12):i207–i214, 2012.

ITAT 2013: Workshops, Posters, and Tutorials, pp. 36–41
ISBN 978-1490952086, © 2013 M. Šimaľová

Nussinov folding based simultaneous alignment and folding of RNA sequences

Mária Šimaľová*

Institute of Computer Science
Pavol Jozef Šafárik University in Košice
Jesenná 5, Košice, Slovak Republic
maria.simalova@gmail.com

Abstract: Multiple sequence alignment and RNA folding are two important tasks in the field of bioinformatics. Solving those problems simultaneously leads to biologically more significant results. In this work we describe our simultaneous alignment and folding algorithm, that is a combination of well known Nussinov folding algorithm and Sankoff alignment algorithm and a speed-up for this algorithm that is inspired by the Carrillo-Lipman algorithm for the multiple sequence alignment problem. Except of that we propose the way of using this algorithm even without knowing any suboptimal solution and some possible ways of parallelization that makes it even faster.

Keywords: multiple sequence alignment, RNA folding, simultaneous alignment and folding, parallelization

1 Introduction

Multiple sequence alignments are an essential tool for protein structure and function prediction, phylogeny inference and other common tasks in sequence analysis. The computation of multiple sequence alignment is not a trivial task, because it is hard to precisely define the properties of biologically optimal alignment. The standard computational formulation of the pairwise problem is to identify the alignment that maximizes sequence similarity, which is typically defined as the sum of substitution matrix scores for each aligned pair of residues, minus some penalties for gaps. This approach is generalized to the multiple sequence case by seeking an alignment that maximizes the sum of similarities for all pairs of sequences (the sum-of-pairs, or SP score)[1].

Until now many sequence alignment methods have been proposed. Algorithms based on the SP scores produce a mathematically, but not necessarily biologically exact alignment. A lot of them is based on the dynamic programming methods. Wang & Jiang in 1994 [2] showed that the minimal time and memory required to find the alignment with maximal SP score grows exponentially with growing number of sequences. The basic dynamic programming algorithm finding the pairwise sequence alignment(alignment of two sequences) from Needleman & Wunsch [3] fills in a two dimensional table D where the value of $D[i, j]$ is the maximal possible value of aligning first i bases of R_1 with first j bases of R_2 and has the time

and space complexity of $O(n^2)$. When generalized for N sequences the space complexity grows up to $O(n^N)$ and the time complexity $O(2^N \cdot N^2 \cdot n^N)$.

Carrillo & Lipman proposed heuristic [4] that significantly reduces the time complexity of Needleman-Wunsch algorithm still producing a mathematically optimal alignment.

Another important sign of RNA sequences is their three-dimensional(secondary) structure. It has a functional role for many molecules and since knowing the sequence is not sufficient to determine the structure, it is important to be able to predict the most probable structures.

The two basic dynamic programming algorithms predicting the secondary structure(folding) of RNA were proposed by Nussinov [5] and Zuker [6]. They both have $O(n^3)$ time and $O(n^2)$ space complexity and especially differ in the scoring system used to determine the value of folding. While Nussinov algorithm maximizes the number of base pairs, the Zuker folding algorithm sums up the energy values of smaller substructures of RNA and finds folding with minimal energy.

We can predict the secondary structure much better if we know the alignment of given sequences. And we can find better multiple alignment if we know the consensus secondary structure. Usually we have only sequences and we know neither the alignment nor the secondary structure. If we want to find them both we can use three different approaches:

- Align sequences using classical multiple alignment tools and then predict the structure for found alignment according to structure neutral mutations. This method can be used only if sequences are well conserved. (RNAalifold [7, 8], Pfold [9, 10, 11], ILM [12, 13])

- If sequences are not well conserved, then predict seconadary structure for each sequence separately and directly align the structures(RNA forester [14, 15], MARNA [16, 17])

- Simultaneous alignment and folding(Sankoff [18])

The first two methods can lead to inaccurate results. This is why more complex algorithms were developed, that solves both problems in one time.

Sankoff in 1985 introduced a dynamic programming algorithm [18] that combines the objective functions for

*Supported by the Slovak Scientific Grant Agency VEGA, Grant No. 1/0479/12

alignment and minimal free energy folding to solve the alignment of finite sequences, their folding and the reconstruction of ancestral sequences on a phylogenetic tree. This algorithm is based on Sankoff alignment algorithm ([19]), distance function for evaluating alignments by Sellers ([20, 21]) and on the Zuker and Sankoff paper [22], who synthesize and advance a series of improvements in algorithmic efficiency including Nussinov algorithm and Zuker algorithm.

Ziv-Ukelson et al. in [23] extended the approach from [24] for speeding up the classical Zuker's folding algorithm to speed up the Sankoff's algorithm for simultaneous folding and alignment and get the time complexity of $O(n^4 \cdot \zeta(n))$ for two sequences, where $\zeta(n)$ goes to n for increasing n.

There is also a few heuristic implementations of Sankoff algorithm. One of them is *Foldalign* [25], which uses a combination of clustal [26] and consensus [27] heuristics to build multiple sequence alignment from pair-wise comparison. Foldaling reduces the time complexity to $O(n^4 \cdot N)$ (N is the number of sequences, n is the length of the longest sequence) by restricting maximum motif size and forbidding multiloops. So it can be used only for short sequences without multiloops.

Another heuristic implementation of Sankoff algorithm is *Dynalign* [28], which restricts the difference in indices i and j of aligned nucleotides to be less than M (i is a position in sequence S_1 and j in sequence S_j). It also limits the size of internal loops to get the complexity of $O(n^3 \cdot M^3)$. The disadvantage is that it is only restricted to pairwise sequence comparison.

There is more heuristic algorithms for simultaneous folding and alignment from recent years, that reduce Sankoff's algorithm computational complexity. They can be found for example in Will et al.([29]), Kiryu et al.([30]) and Torarinsson([31]), all from 2007. But also Dowell, 2006([32]) and Holmes([33]), Uzilov et al.([34]), Havgaard et al.([35]) from 2005 and Hofacker et al.,2004([36]).

In the first part of this work, we describe two known algorithms. The Carrilo-Lipman multiple sequence alignment algorithm and the Nussinov folding algorithm. After this we describe our simultaneous alignment and folding algorithm based on the Nussinov folding scheme and application of Carrillo-Lipman heuristic to this algorithm. In the end we propose the way of using this algorithm without any previously known suboptimal alignment and a parallelization speed-up.

2 Carrillo-Lipman

The Carrillo & Lipman [4] algorithm for multiple sequence alignment is dynamically filling in the matrix D using equations from Needleman & Wunsch algorithm [3], but generalized for N sequences. The value of $D[\vec{i}]$ is the maximal possible value of aligning first i_1 bases of R_1 with first i_2 bases of R_2, ... and first i_N bases of R_N.

Let $Perm_N\{0,1\}$ be the set of all permutations of length N from the set $\{0,1\}$. The generalized equation is:

$$D[\vec{i}] = max_{p \in Perm_N\{0,1\}} \begin{cases} D[\overrightarrow{i-p}] + \sum_{j=1}^N p_j * (N - \sum_{j=1}^N p_j) * y \\ + \sum_{m,l \in \{1,...,N\}, p_m = p_l = 1} C(R_{m,i_m}, R_{l,i_l}) \end{cases}$$

$$(1)$$

The idea of Carrillo-Lipman heuristic is to cut off some computations, which we know will never lead to an optimal solution.

If we compute the value of optimal pairwise alignment for all pairs of sequences such that $d_{m,l}[i_m, i_l]$ will be the maximal value for aligning subsequences $R_m[i_m, ..., n_m]$ and $R_l[i_l, ..., n_l]$, then it is obvious that:

$$D[\vec{n}] - \sum_{m=1}^N \sum_{l=1}^N d_{m,l}[i_m, i_l] \leq D[\vec{i}] \qquad (2)$$

Suppose, we have some suboptimal multiple alignment found by any faster heuristic algorithm. Let U be the value of this suboptimal alignment (U is less or equal to the optimal alignment value). If the cell $D[i_1, i_2, ..., i_N]$ will be a part of the optimal solution, then obviously:

$$D[\vec{i}] + \sum_{m=1}^N \sum_{l=1}^N d_{m,l}[i_m, i_l] >= U \qquad (3)$$

So if the condition 3 is not satisfied, then the cell $D[i_1, i_2, ..., i_N]$ is not a part of the optimal solution. Carrillo & Lipman compute the matrix values in the opposite direction. After improving cell $D[i_1, i_2, ..., i_N]$, they improve all cells that can be affected by this change only if it satisfy the condition 3. That allows them to cut off a lot of unnecessary computations.

3 Nussinov folding algorithm

The Nussinov algorithm predicts the secondary structure of RNA by maximizing of the number of base pairs, according to the assumption that the more base pairs contains the sequence the more stable it is.

Let R be the input RNA sequence of length n. The algorithm fills in the matrix F of size $n \cdot n$, where the value of $F[i, j]$ is the maximum number of possible base pairs in subsequence $R[i...j]$. The best structure for subsequence $R[i...j]$ is calculated from the previously calculated best structures for smaller subsequences [37]. There are four following ways to fill in the value of $F[i, j]$:

- Add unpaired base i to the best secondary structure for subsequence $R[i+1, j]$ ($F[i, j] = F[i+1, j]$).

- Add unpaired base j to the best secondary structure for subsequence $R[i, j-1]$ ($F[i, j] = F[i, j-1]$).

- Add base pair (i, j) to the best secondary structure for subsequence $R[i+1, j-1]$ ($F[i, j] = F[i+1, j-1] + \delta(i, j)$, where $\delta(i, j)$ is value of adding this kind of pair).

- Combination of the best secondary substructures for subsequences $R[i, k]$ and $R[k + 1, j]$ for some $k \in \{i + 1, ..., j - 1\}$. ($F[i, j] = F[i, k] + F[k + 1, j]$)

This leads to following equations, where $1 \leq i \leq n$ and $i < j \leq n$:

$$F(i, j) = max \begin{cases} F[i + 1, j] \\ F[i, j - 1] \\ F[i + 1, j - 1] + \delta(i, j) \\ max_{i < k < j}\{F[i, k] + F[k + 1, j]\} \end{cases} \quad (4)$$

$$F(i, i) = F(i, i + 1) = 0 \quad (5)$$

The matrix is filled, beginning with the initialization according to (5) and then computing the lower half from smaller to longer subsequences [37]. After filling the matrix the solution is recieved via backtracking beginning with $F[1, n]$ what is the maximum number of base pairs for the whole sequence. The time complexity of Nussinov algorithm is $O(n^3)$ because of filling in n^2 cells by looking at $O(n)$ cells filled before. The space complexity is $O(n^2)$.

4 Simultaneous alignment and Nussinov folding

Our objective is to explore, whether it is possible to apply the Carrillo-Lipman approach for multiple sequence alignment to speed up simultaneous alignment and folding. We decided to try it at first with the Nussinov folding algorithm. The first step to this is to design an equation for simultaneous alignment and Nussinov folding.

We combine the Sankoff alignment algorithm with Nussinov folding algorithm like Sankoff[18] combined it with Zuker folding algorithm. For two sequences we distinguish five cases when filling in the value of $F[i, j; k, l]$:

- Add pairs of bases i, j and k, l, base i will be aligned to base k and base j will be aligned to base l. Then the value will be computed as sum of the value $F[i + 1, j - 1; k + 1, l - 1]$, the values of created base pairs $\delta(i, j) + \delta(k, l)$, and the value of aligned bases $C(R_{1,i}, R_{2,k}) + C(R_{1,j}, R_{2,l})$

- Align unpaired nucleotides i and k to the best aligned structures of sequences $R_1[i + 1, ..., j]$ and $R_2[k + 1, ..., l]$.

- Align unpaired nucleotides j and l to the best aligned structures of sequences $R_1[i, ..., j - 1]$ and $R_2[k, ..., l - 1]$.

- There are no base pairs in subsequences $R_1[i, ..., j]$ and $R_2[k, ..., l]$ so we have just to compute the value of aligning those sequences.

- Combine two previously computed substructures $F[i, h; k, p]$ and $F[h + 1, j; p + 1, l]$.

This four cases leads to the following equation:

$$F[i, j; k, l] = max \begin{cases} F[i + 1, j - 1; k + 1, l - 1] + \delta(i, j) + \delta(k, l) \\ \quad + C(R_{1,i}, R_{2,k}) + C(R_{1,j}, R_{2,l}) \\ F[i + 1, j; k + 1, l] + C(R_{1,i}, R_{2,k}) \\ F[i, j - 1; k, l - 1] + C(R_{1,j}, R_{2,l}) \\ D[i, j; k, l] \\ max_{i < h < j; k < p < l} F[i, h; k, p] + F[h + 1, j; p + 1, l] \end{cases}$$

$$\quad (6)$$

$$\forall i, j : F[i, i - 1; j, j - 1] = 0 \quad (7)$$

The space complexity here is $O(n^4)$ and the time complexity goes to $O(n^6)$ because of the fifth case.

We can also generalize it for N sequences (8). It needs $O(n^{2 \cdot N})$ space and $O(n^{3 \cdot N})$ time.

$$F[\overrightarrow{i, j}] = max \begin{cases} F[\overrightarrow{i + 1, j - 1}] \\ \quad + \sum_{k=1}^{N} \delta(i_k, j_k) \\ \quad + \sum_{m=1}^{N} \sum_{k=m+1}^{N} (C(R_{m,i_m}, R_{k,i_k}) + C(R_{m,j_m}, R_{k,j_k})) \\ F[\overrightarrow{i + 1, j}] + \sum_{m=1}^{N} \sum_{k=m+1}^{N} C(R_{m,i_m}, R_{k,i_k}) \\ F[\overrightarrow{i, j - 1}] + \sum_{m=1}^{N} \sum_{k=m+1}^{N} C(R_{m,j_m}, R_{k,j_k}) \\ D[\overrightarrow{i, j}] \\ max_{i_m < h_m < j_m} F[\overrightarrow{i, h}] + F[\overrightarrow{h + 1, j}] \end{cases}$$

$$\quad (8)$$

4.1 Applying Carrillo-Lipman approach to simultaneous alignment and Nussinov folding

Suppose we have some suboptimal alignment and folding of sequences $R_1, R_2, ..., R_n$ with value U. We want to apply the Carrillo-Lipman approach to our algorithm. At first we have to find the upper bound for the value of simultaneous alignment and folding. The upper bound of alignment value for subsequences $R_1[0, ..., i_1], R_2[0, ..., i_2], ... , R_N[0, ..., i_N]$ is the sum of maximal pairwise alignments values for all pairs of sequences, same like in Carrillo-Lipman algorithm. The upper bound for simultaneous algorithm will be equal to sum of the upper bound for alignment and the upper bound for secondary structures. The value of secondary structure is added only in the first case. The value of every base pair in every sequence is added exactly once. Let $f_m(i_m, j_m)$ be the value of best secondary structure of subsequence $R_m[0, ..., i_m - 1, j_m + 1, ..., n_m]$. So we can say, that:

$$F[\overrightarrow{0, n}] - \sum_{m=1}^{N} f_m(i_m, j_m) - \sum_{m=1}^{N} \sum_{l=1}^{N} d_{m,l}[i_m, i_l] - \sum_{m=1}^{N} \sum_{l=1}^{N} d'_{m,l}[j_m, j_l] \leq F[\overrightarrow{i, j}]$$

$$\quad (9)$$

The cell $F[\overrightarrow{i, j}]$ can then be excluded from the computation if its value is so small that even if the alignment and folding value of subsequences $R_1[0, ..., i_1, j_1, ..., n_1]$, $R_2[0, ..., i_2, j_2, ..., n_2], ... , R_N[0, ..., i_N, j_N, ..., n_N]$ are maximal:

$$\sum_{m=1}^{N} \sum_{l=m+1}^{N} d_{m,l}[i_m, i_l] + \sum_{m=1}^{N} f_m(i_m, j_m) + \sum_{m=1}^{N} \sum_{l=m+1}^{N} d'_{m,l}[j_m, j_l]$$

$$\quad (10)$$

U	# computed cells	# skipped cells	time
49.0	457 062	9 600 830	335 s
50.0	392 631	9 522 226	218 s
51.0	329 429	9 447 505	163 s
52.0	282 894	9 383 973	126 s
53.0	207 882	9 280 084	97 s
54.0	175 322	9 236 203	84 s
55.0	143 061	9 196 462	75 s
56.0	117 202	9 159 881	68 s
57.0	88 778	9 118 067	65 s
58.0	58 340	9 076 604	61.7 s
59.0	45 948	9 058 582	60.5 s
60.0	36 410	9 046 724	60.2 s
61.0	27 773	9 035 099	60 s
62.0	14 069	9 016 420	59.7 s
63.0	9 301	9 009 240	59.2 s
65.0	3 889	9 002 811	59.1 s
66.0	1 859	9 000 656	59.3 s
67.0	424	8 999 232	59.28 s
69.0	185	8 999 003	59.2 s

Table 1: Computation times for 3 sequences from HIV-1_SD family without parallelization.

then the whole alignment and folding value will be less than U:

$$F[\overrightarrow{i,j}] + \sum_{m=1}^{N} f_m(i_m, j_m) + \sum_{m=1}^{N} \sum_{l=m+1}^{N} d_{m,l}[i_m, i_l] + \sum_{m=1}^{N} \sum_{l=m+1}^{N} d'_{m,l}[j_m, j_l] < U$$
(11)

The preprocessing complexity depends on the heuristical method used for finding the suboptimal alignment and folding. Except of that it needs $O(2 \cdot N^2 \cdot n^2) = O(N^2 \cdot n^2)$ space and $O(2 \cdot N^2 \cdot n^2) = O(N^2 \cdot n^2)$ time for pairwise alignment using Needleman-Wunsch algorithm, and $O(N \cdot n^2 \cdot n^2) = O(N \cdot n^4)$ space and $O(N \cdot n^3)$ time for finding best secondary structure for each sequence using Nussinov algorithm. The most expensive part is computing the Sankoff multiple alignment matrix D. It needs $O(n^{2 \cdot N})$ space and $O(n^{2 \cdot N} \cdot 2^N \cdot N^2)$ time, but it is also a part of the computation of unimproved algorithm.

This approach allows us to simultaneously align and fold sequences in more reasonable time. Testing results for 3 sequences from RNA family HIV-1_SD are in following table. The length of the test sequences was about 19 nucleotides. The algorithm was implemented in Java and tested on 2.30GHz Intel i7 processor with 8 threads.

We can see, that increasing the value of U rapidly decreased the number of computed cells in F. First used value of U (49.0) was the value of multiple alignment($D[\overrightarrow{0,n}]$) computed in preprocessing phase. The value of simultaneous alignment and folding is never less than $D[\overrightarrow{0,n}]$. The best value of simultaneous alignment and folding received was in every case equal to 71.0. The value received by previous algorithm was also equal to 71.0. The preprocessing time was about 45 seconds.

In the beginning of the main computation all cells of D must be checked and all of them that satisfy the condition 11 are inserted to the list of cells to be processed. According to the way of filling the matrix F cells from this list have to be processed in an order of increasing subsequences length. We can obtain this if we use a heap to store cells that have to be processed. That makes the time needed to process one cell $log(M)$ times bigger, where M is the number of cells in heap. But we can see from the table 4.1, that the number of processed cells is decreasing rapidly with increasing U.

Using Carrillo-Lipman approach to simultaneous alignment and Nussinov folding without given bound In table 4.1 we can see, that the main computation time is much smaller than the time of preprocessing for bound close to the result value. Also the number of processed cells in heap is really small for such bound.If we use a bound bigger than the expected result value, then the number of cells in heap will be even smaller and the result value $F[\overrightarrow{0,n}]$ will be null. As we mentioned before, the value of $F[\overrightarrow{0,n}]$ will never be less than the value of $D[\overrightarrow{0,n}]$. That means if we do not have a good bound, we can still use $U = D[\overrightarrow{0,n}]$. But the computation time will not be so good. So we can try it with some bigger bound and if the result is null try it with a bit smaller one like this:

- Preprocessing

- Set $U = C_1 \cdot D[\overrightarrow{0,n}]$, where C_1 is some constant number bigger than one. For example $C_1 = 2$

- Main computation

- If $F[\overrightarrow{0,n}]$ is null, then end. Else $U = U - C_2 \cdot D[\overrightarrow{0,n}]$, where $0 < C_2 < 1$ is some constant number(for example $C_2 = 0.2$) and go back to previous step.

The preprocessing part is done just once. If the value of U is too big, then the number of processed cells is really small, so the time of main computation is not so big. From table 4.1 we can see, that the main computation time for $U \geq 63$ was about 14 seconds. If we use $C_1 = 2$ and $C_2 = 0.2$ then we will try the main computation for $U = 98.0, 78.4$ and 68.8 until we get the result. So the computation time is about $45s + 3 \cdot (14s) = 87s$ and this is a few times smaller than computation time for $U = D[\overrightarrow{0,n}] = 49.0$.

Preprocessing parallelization To speed up the computation it is possible to parallelize each part of preprocessing and the first step of main computation.

- The best secondary structure for each sequence using Nussinov algorithm can be done separately in $O(n^5)$ time.

preprocessing phase	without parallelization	with parallelization
D	44 s	7 s
d, d'	< 1 s	< 1 s
f	< 1 s	< 1 s
adding D	15 s	3 s

Table 2: Preprocessing computation times for 3 sequences from HIV-1_SD family.

- The pairwise alignment using Needleman-Wunsch algorithm, can also be computed separately for each pair of sequences in time $O(n^4)$.

- The Sankoff alignment algorithm used for computing D, can also be parallelized, because the value of $D[\overrightarrow{i,j}]$ depends only on values of $D[\overrightarrow{i,X}]$, where $X \in \{1,..,n\}^N$. So each processor can compute values for different fixed $\overrightarrow{i}$.

- Adding cells from D to heap of cells that have to be processed, can be parallelized by creating more smaller heaps and merging them togehter.

5 Conclusion

In this work we described our algorithm for simultaneous alignment and folding using the Nussinov folding algorithm and a speed-up of this algorithm that cuts off unnecessary computations according to Carrillo-Lipman multiple sequence alignment algorithm. We proposed possible ways of parallelization and using of this algorithm. Our approach leads to an optimal solution of alignment and folding for more than two sequences using the Nussinov scoring scheme for folding in better time than the Sankoff simultaneous alignment and folding algorithm. In our future work we want to find out whether it is possible to use this approach with more complex Zuker folding scheme [22].

References

[1] Edgar R.C., Batzoglou S.: Multiple sequence alignment. Current Opinion in Structural Biology, 16: 368-373, 2006

[2] Wang L., Jiang T.: On the complexity of multiple sequence alignment. J Comput Biol, 1:337-348, 1994

[3] Needleman S.B., Wunsch Ch.D.: A general method applicable to the search for similarities in the amino acid sequence of two proteins. Journal of Molecular Biology, 48: 443-53, 1970

[4] Carrillo H., Lipman D.: The multiple sequence alignment problem in biology. SIAM Journal on Applied Mathematics, 48, 1988

[5] Nussinov, R., et al.: Algorithm for Loop Matching. SIAM Journal on Applied Mathematics 35(1), 1978, p. 68-82

[6] Zuker M., Stiegler P.: Optimal computer folding of large RNA sequences using thermodynamics and auxiliary information., Nucleic Acids Res., 1981, p. 133-148

[7] Hofacker I., Fekete M., Stadler P.: Secondary structure prediction for aligned RNA sequences. Journal of Molecular Biology, 319(5):1059-1066, 2002

[8] RNAalifold: http://www.tbi.univie.ac.at/ ivo/RNA/

[9] Knudsen B., Hein J.: Pfold: RNA secondary structure prediction using stochastic context-free grammars. Nucleic Acids Research, 31(13):3423-3428, 2003

[10] Knudsen B., Hein J.: RNA secondary structure prediction using stochastic context-free grammars and evolutionary history.Bioinformatics, 15(6):446-454, 1999

[11] Pfold: http://www.daimi.au.dk/ compbio/rnafold/

[12] Ruan J., Stormo G., Zhang W: An iterated loop matching approach to the prediction of RNA secondary structures with pseudoknots. Bioinformatics, 20:58-66, 2004

[13] ILM: http://www.cs.wustl.edu/ zhang/projects/rna/ilm/

[14] Hochsmann M., Toller T., Giegerich R., Kurtz S.: Local similarity of RNA secondary structures. Proc of the IEEE Bioinformatics Conference, p.159-168, 2003

[15] RNAforester: http://bibiserv.techfak.uni-bielefeld.de/rnaforester/

[16] Siebert S., Backofen R.: MARNA A server for multiple alignment of RNAs. In Proceedings of the German Conference on Bioinformatics, p.135-140, 2003

[17] MARNA: http://www.bio.inf.uni-jena.de/Software/MARNA/index.html

[18] Sankoff D.: Simultaneous solution of the RNA folding, alignment, and protosequence problems. SIAM J Appl Math 1985, Vol. 45, p. 810-825

[19] Sankoff D.: Matching sequences under deletion/insertion constraints, Proceedings of the National Academy of Sciences (U.S.A.), 1972, Vol. 69, p. 4-6

[20] Sellers P. H.: An algorithm for the distance between two finite sequences, J. Combin. Theory, 1974, Vol. 16, p. 252-258

[21] Sellers P. H.: On the theory and computation of evolutionary distances, SIAM J Appl Math, 1974, Vol. 26, p. 787-793

[22] Zuker M., Sankoff D.: RNA secondary structure and their prediction, Bull. Math. Biol., 1984, Vol. 46, p.591-621

[23] Ziv-Ukelson M., Gat-Viks I., Wexler Y., Shamir R.: A Faster Algotihm for Simultaneous Alignment and Folding of RNA, Journal of Computational Biology, 2010, Vol. 17, Nr. 8

[24] Wexler Y., Zilberstein C., Ziv-Ukelson M.: A Study of Accessible Motifs and RNA Folding Complexity. Journal of Computational Biology, 2007, Vol. 14

[25] Gorodkin J., Heyer L., Stormo G.: Finding the most significant common sequence and structure motifs in a set of RNA sequences. Nucleic Acids Research, 25(18): 3724-3732, 1997

[26] Thompson J.D., Higgins D.G., Gibson T.J.: CLUSTALW: improving the sensitivity of progressive multiple sequence alignment through sequence weighting, position-specific gap penalties and weight matrix choice. Nucleic Acids Res, 22:4673-4680, 1994

[27] Hertz G., Hartzell G., Stormo G.: Identification of consen-

sus patterns in unaligned DNA sequences known to be functionally related. Comput Appl Biosci, 6: 81-92, 1990

[28] Mathews D., Turner D.: Dynalign: An algorithm for finding the secondary structure common to two RNA sequences. Journal of Molecular Biology, 317(2):191-203, 2002

[29] Will S., Reiche K., Hofacker I.L., et al.: Inferring noncoding RNA families and classes by means of genome-scale structure-based clustering. PLOS Comput. Biol, Vol. 3, 2007

[30] Kiryu H., Tabei Y., Kin T., et al.: MURLET: a practical multiple alignmetn tool for structural alignment sequences. Bioinformatics, 23: 1588-1598, 2007

[31] Torarinsson E., Havgaard J.H., Gorodkin J.: Multiple structural alignment and clustering of RNA sequences. Bioinformatics 23:926-932,2007

[32] Dowel R.D., Eddy S.: Efficient pairwise RNA structure prediction and alignment using sequence alignment constraints. BMC Bioinform. 7: 400, 2006

[33] Holmes I.: Accelerated probabilistic inference of RNA structure evolution. BMC Biooinform. 6:73, 2005

[34] Uzilov A.V., Keegan J.M., Mathews D.H.: Detection of non-coding RNAs on the basis predicted secondary structure formation free energy change. BMC Bioinform. 7:173, 2005

[35] Havgaard J.H., Lyngso R.B., Stormo G.D., et al.: Pairwise local structural alignment of RNA sequences with sequence similarity less than 40%. Bioinformatics 21: 1815-1824, 2005

[36] Hofacker I.L., Bernhart S., Stadler P.: Alignment of RNA base pairing probability matrices. Bioinformatics 20: 2222-2227, 2004

[37] Sperschneider V., Sperschneider J., Scheubert L.: Bioinformatics: problem solving paradigms. Springer, 2008

ITAT 2013: Workshops, Posters, and Tutorials, pp. 42–46
ISBN 978-1490952086, © 2013 M. Brázdová, T. Martínek, M. Lexa

In silico search for secondary structures in p53 target genes using R/Bioconductor

Marie Brázdová[1], Tomáš Martínek[2], and Matej Lexa[3]

[1] Biophysical Institute of the Czech Academy of Sciences, Královopolská 135, 61265 Brno, Czech Republic
maruska@ibp.cz
[2] Faculty of Informatics, Masaryk University, Botanická 68a, 60200 Brno, Czech Republic, lexa@fi.muni.cz
[3] Faculty of Information Technology, Brno Technical University, Božetěchova 1/2, 61266 Brno, Czech Republic,
martinto@fit.vutbr.cz

Abstract: p53 is a well-known transcription factor and tumor suppressor, regulating among other processes, the commitment of cells to apoptosis and DNA repair. p53 mutants are often found in cancers of different kinds, either as mutant or misregulated p53. p53 is involved in many other processes and we currently do not understand the full range of its functions. It is known to recognize the p53con sequence by its specific DNA-binding domain (DBD). It is also known to bind DNA non-specifically. This binding has been shown to involve superhelical DNA, more specifically, cruciform, triplex and quadruplex structures. In our laboratories we were intrigued by the possible interplay between non-canonical DNA structure binding and regular p53con binding. In an attempt to clarify this interplay and discover suitable candidate genes for further study, we carried out an in silico study on the human genome. We identified all the occurences of potential cruciform DNA, triplex DNA, quadruplex DNA and p53con recognition sequences in +/-40000 bp regions of known genes. We analyzed this data for statistically significant patterns and combinations of patterns using a small set of available R/Bioconductor packages. This paper describes the computational pipeline designed for this type of studies. We also show preliminary results for selected human sequences.

1 Introduction

The existence of non-canonical DNA (also non-B DNA) with secondary structure different from the B-DNA form described by Crick and Watson [1] has been known for som time now. Cruciform, slipped, triplex or quadruplex DNA has been recognized as a factor in several important biological processes or functions. The structures have the ability to modulate replication [2], transcription [3] or translation [4] of DNA/RNA by mechanisms that may have their origins in times when nucleic acids dominated all life processes [5]. Their possible functions may be globally regulated by the overall topology of DNA in cells, since their existence is thermodynamically possible only above/below certain superhelicity thresholds.

p53 belongs to a small group of proteins capable of non-specifically binding non-B DNA, such as cruciform or quadruplex DNA [6]. Because of its importance as a tu-

mor supressor (in its wt-p53 form) or tumor activator (mut-p53), we would like to better understand the relationship between human p53 function and non-B DNA structures present in the human genome. While many experiments have previously addressed this issue [6][7], we still do not properly understand the interplay between DNA topological status, gene regulation, cell fate and p53.

In this paper, we describe the possibilities for in silico studies of possible relationships by analyzing the human genome sequence or sequences of selected genes and their immediate surroundings. To carry out such study, we take advantage of our own software for detecting potential intramolecular triplexes (H-DNA) and the existing R/Bioconductor framework, to efficiently locate and evaluate all sequences capable of forming non-B DNA or attracting p53 in a more sequence-specific manner.

Using this approach we were able to find over- or under-representation of sequence patterns in the vicinity of gene transcription start sites (TSS) and p53con sequences.

2 Software

2.1 R/Bioconductor

To analyze the human genome, or other sequence set, we employ the R/Bioconductor framework, which has now matured to the point, where we can use R to represent biological sequences, search these sequences, represent the search results, analyze them statistically and visualize the results of the searchs and the statistical analysis. All this can be done with relatively straightforward scripts, using a handful of well integrated R/Bioconductor software packages.

Packages used in this study include:

Biostrings String objects representing biological sequences, and matching algorithms[8]

BSgenome Infrastructure for Biostrings-based genome data packages[9]

BSgenome.Hsapiens.UCSC.hg19 Homo sapiens (Human) full genome (UCSC version hg19)

biomaRt Interface to BioMart databases (e.g. Ensembl, COSMIC ,Wormbase and Gramene)[10]

triplex Search and visualize intramolecular triplex-forming sequences in DNA[11]

GenomicRanges Representation and manipulation of genomic intervals[12]

rtracklayer R interface to genome browsers and their annotation tracks[13]

GenomeGraphs Plotting genomic information from Ensembl[14]

Gviz Plotting data and annotation information along genomic coordinates[15]

Examples of operations that can be carried out in R/Bioconductor to perform non-B DNA structure prediction:

To load a genome we use one of the Bioconductor genome sequence packages.

```
library(BSgenome.Hsapiens.UCSC.hg19)
```

To find all triplexes with score > 24 and length > 7 on chromosome X we call the *triplex.search()* function

```
library(triplex)
t <- triplex.search(Hsapiens[["chrX"]],min_
    score=25,min_len=8)
```

and display the best of them as 2D diagram showing nucleotide connections (triplets).

```
ts <- t[order(score(t),decreasing=TRUE)]
triplex.diagram(ts[1])
```

To export the identified triplexes into a GFF3 file we use the *export()* function from the *rtracklayer* package.

```
gr <- as(t, "GRanges")
library(rtracklayer)
export(gr,"test.gff", version="3")
```

Results can be displayed using *GenomeGraphs* or *Gviz*.

```
plot(coverage(ts[0:length(t)]), type="s", col
    ="grey75")
library(GenomeGraphs)
library(biomaRt)
mart <- useMart("ensembl", dataset = "
    hsapiens_gene_ensembl")

# Set up basic GenomeGraphs annotation tracks
ideog <- makeIdeogram(chromosome = "X")
genomeAxis <- makeGenomeAxis()
genesplus <- makeGeneRegion(start = 0, end =
    62000, strand = "+",
    chromosome = "X", biomart = mart)
genesminus <- makeGeneRegion(start = 0, end =
    62000, strand = "-",
    chromosome = "X", biomart = mart)
```

```
# Set up triplex annotation tracks
tall <- as(t,"GRanges")
ta <- makeAnnotationTrack(
  start = start(tall[which(end(tall)<62000)])
    ,
  end = end(tall[which(end(tall)<62000)]),
  feature = "gene_model",
  dp = DisplayPars(gene_model = "grey")
)

# Plot the entire thing
gdPlot(list(fwd = genesplus, GENES =
    genomeAxis, rev = genesminus,
  h-dna = ta, chrX = ideog), minBase = 0,
  maxBase = 62000, labelRot = 0)
```

2.2 Triplex

Searching for sequences supporting quadruplexes or representing a potential p53con binding site can be acheived by employing regular expression matching already present in R/Bioconductor packages. However, identification of palindromes and intramolecular triplexes (H-DNA) requires specialized algorithms based on dynamic programming (DP) not previously existent as R packages.

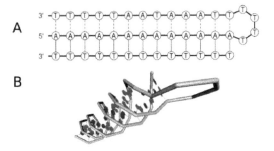

Figure 1: (A) 2D diagram and (B) 3D model of one of the best scored triplex

Recognizing the need for specialized triplex-searching software, we previously designed an algorithm for this purpose and implemented it in the *triplex* program [16]. Recently, we transformed this software into a fully integrated R/Bioconductor package of the same name [11]. The package can be freely downloaded from the Bioconductor web site (http://bioconductor.org/packages/release/bioc/ html/triplex.html). The *triplex.search()* function applies a DP algorithm to DNA sequences to identify mirror repeats and similar structures with the maximal possible number of valid nucleotide triplets. The most common triplets in known H-DNA structures are T.A:T, G.T:A and C.G:C for parallel triplexes and T.A:T, A.A:T and G.G:C for antiparallel triplexes (. - Hoogsteen pair; : - Watson-Crick pair). Identified sequences with high score are likely to form intramolecular triplexes (H-DNA). They can be displayed as diagrams or 3D models with appropriate visualization functions from the *triplex* package (Figure 1).

3   Methods

In this particular study, the following code was used to search for p53con sites in the entire human genome

```
hgenome <- BSgenome.Hsapiens.UCSC.hg19
gr_p53cons <- GRanges()
for (i in c(seq(22), "Y", "X")) {

  chr_name <- paste("chr",i,sep="")
  print(chr_name)
  chr <- hgenome[[chr_name]]

  p53_half <- matchPattern("RRRCWWGYYY", chr,
      max.mismatch=1, fixed=FALSE)
  p53_gaps <- gaps(p53_half)
  hits <- which(width(p53_gaps) <= 18)
  if(length(hits) > 0) {
    p53 <- p53_gaps[hits]
    start(p53) <- start(p53)-10
    end(p53) <- end(p53)+10
    gr <- GRanges(seqnames=chr_name, ranges=
        ranges(p53), strand="*")
    print(length(gr))


    gr_p53cons <- c(gr_p53cons, gr)
  }
}
save(gr_p53cons, file="p53cons.RData")
```

To search for quadruplexes, we applied the following function to both strands of every human chromosome. The constructed regular expression matches consecutive runs of Gs with adequate spacing (*loop_min, loop_max*).

```
get_strand_quadruplexes <- function(seq,
   seqname, strand, g_min, g_max, loop_min,
   loop_max) {
  symbol <- if (strand == "+") "G" else "C"
  gr_gg <- GRanges()
  for (g_len in seq(g_min, g_max)) {
    pattern <- paste("(",symbol,"{",g_len,"
        }.{",loop_min,",",loop_max,"}){3,}",
        symbol,"{",g_len,"}",sep="")

    ggroups <- gregexpr(pattern, seq, ignore.
        case=T)
    if(as.vector(ggroups[[1]])[1] != -1) {
      ir_gg <- IRanges(start=as.vector(
          ggroups[[1]]), width=attr(ggroups
          [[1]], "match.length"))

      gr_gg <- union(gr_gg, GRanges(seqnames=
          seqname, ranges=ir_gg, strand=
          strand))
    }
  }
  gr_gg
}
```

To limit the sets only to matches in close vicinity of annotated genes, we used the following code.

```
load("bm_genes.RData")
gr_tss <- get_tss_gr(bm_genes)
tss_p53con_hits <- distanceToNearest(gr_tss,
    gr_p53cons, ignore.strand=TRUE)
tss_p53con_dist <- as.data.frame(tss_p53con_
    hits)$distance
gr_p53cons_genes <- gr_p53cons[subjectHits(
    tss_p53con_hits)[which(tss_p53con_dist <
    40000)]]
save(gr_p53cons_genes, file="p53cons_genes.
    RData")
```

A special function was used to ranomize positions and save them in the same GRanges format used above for triplexes and quadruplexes.

```
gr_randomize <- function(gr) {
  gr_rand <- GRanges()
  for(i in c(seq(22), "X", "Y")) {
    chr_name <- paste("chr",i,sep="")
    gr_chr <- gr[seqnames(gr) == chr_name]
    if (length(gr_chr) > 0) {
      chr_len <- seqlengths(hgenome)[which(
          names(seqlengths(hgenome)) == chr_
          name)]
      new_start <- sample(1:chr_len, length(
          gr_chr))
      gr_chr_rand <- shift(gr_chr, new_start-
          start(ranges(gr_chr)))
      gr_rand <- c(gr_rand, gr_chr_rand)
    }
  }
  gr_rand
}
```

Supporting functions and additional source code used in plotting and summarizing the results, including data files with genome search results are available at http://www.fi.muni.cz/ lexa/itat_2013.

4   Results

In a preliminary test we applied the approach and code listed above to gene-neighboring regions of known human genes. We used *biomaRt* to download annotation data for human genes and determine the most likely transcription start site (TSS). We searched the +/-40000bp of the human genome surrounding the TSS for occurrences of p53con sequences and close-by sequences supporting the formation of non-B DNA (palindromes, triplexes, quadruplexes). When distribution of these sites was compared with the corresponding random distributions, we recognized differences between the two in the case of quadruplexes and triplexes. While triplex-supporting sequences were depleted in the immediate vicinity (+/- 1000 bp) of the respective p53con (Figure 2), quadruplexes behaved in the opposite way. They were more frequently found close to p53con or the TSS (Figure 3).

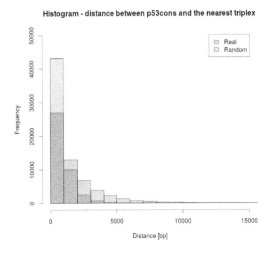

Figure 2: Statistical distribution of p53con site distances from the nearest potential triplex DNA. There is a depletion of triplex DNA in the +/- 1000 bp neighborhood of p53con.

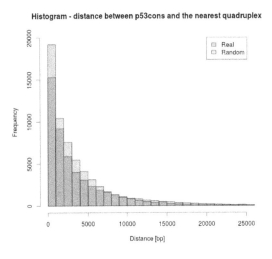

Figure 3: Statistical distribution of p53con site distances from the nearest potential quadruplex DNA. There is an enrichment of quadruplex DNA in the +/- 1000 bp neighborhood of p53con.

5 Discussion

We have reviewed the problem of non-B DNA prediction from sequence by computational means using R/Bioconductor. With a combination of available packages, we were able to identify the most likely candidates for non-B DNA structure formation in DNA sequences of our choice. The R/Bioconductor framework provides a convenient environment for the necessary searches and visualization of the results.

When applied to genes of the entire human genome, we witnessed a non-random distribution of some of the potential non-B DNA structures in gene regulatory regions, es-

pecially the promoter and the 1st intron (data not shown). We are particularly interested to see if any such patterns prove to be associated with p53-regulated genes. Studies like the one outlined here provide biologically interesting hypotheses that can be tested experimentally or in a more elaborate *in silico* study. A good selection of appropriate R/Bioconductor packages allows us to concentrate on identification of ad-hoc patterns without the need of writing excessive amounts of code.

6 Acknowledgements

This work was supported by 13-36108S (Grant Agency of Science of CR) to M.B., by the project "CEITEC - Central European Institute of Technology" (CZ.1.05/1.1.00/02.0068) from European Regional Development Fund to M.L., by IT4Innovations project, reg. no. CZ.1.05/1.1.00/02.0070 funded by the EU Operational Programme 'Research and Development for Innovations', by MSMT Grant No.0021630528 "Security-Oriented Research in Information Technology" and by BUT grant FIT-S-11-1 "Advanced secured, reliable and adaptive IT".

References

[1] Watson, J.D. and Crick, F.H.C.: A structure for deoxyribose nucleic acid. Nature **171** (1953) 737-738

[2] Dixon, B.P., Lu, L., Chu, A. and Bissler, J.J.: RecQ and RecG helicases have distinct roles in maintaining the stability of polypurine.polypyrimidine sequences. Mutat Res **643** (2008) 20–28

[3] Rich, A. and Zhang, S.: Timeline: Z-DNA: the long road to biological function. Nat Rev Genet **4** (2003) 566-72.

[4] Arora,A., Dutkiewicz, M. and Scaria, V.: Inhibition of translation in living eukaryotic cells by an RNA G-quadruplex motif. RNA **14** (2008) 1290–1296

[5] Bacolla, A. and Wells, R.D.: Non-B DNA Conformations, Genomic Rearrangements, and Human Disease. Journal of Biological Chemistry **279** (2004) 47411-47414.

[6] Göhler, T., Jäger, S., Warnecke, G., Yasuda, H., Kim, E. and Deppert, W.: Mutant p53 proteins bind DNA in a DNA structure-selective mode Nucleic Acids Research **33** (2005) 1087-1100.

[7] Quante, T., Otto, B., Brázdová, M., Kejnovská, I., Deppert, W., Tolstonog, G.V.: Mutant p53 is a transcriptional cofactor that binds to G-rich regulatory regions of active genes and generates transcriptional plasticity. Cell Cycle **11** (2012) 3290-3303.

[8] Pages, H., Aboyoun, P., Gentleman, R. and DebRoy, S.: Biostrings: String objects representing biological sequences, and matching algorithms. R package version 2.26.3.

[9] Pages, H.: BSgenome: Infrastructure for Biostrings-based genome data packages. R package version 1.26.1

[10] Durinck, S., Spellman, P.T., Birney, E. and Huber, W.: Mapping identifiers for the integration of genomic datasets with the R/Bioconductor package biomaRt. Nature Protocols **4** (2009) 1184-1191.

[11] Hon, J., Martinek, T., Rajdl, K. and Lexa, M.: Triplex: an R/Bioconductor package for identification and visualization of potential intramolecular triplex patterns in DNA sequences. Bioinformatics (in press).

[12] Aboyoun, P., Pages, H. and Lawrence, M.: GenomicRanges: Representation and manipulation of genomic intervals. R package version 1.10.7.

[13] Lawrence, M., Gentleman, R. and Carey, V.: rtracklayer: an R package for interfacing with genome browsers. Bioinformatics **25** (2009) 1841-1842.

[14] Durinck, S. and Bullard, J.: GenomeGraphs: Plotting genomic information from Ensembl. R package version 1.18.0.

[15] Hahne, F., Durinck, S., Ivanek, R., Mueller, A. and Lianoglou, S.: Gviz: Plotting data and annotation information along genomic coordinates. R package version 1.2.1.

[16] Lexa, M., Martinek, T., Burgetova, I., Kopecek, D. and Brazdova, M.: A dynamic programming algorithm for identification of triplex-forming sequences. Bioinformatics **27** (2011) 2010-2017.

ITAT

RNArobo: Fast RNA Motif Search
(Abstract)

Ladislav Rampášek[1,3], Andrej Lupták[2], Tomáš Vinař[3], and Broňa Brejová[3]

[1] Department of Computer Science, University of Toronto, Toronto, ON M5R 3G4 Canada
[2] Department of Pharmaceutical Sciences, Chemistry and Molecular Biology, University of California, Irvine,
2141 Natural Sciences 2, Irvine, CA 92697
[3] Faculty of Mathematics, Physics, and Informatics, Comenius University, Mlynská Dolina, 842 48 Bratislava, Slovakia

RNA sequences are generally more conserved in their structure than in sequence. Thus to find RNAs related to a known example, we look for sequences capable of assuming appropriate secondary structure. We investigate the problem of RNA motif search based on user-defined descriptors. RNA motif descriptors specify restrictions on base-pairing structure of the target RNA, as well as sequence constraints characterizing conserved functional sites. As opposed to popular fully-automated systems based on probabilistic models, this approach allows expert human users to handcraft motif descriptors and highlight the most important features of the target RNAs, thus better targeting a particular biological phenomenon.

The problem of descriptor-based RNA-motif search is NP-hard [1]. Nevertheless, effective search methods have been developed using either backtracking (e.g., RNAMot [2]), non-deterministic finite-state automata with node rewriting (e.g. RNAbob [3]), or dynamic programming for structures without pseudoknots (e.g. Locomotif [4]). Most of the other tools are based on one of these ideas, differing in descriptor capabilities and post-processing options; extensive review can be found in [5].

Our new tool, RNArobo, builds on the descriptor format of RNAbob and employs the backtracking algorithm of RNAMot. We improve these tools in two ways. First, we extend the RNAbob descriptor format to allow insertions, which is very useful for RNA structures that tolerate bulges in their helices. Our main contribution, however, is a technique for improving the running time of the backtracking algorithm.

The performance of backtracking depends greatly on ordering of elements in the search. Each RNA structure descriptor consists of several structural elements. In our algorithm, individual elements are aligned to the DNA sequence by dynamic programming, with backtracking guiding the search for successive elements to appropriate locations with respect to the already matched elements.

Ideally, the first elements will have few matches, filtering out most of the sequence from further processing. Such filtering is a common theme in many text search methods, such as the popular sequence similarity search tool BLAST [6]. Different element orderings in the backtracking search result in significant differences in running time. Finding the best ordering is an interesting and non-trivial problem, due to complex dependencies between locations of individual element. We approach this as an on-line problem, using the observed performance of the search so far to adjust ordering on-the-fly.

Using several realistic motif descriptors on the whole human genome, we demonstrate that for complex descriptors our strategy leads to a significant reduction in running time compared to existing tools RNAbob 2.2 (1999) [3] and RNAmotif 3.0.7 (2010) [7]. Our software tool RNArobo is available at http://compbio.fmph.uniba.sk/rnarobo

Acknowledgments. This research was supported by VEGA grant 1/1085/12.

References

[1] L. Rampášek. RNA structural motif search is NP-complete. In *Proceedings of the Student Science Conference 2011, Faculty of Mathematics, Physics and Informatics, Comenius University in Bratislava*, pages 341–348, 2011. http://compbio.fmph.uniba.sk/svk2011/svk2011-zbornik.pdf.

[2] D. Gautheret, F. Major, and R. Cedergren. Pattern searching/alignment with RNA primary and secondary structures: an effective descriptor for tRNA. *Comput Appl Biosci*, 6(4):325–31, 1990.

[3] S.R. Eddy. RNABob: a program to search for RNA secondary structure motifs in sequence databases. unpublished, 1996.

[4] J. Reeder, J. Reeder, and R. Giegerich. Locomotif: from graphical motif description to RNA motif search. *Bioinformatics*, 23(13):i392–i400, 2007.

[5] A. D. George and S. A. Tenenbaum. Informatic resources for identifying and annotating structural RNA motifs. *Mol Biotechnol*, 41(2):180–93, 2009.

[6] S. F. Altschul, W. Gish, W. Miller, E. W. Myers, and D. J. Lipman. Basic local alignment search tool. *Journal of Molecular Biology*, 215(3):403–410, 1990.

[7] T. J. Macke, D. J. Ecker, R. R. Gutell, D. Gautheret, D. A. Case, and R. Sampath. RNAMotif, an RNA secondary structure definition and search algorithm. *Nucl. Acids Res.*, 29(22):4724–4735, 2001.

ITAT 2013: Workshops, Posters, and Tutorials, pp. 48–55
ISBN 978-1490952086, © 2013 M. Anděl, J. Kléma, Z. Krejčík

Integrating mRNA and miRNA expression with interaction knowledge to differentiate myelodysplastic syndrome

Michael Anděl[1], Jiří Kléma[1], and Zdeněk Krejčík[2]

[1] Department of Computer Science and Engineering, Prague, Czech Republic,
{andelmi2,klema}@fel.cvut.cz,
[2] Institute of Hematology and Blood Transfusion, Prague, Czech Republic,
zdenek.krejcik@uhkt.cz

Abstract: Onset and progression of a genetically conditioned disease depend not only on genes themselves, but mainly on their expression during transcriptional and proteosynthetic process. Monitoring gene expression merely at its transcription level often proves insufficient for an automated disease understanding and prediction. An integration of diverse high-throughput measurements and prior knowledge is needed to capture gene expression in a holistic way. In this paper, we apply a recent matrix factorization integration method to build a plausible and comprehensive predictive model of an outcome or progress of myelodysplastic syndrome, a blood production disease often progressing to leukemia. We propose an efficient learning methodology that enables to maximize predictive performance and keep the main assets of the original method. The resulting model shows a comparable predictive accuracy with a straightforward data integration method while being more understandable and compact. The identified gene expression regulatory units with the best predictive performance will be subject of further biological analysis.

1 Introduction

A lot of severe diseases are genetically conditioned. The outcome or progress of such a disease depends not only on the patient's genome, but also on the manifestation of certain genes. The overall gene activity during the transcriptional-translational process is called *gene expression* (GE). It is the process through which genes synthesize their products and afflict the phenotype. It is possible to sense the activity of a gene as the measured amount of gene transcripts during its expression process. Current technological progress enables to measure the activity of thousands of genes simultaneously in one tissue sample. One may so feel being capable of predicting the disease outcome, progress or related issues based on acquired *gene expression data* [7]. In other words, to build a molecular classifier with particular genes as features, gene expression levels as feature values and phenotype as target variable.

Nevertheless, recent studies suggest that such a molecular classifier based solely on GE data is often not sufficiently accurate nor understandable [5]. The lack of accuracy can be caused by technical difficulties such as the noise in data as well as immense number of features. Too many features may lead to overfitting, not to mention the features are often redundant, irrelevant or highly dependent. As a reaction to this observation, the prevailing trend in GE data classification is focused on considering entire sets of genes rather than particular genes as the features [1, 8, 11, 15]. The gene sets are related to known or yet unknown biological processes as gene transcription regulation or metabolic pathways. Current effort is to reformulate GE features to gene sets and build models upon whole biological processes. Resulting models should be more precise, robust and, of course, biologically meaningful and more understandable for the experts.

But still, the results of set-level models may turn out disappointing. Gene expression is a complex process with multiple phases and components, which makes measurement of gene activity non-trivial. The acquired data are often confusing in their nature and difficult to interpret and apply. Current molecular biology addresses this difficulty through monitoring the activity of gene expression within multiple components at more stages of the process. The multilevel measurement of GE results in potentially more informative, but much larger data. Therefore another challenge for data analysis raises. A meaningful and comprehensive integration of multiple measurements or multiple data sources is desirable.

In this work we propose a robust classification framework for knowledge-based integration of molecular expression data. Currently, our quantitative measurements cover two fundamental transcript types: messenger RNA (mRNA) and microRNA (miRNA), both the crucial components of the overall gene expression process. mRNA serves as a carrier of genetic information from DNA to proteins. miRNA is a small non-coding molecule acting in transcriptional and post-transcriptional regulation, often hastening mRNA degradation and inhibiting translation of a complementary mRNA into protein. Our challenge is to integrate the measurements of these different types of ribonucleic acids in a biologically meaningful way with great regard to the predictive accuracy of resulting models. The integration is driven by the existing knowledge on miRNA targets and gene-gene interactions. The ultimate goal is a valid and robust decision support tool for immediate use in clinical or experimental practice.

The framework is tested on a particular domain of *myelodysplastic syndrome* (MDS) [23]. The data were provided by the Institute of Hematology and Blood Transfusion in Prague. MDS obstructs blood stem cells in bone marrow from maturation, resulting in shortage of healthy blood cells. Consequent symptoms are anemia, increased susceptibility to bleeding and infection. What is more, great deal of MDS patients progress to treatment resistant acute myeloid leukaemia. Although many patients are asymptotic, the leukaemia may come out, though. Another issue, reflected in the data is the *chromosome 5q deletion syndrome (del(5q))*. del(5q) has similar symptoms as MDS, but mostly does not result in leukaemia. Therefore the del(5q) patients without MDS require different treatment than those with MDS. If this is not confusing enough, del(5q) may progress in MDS. It is evident, that sharp discrimination between healthy and afflicted patients and between the above-mentioned syndromes is needed.

2   Domain description and formalization

Gene expression is the overall process of transferring information from the genome towards the tangible signs of the individual, which are generally called *phenotype*. During the process, the gene is firstly transcribed into the molecule of *messenger* RNA (mRNA), which subsequently migrates towards the ribosomes, where it is translated to a protein. The protein levels determine the final phenotype. GE is most often monitored in its transcriptional phase since the transcript level is easiest to measure. The phenotype prediction stems from the basic assumption that a higher amount of detected mRNA implies a higher amount of translated protein, and therefore higher manifestation of respective gene. Currently the most popular methods for measuring expression level of the genes are the *microarray* and *RNA-Seq* technologies, which enable measuring the activity of thousands of genes in parallel.

As mentioned before, cellular pathology is still not well explored, and therefore it is often unclear which of the thousands of genes are disease related. Analyzing them all may lead to overfitting. What is more, the phenotype is not afflicted by the genes separately, but there is a complex synergy of involved genes. The expression activities of particular genes are often linked together, while *transcription factor* (proteomic functional product), synthesized according to one gene, may control, i.e. *upregulate* or *downregulate*, the transcription of several other genes. That is why one aims at analyzing GE data in terms of *gene sets* or *functional units*, based on gene regulatory networks. The gene-gene interaction networks are *partially* discovered and stored in genomic knowledge bases. The GE data are reformulated in new features, corresponding to the gene sets or heterogeneous biological process units, with the aid of certain genes function already known. The prior (background) knowledge is utilized to control or validate the discovery of novel knowledge. Its application results in more accurate, robust and biologically plausible predictive and descriptive models.

However, correlation between the amount of mRNA as the gene transcription product and the amount of protein as the gene translation product is often much weaker than expected [17, 25]. For that reason the attempt to improve model accuracy through gene set features may often fail. Gene expression process is subdued to more regulatory mechanisms than protein-gene *pre-transcriptional* regulation mentioned above. One of the essentials is gene *post-transcriptional* inhibition through *miRNA*. miRNA regulators are short (22-nt long RNA) sequences of noncoding RNA with crucial role in GE process. Despite its undeniable impact, miRNA was discovered not long ago [16], hence it is subject of intensive biological interest. The molecule of miRNA binds to mRNA molecule, suppressing its further functions. The amount of transcribed mRNA is thus reduced, and the expression of corresponding gene is put down. Malfunction of even one miRNA sequence regulator may cause a severe disease [19]. It is not an easy quest for molecular biologists [12] and bioinformaticians [26] to determine which mRNA sequences target a particular gene. This research is referred to as *target prediction*, an increasing number of the validated and predicted miRNA-gene interactions is available in public target databases such as [6, 24]. The amount of miRNA is measured by miRNA microarrays working in the analogous way as mRNA microarrays. Still more labs issue the miRNA measurements along with the common mRNA profiles in order to capture GE process at more levels and in a broader systematic view [18].

Nevertheless, in order to exhaustively utilize all the advantages contained in simultaneous measurement of mRNA and miRNA expression levels (features) on the same set of samples, one needs to engage the prior knowledge about the *interaction* between particular miRNA and mRNA molecules respectively. One miRNA sequence can target a mRNA code associated with more genes and contrariwise, one gene can be regulated by more miRNAs. Henceforth, the analysis of GE data must be led through entire gene-miRNA *modules* (regulatory units). The integration of mRNA and miRNA features is a non-trivial task due to several reasons: a) the relationship between miRNAs and genes is many-to-many, so the brute force search in known or possible interactions would lead to combinatorial explosion, b) many miRNA-gene interactions are false positive, all the miRNA sequences have not even been discovered, c) little is known about the shape, role and occurrence of modules in the miRNA-gene regulation system. Accordingly, an intelligent method of miRNA and mRNA feature integration should consider the known miRNA-gene interactions and confirm them based on measured data. Finally, based on relevant interactions it would identify present GE regulatory modules. As for the purpose of classification, the last but not least task is to reformulate the data samples in terms of learned modules.

Our challenge is to provide such an integration method for the myelodysplastic syndrome data, acquired through mRNA and miRNA microchips. The method should take into account the recent knowledge and model the regulatory function units with subsequent use in diagnostic or treatment classification tasks. Let $\mathscr{G} = \{g_1, ..., g_{M^g}\}$ be a the genes, whose expression activity is sensed through the mRNA microarray platform, $\mathscr{R} = \{r_1, ..., r_{M^\mu}\}$ be known miRNA sequences detected through the miRNA platform, $\mathscr{S} = \{s_1, ..., s_N\}$ be the interrogated samples (tissues, patients) and $\mathscr{U} = \{u_1, ..., u_K\}$ be GE regulatory units or biological processes. Then $x^g : \mathscr{G} \times \mathscr{S} \to \mathbb{R}$ is the activity of measured genes within particular samples *in terms of mRNA*, $x^\mu : \mathscr{R} \times \mathscr{S} \to \mathbb{R}$ is the activity of measured miRNA regulators within the samples. $\mathscr{I} : \mathscr{G} \times \mathscr{G} \to \mathbb{B}$ represents known protein-gene regulatory network. The network can be seen as a graph with the genes as vertices and the *known* interactions as edges. $\mathscr{C} : \mathscr{R} \times \mathscr{G} \to \mathbb{B}$ represents the known miRNA-gene control system. It can be interpreted as a bipartite graph, with the genes and miRNAs as vertices and interactions between miRNA regulators and targeted genes. The integration method should take into account these four data sources and knowledge inputs respectively and provide an output in the form $z : \mathscr{R} \times \mathscr{G} \times \mathscr{S} \times \mathscr{U} \to \mathbb{R}$, i.e. the *virtual expression* of the entire set of miRNA-gene regulatory modules.

3 Related work

The most straightforward and intuitive way to integrate the data from mRNA and miRNA platforms, measured on the *same* set of samples, is a mere concatenation of these two sets of RNA profiles for each sample [13]. The miRNA measurements are viewed as just another kind of features besides the mRNA profiles. But the data integrated in such a *blind* way are unsurprisingly larger than simple mRNA data sets, and thus liable to overfitting or noise as mentioned above, not to mention poor interpretability of the resulting model. Additionally, certain gene features (mRNA) and miRNA features are highly associated as miRNA performs the regulation of gene expression. But these relations may not be visible in the data, as miRNA inhibition of a gene displays more in the amount of the synthesized protein, rather than in the momentary concentration of its transcript (mRNA). Therefore the utilization of the known miRNA-gene interactions is advisable.

[9] presents an interesting tool for inferring a disease specific miRNA-gene regulatory network, based on prior knowledge and user data (miRNA and mRNA profiles). However, this method does not address the way to break down the large inferred network into smaller regulatory units, which are essential for subsequent classification. The method of *data specific* identification of miRNA-gene regulatory modules is proposed in [20] and [22], where the modules are searched as maximal bi-cliques or induced as decision rules respectively. But none of these methods gives an intuitive way to *express* the identified modules within the sample set. Contrariwise, [10] provides a black box integration procedure for several data sources

as mRNAs, miRNAs, methylation data etc., with an immediate classification output. Nevertheless, this method has no natural interpretation of the learned predictive models, which is unsuitable for an expert decision-making tool. [27] presents a computational framework for integration of multiple types of genomic data to identify miRNA-gene regulatory units by the means of multiple *nonnegative matrix factorization* (NMF). Unlike the other above-mentioned methods, the multiple NMF-based framework utilizes the gene-gene interaction knowledge as well as the miRNA-gene interactions. The identified GE regulatory units thus consist both of the miRNA-gene regulatory module and the gene-gene regulatory module. The authors evaluate their resulting *co-modules* in terms of biological relevance, enrichment analysis but not as to the predictive accuracy. However, NMF is an intuitive method of data modeling with a direct sample transformation to the new feature space.

4 Materials and methods

For the reasons mentioned above, the first step in seeking a way for integration and classification of MDS data will be *sparse network regularized multiple nonnegative matrix factorization* (SNMNMF) from [27]. This section briefly describes the family of NMF methods in general and specifies the applied SNMNMF method. Finally, the SNMNMF application in classification is explained.

4.1 NMF

NMF [14] is a class of methods for data modeling and approximation widely used in other machine learning applications such as computer vision, text mining. Let $\mathbf{X}^g \in \mathbb{R}^{N \times M^g}$ be a data matrix of gene expression, measured as amount corresponding mRNAs, with N samples and M^g features (genes), x_{ij} be expression of gene g_j in sample s_i. NMF then approximates the data as a linear combination of K feature subsets $\mathbf{X}^g \approx \mathbf{WH}$, with $\mathbf{H} \in \mathbb{R}^{K \times M^g}$ a soft membership assigning the features into K feature subsets or modules and $\mathbf{W} \in \mathbb{R}^{N \times K}$ the weight matrix assigning a weight w_{ij} to each j-th feature subset within i-th sample. The of $\mathbf{W}$ are commonly understood as the data samples in the new feature (module) representation [21].

Computation of the matrices W and H is formulated as an optimization problem. The objective is some kind of metric between the original data matrix $\mathbf{X}$ and its approximation $\mathbf{WH}$. The basic constraint is the nonnegativity $\mathbf{W}, \mathbf{H} \geq 0$. Due to such a vague definition of NMF there is really huge amount of factorization methods and appropriate optimization algorithms.

4.2 SNMNMF

Let $\mathbf{X}^g \in \mathbb{R}^{N \times M^g}$ be a data matrix of gene (mRNA) expression and $\mathbf{X}^\mu \in \mathbb{R}^{N \times M^\mu}$ be a data matrix of miRNA activity, with N samples and M^g genes and M^μ miRNA regulators. The multiple matrix factorization models these data as a linear combination of K gene-gene regulatory modules $\mathbf{H}^g \in \mathbb{R}^{K \times M^g}$ and K miRNA-gene regulatory modules $\mathbf{H}^\mu \in \mathbb{R}^{K \times M^\mu}$ [27], i.e. $\mathbf{X}^\mu = \mathbf{WH^g}$ and $\mathbf{X}^\mu = \mathbf{WH}^\mu$ respectively. The unification of k-th gene-gene module and k-th miRNA-gene module constitutes a miRNA-gene regulatory *comodule*. The weight of k-th comodule in n-th data sample encodes matrix $\mathbf{W} \in \mathbb{R}^{N \times K}$.

SNMNMF factorizes both data matrices in parallel, while the prior knowledge is incorporated to the factorization through network regularization constraints. The overall minimized objective function looks as follows [27]:

$$\|\mathbf{X}^g - \mathbf{WH}^g\|_F^2 + \|\mathbf{X}^\mu - \mathbf{WH}^\mu\|_F^2$$
$$-\lambda_g Tr\left(\mathbf{H}^g \mathbf{AH}^{gT}\right) - \lambda_\mu Tr\left(\mathbf{H}^\mu \mathbf{BH}^{gT}\right)$$
$$+\gamma_1 \|\mathbf{W}\|_F^2 + \gamma_2 \left(\sum \left\|h_j^\mu\right\|_F^2 + \sum \left\|h_j^g\right\|_F^2\right),$$

where $\mathbf{A} \in \mathbb{B}^{M^g \times M^g}$ is the gene-gene regulatory network matrix, with $a_{ij} = 1$ if and only if the i-th gene and j-th gene interact, $\mathbf{B} \in \mathbb{B}^{M^\mu \times M^g}$ is the miRNA-gene regulatory network matrix, with $b_{ij} = 1$ if and only if i-th miRNA regulates j-th gene, h_j^μ and h_j^g are the j-th column of $\mathbf{H}^\mu$ and $\mathbf{H}^g$ respectively. The third and fourth terms of the objective introduce the prior knowledge, i.e. λ_μ and λ_g encode the strength of *known* miRNA-gene ($\mathbf{B}$) and gene-gene ($\mathbf{A}$) interactions, respectively. The fifth term limits the growth of $\mathbf{W}$, while the last one encourages sparsity. The objective function is minimized by gradient descent through alternating updates of $\mathbf{W}$ and $\mathbf{H}$s [27]. λ_μ, λ_g, γ_1 and γ_2 are the unknown parameters of the model.

4.3   Classification framework

Although SNMNMF was not primarily intended as a *feature extraction* method with subsequent classification, its use in predictive modeling is intuitive. As the weight matrix $\mathbf{W}$ represents activity of the comodules in particular sample, it may be considered as a projection onto a new feature (comodule) space. Nevertheless, in order to avoid selection bias, while estimating the classification error over the transformed data, one must not incorporate the testing samples into the process of integration parametrization. In the other words, matrix factorization has to be performed on training data only, whereas the testing data are projected into the factorization just learned. Therefore a projection of testing data into the existing transformation (factorization) is needed. Such a projection, we used, is quite intuitive, though. The comodules encoded in matrices $\mathbf{H}^g$ and $\mathbf{H}^\mu$, are learned on training data through the iterative updates, alternating with updates of weight matrix $\mathbf{W}$. Subsequently, the comodule matrices learned are fixed and freshly initialized weight matrix $\mathbf{W}_{test}$ is computed by updating *only* $\mathbf{W}_{test}$ based on *test* data and fixed matrices $\mathbf{H}^g$ and $\mathbf{H}^\mu$. $\mathbf{W}_{test}$ is then considered as the test data in comodule feature space.

SNMNMF seems to be suitable for classification tasks thanks to its natural interpretability, intuitive test data pro-

jection and plausible incorporation of prior knowledge. However, its stability with regards to the random initialization of matrix factors and parameter settings remains debatable. Another challenge is the choice of proper number of comodules K, the metaparameter of the algorithm. We set K as the number of "natural" clusters in the miRNA profiles. In order to find this number, we clustered the miRNA profiles by k-means algorithm and set the number of clusters based on Hartigan heuristic, i.e. the sharpest decline of clustering homogeneity. This choice was done independently in each of 10 tasks.

5   Experiments

In this section, we describe the available MDS data and specify the experimental protocol that allows us to set the internal parameters of SNMNMF and evaluate its predictive potential in an unbiased way. Finally, the results and their possible biological interpretation will be discussed.

5.1   Data

The data provided by the Institute of Hematology and Blood Transfusion in Prague consist of microarray measurements of mRNA and miRNA profiles. The measurements were realized using Illumina chips. The mRNA dataset has 16,666 attributes representing the GE level through the amount of corresponding mRNA measured, while the miRNA dataset has 1,146 attributes representing the activity of particular miRNA regulators.

The measurements were conducted on 75 tissue samples categorized according to the several conditions: 1) tissue type: peripheral blood (PB) CD14+ monocytes vs. bone marrow (BM) CD34+ progenitor cells, 2) presence of MDS or del(5q), 3) treatment stage: before treatment (BT) vs. during treatment (DT). Henceforth the samples can be broken into 10 categories. The categories with the actual number of samples are shown in Table 1.

	Healthy		10
PB	5q-	BT	9
		DT	13
	non 5q-	BT	4
		DT	5
	Healthy		10
BM	5q-	BT	11
		DT	5
	non 5q-	BT	6
		DT	2

Table 1: The overview of MDS classes

The domain experts defined 10 binary classification tasks with a clear diagnostic and therapeutic motivation. There are 5 tasks for each tissue type, the numbers of samples are shown in parentheses:

1. **PB1**: healthy (10) vs. afflicted in PB (31),

2. **BM1**: healthy (10) vs. afflicted in BM (24),

3. **PB2**: healthy vs. untreated in PB (13),

4. **BM2**: healthy vs. untreated in BM (17),

5. **PB3**: healthy vs. untreated with del(5q) in PB (9),

6. **BM3**: healthy vs. untreated with del(5q) in BM (11),

7. **PB4**: healthy vs. treated in PB (18),

8. **BM4**: healthy vs. treated in BM (7),

9. **PB5**: afflicted with del(5q) (9) vs. afflicted without del(5q) in PB (22),

10. **BM5**: afflicted with del(5q) (8) vs. afflicted without del(5q) in BM (16).

Considering the prior knowledge, we had downloaded the interactions between genes and miRNAs from miR-Walk database [6], while the knowledge about interactions between particular genes we obtained as the interactions of their corresponding proteins from [2].

5.2 Experimental procedure

We used three different classification algorithms to learn on resulting comodules: 1) naïve Bayes, 2) support vector machine (SVM) and 3) k-nearest neighbor (kNN). This selection is to avoid dependence of experimental results on a specific choice of a learning method.

For each task, SNMNMF needs to be correctly parametrized first. When the parametrization is available, the raw data can be projected onto comodules. Finally, the three learners are applied in the transformed comodule space and evaluated using 5-fold cross-validation.

The proper parameter configuration of SNMNMF was reached as follows. The parameters γ_1 and γ_2 were set to 5 as recommended by [27]. The "knowledge-strength" parameters λ_μ and λ_g, which seemed crucial for predictive accuracy, were tuned through 5-fold internal cross-validation for each particular experiment. For each parameter configuration, a factorization process was run on training subsets of the *internal* cross-validation and the predictive accuracy of learned comodules was estimated on testing subsets for each of the learners. The locally optimal parameter configuration has been validated for each of the learners by *external* 5-fold cross-validation. Eventually, this validated accuracy was considered as the final accuracy estimate reached by the optimized matrix factorization. The values of parameters were chosen from $\left\{5 \cdot 10^{-5}, 5 \cdot 10^{-4}, 10^{-3}, 0.01\right\}$ for λ_g and $\left\{10^{-3}, 0.01, 0.05, 0.1, 0.2\right\}$ for λ_μ. The number of iterations of SNMNMF factorization was set to 50. For each classification task the experiment was rerun from 15 initializations.

To ensure equal conditions within the course of each experiment, the matrix factors $\mathbf{H}^g$, $\mathbf{H}^\mu$ and $\mathbf{W}$ were randomly initialized only once, on the experiment beginning. The initialized matrix factors were subsequently passed to the folds of cross-validation as follows. The sample-size invariant comodule matrices $\mathbf{H}^g$ a $\mathbf{H}^\mu$ were passed unchanged. In the weight matrix $\mathbf{W}$ representing the data samples in the comodule space, only the rows that link to the particular validation fold were passed.

To sum up, $4 \times 5 = 20$ different parameter configurations were evaluated. Each parametrization was run 15 times for each of 5 internal folds. This process was repeated in each of 5 external folds. Having 10 tasks, we performed 75,000 individual factorizations. The best parametrization was found for each task, external fold and random initialization, which gives 750 λ_g and λ_μ pairs.

The SNMNMF predictive accuracy was compared with accuracy of its several straightforward alternatives. Firstly, we used only mRNA features to classify the samples. The goal was to compare SNMNMF with the most common GE classification technique. Secondly, we used only miRNA features to classify the samples in order to see direct applicability of miRNA for MDS prediction. Eventually, we evaluated the blind *merged* integration method, concatenating the mRNA and miRNA features. This reference allows us to study the asset of the advanced knowledge-driven feature extraction taken in SNMNMF. All these classification techniques were assessed through the three learners and 5-fold cross-validation.

The experiments were implemented in Python with the aid of numerical library NumPy [4] and machine learning library Orange Biolab [3].

5.3 Results

We obtained 450 predictive accuracy values (PAs) for SNMNMF integration method (10 tasks, 3 learners, 15 initializations). To compare it with the reference techniques we used the median PAs taken over the initializations. For the three reference techniques we obtained 30 PAs (10 tasks, 3 learners). The absolute accuracy of the compared classification techniques is summarized in Tables 2-4. The relative accuracy comparison of SNMNMF integration and the blind merged integration method is in Figures 1-3.

5.4 Discussion

The individual methods were evaluated for 10 classification tasks and 3 different learners, i.e., in 30 experiments. The results suggest that none of the methods shows clear dominance over the others. To obtain a global picture, each pair of the methods is mutually compared in every single experiment. The overall pairwise accuracy comparison of particular methods is graphically represented in Figure 4. To exemplify, the miRNA features dominate the mRNA features in 15 experiments, tie on 5, and surrender

task	mRNA	miRNA	merged	SNMNMF
PB1	0.85	**0.88**	**0.88**	**0.88**
BM1	0.94	**0.97**	**0.97**	**0.97**
PB2	0.75	0.76	0.70	**0.80**
BM2	0.97	**1.00**	**1.00**	**1.00**
PB3	**0.85**	0.80	**0.85**	**0.85**
BM3	**1.00**	0.95	0.95	0.95
PB4	**0.83**	0.78	0.78	0.78
BM4	**0.95**	0.87	0.87	0.93
PB5	0.93	**1.00**	0.97	0.94
BM5	0.87	**0.96**	**0.96**	0.95

Table 2: Absolute PAs for evaluated classification techniques in the view of naïve Bayes classifier

task	mRNA	miRNA	merged	SNMNMF
PB1	**0.98**	0.80	**0.98**	0.91
BM1	0.89	**0.97**	0.89	0.94
PB2	0.88	0.73	0.88	**0.90**
BM2	0.90	**0.97**	0.90	**0.97**
PB3	0.85	0.75	**0.95**	0.85
BM3	0.95	**1.00**	0.95	0.95
PB4	0.78	0.57	0.77	**0.81**
BM4	0.88	**0.93**	0.83	**0.93**
PB5	0.97	0.97	0.97	**1.00**
BM5	0.92	**1.00**	0.92	0.96

Table 4: Absolute PAs for evaluated classification techniques in the view of kNN classifier

task	mRNA	miRNA	merged	SNMNMF
PB1	**0.76**	**0.76**	**0.76**	**0.76**
BM1	0.74	**0.77**	0.74	**0.77**
PB2	**0.90**	0.77	**0.90**	**0.90**
BM2	0.93	1.00	0.96	**1.00**
PB3	**1.00**	0.90	**1.00**	0.88
BM3	0.95	**1.00**	0.95	**1.00**
PB4	0.76	0.76	**0.80**	0.72
BM4	**0.95**	**0.95**	**0.95**	0.93
PB5	**0.71**	**0.71**	**0.71**	**0.71**
BM5	0.79	**0.87**	0.79	**0.87**

Table 3: Absolute PAs for evaluated classification techniques in the view of SVM classifier

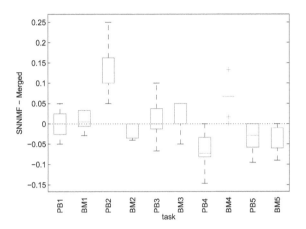

Figure 1: naïve Bayes

in 10. This observation indicates that miRNA measurements have a real merit compared to the standard GE classification based on mRNA features. This may be caused by the key role of miRNA regulation in the examined disease or by the substantially smaller number of features in case of miRNA classification, which fundamentally prevents overfitting. However, the tight miRNA win confirms that mRNA information also has its worth. Concatenating miRNA and mRNA features together does not improve the accuracy, though. The blind mRNA concatenation to the auspicious miRNAs immensely increases feature space, which probably leads to overfitting.

Technically, the SNMNMF-based classification surpasses the reference techniques. But still, there are frequent cases, when namely the merged integration or miRNA model outperforms it. We conclude that the integrative SNMNMF yields predictive results clearly not worse than its counterparts. The SNMNMF results seem hopeful with respect to its biologically sound feature compression and locally-optimal parameter configuration only.

Of the different tasks and comodules given, biological relevance can be observed in several cases. miR-451 was previously reported as positive regulator of erythroid cell maturation and recently we have detected increased ex-

pression of miR-451 that was not affected by lenalidomide treatment in both BM CD34+ cells and PB monocytes of MDS patients with del(5q). In task PB1 a link of miR-451 to *hbb* (hemoglobin, beta), *hbe1* (hemoglobin, epsilon 1) and *hbq1* (hemoglobin, theta 1) genes has been found in the same comodule. miR-451 appears also in task PB3, where the interaction of jointly (in the same comodule) reported entities, namely *bax* and *cd82* (p53 signaling pathway), *rab11b* (member of RAS oncogene family), *cdkn2d* (cell cycle), *grb2* and *mapk11* (MAPK signaling pathway) and *pim1* (acute myeloid leukemia), could act in development of MDS.

miR-150 and miR-146a are known to be involved in hematopoiesis and MDS with del(5q), respectively. So called minor versions of those, miR-150* and miR-146a*, are coexpressed in the same comodule in task BM2; and downregulation of miR-150* has also been detected in BM CD34+ cells of del(5q) MDS patients before treatment compared to healthy donors. Of the genes expressed in that comodule, *bcl11a* (B-cell lymphoma/leukaemia 11A), which encodes zinc finger protein, is of importance as it functions as a myeloid and B-cell proto-oncogene and

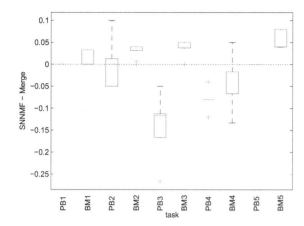

Figure 2: SVM

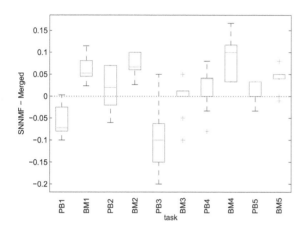

Figure 3: kNN

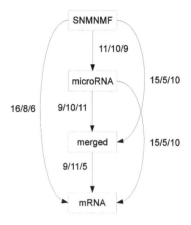

Figure 4: Pairwise accuracy comparison graph. The nodes represent particular feature sets, an edge from node *a* to node *b*, annotated as *x/y/z* means that method *a* outperforms method *b* in *x* experiments, in *y* ties and in *z* looses.

therefore may play an important role in leukaemogenesis and hematopoiesis. Gene functional classification analysis of the genes of that comodule revealed some other genes (*znf319, zscan2, znf467, znf585a, znf32*) coding for yet unidentified zinc finger proteins which may be involved in transcriptional regulation, however, their role remains speculative.

Of the miRNAs jointly appeared in task BM4, miR-154 and miR-381 were significantly upregulated in BM cells of MDS del(5q) and their link to *rab23* (member of RAS oncogene family) and *wnt9b* (wingless-type MMTV integration site family, member 9B), both involved in Hedgehog signaling pathway, which has also been implicated in the growth of some cancers, is to be further explored.

6 Conclusion

The increasing amount of genomic data measured on different stages of expression process, along with the rising availability of prior knowledge about GE regulation, give

us the challenging opportunity to build robust predictive models based on entire biological processes. Such models should be more comprehensible and potentially more accurate than standard GE classification based solely on one type of measurement, mostly the amount of mRNA. The integration of heterogeneous measurements and prior knowledge is non-trivial, though.

In this work we classify myelodysplastic syndrome patients. Two types of measurements are available for each sample: the amount of mRNA corresponding to gene transcription and the amount of miRNA corresponding to gene translation regulation. We investigate the possibility to utilize the biggest deal of information contained in the provided data through their integration with available prior knowledge, namely miRNA targets and protein-protein interactions. We propose the classification framework based on multiple matrix factorization. The result is a knowledge-enriched predictive model.

A large number of experiments was run to obtain an unbiased accuracy of the integrated model. The results indicate that integration of the heterogeneous measurements together with prior knowledge has its merit and prospects. The knowledge-based classification yields possibly better but clearly not worse results than simple data concatenation or omitting of one type of measurement. What is more, the integrated models are more comprehensive and interpretable. It is obvious that predictive accuracy of the SNMNMF and any other integrated model can further be increased by utilization of the most prospective raw features, in the case of MDS it would namely be the most predictive miRNAs.

But still, there is a lot of future work. The first field of improvements concerns algorithmic enhancements. Within SNMNMF it is desirable to employ an informed parameter search instead of the actual non-informed complete search. Another possibility is to develop a less parameter dependent integration method. We intend to use the prior knowledge to control pseudorandom construction of weak classifiers vaguely corresponding to the individual biological processes. The weak classifiers will later be merged into an ensemble classifier.

Further, the gene regulatory network shall be extended. Currently it contains protein-protein interactions only, not considering the interactions between genes and their transcription factors. Another challenge is to employ epigenomic data, namely DNA methylation.

Acknowledgments

This research was supported by the grants NT14539, NT14377 and NT13847 of the Ministry of Health of the Czech Republic.

References

[1] G. Abraham, A. Kowalczyk, S. Loi, I. Haviv, et al. Prediction of breast cancer prognosis using gene set statistics provides signature stability and biological context. *BMC Bioinformatics*, 11:277, 2010.

[2] A. Bossi and B. Lehner. Tissue specificity and the human protein interaction network. *Molecular systems biology*, 5(1), Apr. 2009.

[3] T. Curk, J. Demšar, Q. Xu, G. Leban, et al. Microarray data mining with visual programming. *Bioinformatics*, 21:396–398, Feb. 2005.

[4] P. F. Dubois, K. Hinsen, and J. Hugunin. Numerical python. *Computers in Physics*, 10(3), May/June 1996.

[5] A. Dupuy and R. M. Simon. Critical Review of Published Microarray Studies for Cancer Outcome and Guidelines on Statistical Analysis and Reporting. *JNCI Journal of the National Cancer Institute*, 99(2):147–157, Jan. 2007.

[6] H. Dweep, C. Sticht, P. Pandey, and N. Gretz. miRWalk-database: prediction of possible miRNA binding sites by "walking" the genes of three genomes. *Journal of biomedical informatics*, 44(5):839–847, Oct. 2011.

[7] T. R. Golub, D. K. Slonim, P. Tamayo, C. Huard, et al. Molecular classification of cancer: class discovery and class prediction by gene expression monitoring. *Science*, 286(5439):531–537, Oct. 1999.

[8] M. Holec, J. Kléma, F. Železný, and J. Tolar. Comparative evaluation of set-level techniques in predictive classification of gene expression samples. *BMC Bioinformatics*, 13(Suppl 10):S15, 2012.

[9] G. T. Huang, C. Athanassiou, and P. V. Benos. mirConnX: condition-specific mRNA-microRNA network integrator. *Nucleic acids research*, 39(Web Server issue):W416–W423, July 2011.

[10] D. Kim, H. Shin, Y. S. Song, and J. H. Kim. Synergistic effect of different levels of genomic data for cancer clinical outcome prediction. *J. of Biomedical Informatics*, 45(6):1191–1198, Dec. 2012.

[11] M. Krejník and J. Kléma. Empirical evidence of the applicability of functional clustering through gene expression classification. *IEEE/ACM Trans. Comput. Biol. Bioinformatics*, 9(3):788–798, May 2012.

[12] M. Lagos-Quintana, R. Rauhut, Meyer, et al. New microRNAs from mouse and human. *RNA (New York)*, 9(5):175–9, 2003.

[13] G. Lanza, M. Ferracin, R. Gafà, et al. mRNA/microRNA gene expression profile in microsatellite unstable colorectal cancer. *Molecular cancer*, 6:54+, Aug. 2007.

[14] D. Lee and H. Seung. Learning the parts of objects by non-negative matrix factorization. *Nature*, 401:788–791, 1999.

[15] E. Lee, H.-Y. Chuang, J.-W. Kim, et al. Inferring pathway activity toward precise disease classification. *PLoS Computational Biology*, 4(11), 2008.

[16] R. C. Lee, R. L. Feinbaum, and V. Ambros. The C. elegans heterochronic gene lin-4 encodes small RNAs with antisense complementarity to lin-14. *Cell*, 75(5):843–854, Dec. 1993.

[17] E. Lundberg, L. Fagerberg, D. Klevebring, I. Matic, et al. Defining the transcriptome and proteome in three functionally different human cell lines. *Molecular systems biology*, 6(1), Dec. 2010.

[18] J. Nunez-Iglesias, C.-C. Liu, T. E. Morgan, et al. Joint genome-wide profiling of miRNA and mRNA expression in Alzheimer's disease cortex reveals altered miRNA regulation. *PloS one*, 5(2):e8898+, Feb. 2010.

[19] K. V. Pandit, D. Corcoran, H. Yousef, M. Yarlagadda, et al. Inhibition and role of let-7d in idiopathic pulmonary fibrosis. *Am J Respir Crit Care Med*, 182(2):220–9, 2010.

[20] X. Peng, Y. Li, K. A. Walters, and E. a. o. Rosenzweig. Computational identification of hepatitis C virus associated microRNA-mRNA regulatory modules in human livers. *BMC Genomics*, 10(1):373+, Aug. 2009.

[21] R. Schachtner, D. Lutter, P. Knollmüller, A. M. Tomé, et al. Knowledge-based gene expression classification via matrix factorization. *Bioinformatics*, 24(15):1688–1697, 2008.

[22] D. H. Tran, K. Satou, and T. B. Ho. Finding microRNA regulatory modules in human genome using rule induction. *BMC Bioinformatics*, 9(S-12), 2008.

[23] A. Vašíková, M. Běličková, E. Budinská, and J. Čermák. A distinct expression of various gene subsets in cd34+ cells from patients with early and advanced myelodysplastic syndrome. *Leuk Res*, 34(12):1566–72, 2010.

[24] T. Vergoulis, I. S. Vlachos, P. Alexiou, G. Georgakilas, et al. TarBase 6.0: capturing the exponential growth of miRNA targets with experimental support. *Nucleic acids research*, 40(Database issue):D222–D229, Jan. 2012.

[25] C. Vogel and E. M. Marcotte. Insights into the regulation of protein abundance from proteomic and transcriptomic analyses. *Nature reviews. Genetics*, 13(4):227–32, Apr. 2012.

[26] B. Zhang, X. Pan, Q. Wang, et al. Review: Computational identification of microRNAs and their targets. *Comput. Biol. Chem.*, 30(6):395–407, Dec. 2006.

[27] S.-H. Zhang, Q. Li, J. Liu, and X. J. Zhou. A novel computational framework for simultaneous integration of multiple types of genomic data to identify microRNA-gene regulatory modules. *Bioinformatics [ISMB/ECCB]*, 27(13):401–409, 2011.

ITAT 2013: Workshops, Posters, and Tutorials, pp. 56–61
ISBN 978-1490952086, © 2013 I. Ihnátová

Topology Incorporating Pathway Analysis of Expression Data: An Evaluation of Existing Methods

Ivana Ihnatova[1]

Bioinformatics In Translational Research Team, Institute of Biostatistics and Analyses, Brno, Czech Republic,
WWW home page: http://btr.iba.muni.cz ihnatova@iba.muni.cz,

Abstract: Pathway analysis of expression data aims to assess the overall evidence of association of a biological pathway with a binary phenotype. Recently, a new approach for this type of analysis has been proposed. These methods use pathway topology to compute pathway-level statistics. Seven such methods are reviewed and compared their performance via an extensive simulation study, in which the scenarios vary according to: the proportion of differentially expressed genes, effect sizes and the location of the differentially expressed genes in the pathway topology.

The results demonstrate that Pathway regulation score, TopologyGSA and SPIA have the highest power for scenarios with small proportion of the differentially expressed genes. On the other hand, when the proportion of differentially expressed genes is high, TAPPA and DEGraph outperform the other methods. TopologyGSA and Pathway regulation score are the least sensitive to the positions of differentially expressed genes in the pathway.

1 Introduction

Gene expression microarrays are a popular tool for detecting differences in gene activity across biological samples. Analysis of microarray data typically yields a list of differentially expressed genes. This list is extremely useful in identifying genes that may have a role in given phenotype. However, biological processes are generally the result of interactions between multiple genes (pathways). To facilitate such analyses, statistical methods have been developed which focus on detecting changes in groups in functionally related genes, thus allowing additional biological information to be incorporated into the analysis process. This approach is called pathway analysis and the result of it is a list of differentially expressed pathways.

An increasing number of publicly available databases (KEGG, Biocarta, Reactome, PID) provide not only a simple lists of genes for each pathway, but also the interactions between them. Pathway topology (PT)-based methods have been developed to utilize this additional information. PT-based methods were introduced in [1] and they usually contain three steps: 1) calculation of gene-level statistics, 2) the gene-level statistics for all genes in a pathway are aggregated into a single pathway level statistic (univariate or multivariate approaches), 3) assessing the statistical significance of the pathway-level statistics (usually by permutations).

Since PT-based methods are relatively new, a comparative review of them has not been published yet. The goals of this paper are to describe the existing pathway topology-based methods and examine their performance through the analysis of simulated data. Methods were selected according to their available implementation. For four out of seven methods there is a package available through Bioconductor or CRAN. The remaining three methods were implemented in R by authors.

2 Material and Methods

2.1 Methods

In this section, the seven methods are briefly described. The phenotype of interest is assumed to be binary. Unless stated otherwise, x_{is} represents the expression value of gene i in sample s and N denotes the number of genes in the pathway. A pathway is represented as directed graph $G(V,E)$, V and E refer to set of nodes (vertices) and edges, respectively.

TAPPA TAPPA was introduced in [2]. The pathway-level statistic is called a Pathway Connectivity Index (PCI). The index is inspired by the second-order molecular connectivity index from chemoinformatics. The PCI is defined as

$$PCI = \sum_{i=1}^{N} \sum_{j=1}^{N} sgn(x_{is}+x_{js})|x_{is}|^{0.5} a_{ij}|x_{js}|^{0.5},$$

where $a_{ij} = 1$ if there is an edge between genes i and j and $a_{ij} = 0$ otherwise, x_{is} denotes the expression value of gene i in sample s and $sgn(x_{is}+x_{js})$ represents the overall expression status of the gene pair (up- or down-regulation). PCI normalized to the pathway size follow the normal distribution, therefore the Mann-Whitney test can be applied to test the hypothesis of equal medians of PCI in two groups. The pathway topology is incorporated as the higher contribution of the hub genes to PCI.

SPIA Signaling pathway impact analysis (SPIA) was developed by *Tarca et al.* [3]. In the impact analysis, two independent aspects of the pathway expression are captured by two p-values P_{NDE} and P_{PERT}. The first one refers to the significance of a pathway as provided by regular gene set analysis method (it is based on the number of DEG observed in the pathway). The second probability is calculated from the amount of perturbation measured. It is assumed that the difference in the expression of the entry nodes has greater impact on the rest of the pathway than the difference in the expression of the leaf nodes. The set of linear equations is used to calculate a perturbation factor for each node. The two p-values are finally combined into a overall probability

$$P = c - c\ln(c) \text{ where } c = P_{NDE}.P_{PERT}$$

that tests the hypothesis that the pathway is significantly perturbed between two groups.

TopologyGSA TopologyGSA [4] is a multivariate method based on the Gaussian Graphical Models. After the pathway topology was converted into a directed acyclic graph and moralized, the concentration matrices can be estimated via Iterative Proportional Scaling algorithm [5]. First, the question of the equality of the concentration matrices must be addressed via likelihood test. If the null hypothesis is rejected, the Behrens-Fisher test [6] is used to assess the differential expression of the pathway. Otherwise, a multivariate analysis of variance is applied.

DEGraph DEGraph [7] belongs also to the multivariate methods. It assumes a smooth distribution shift of the gene expression on the graph. The smoothness is defined and controlled through spectral analysis of the graph Lapacian. In particular, the eigenvectors of the Laplacian provide a basis of functions which vary on the graph at increasing frequencies (corresponding to the increasing eigenvalues). Two groups can be therefore compared in terms of the first k components of the graph-Fourier basis, or in the original space after filtering out k high-frequency components. Hotelling's T^2-test is used for the comparison and a p-value is assigned to each connected component of the pathway topology.

PWEA PWEA [8] is GSEA-based method. The topological information is included by the so called topological influence factor (TIF). TIF for a gene is defined as the geometric average mutual influence that the gene imposes on the rest of the genes in the pathway. The mutual influence between two genes i and j is

$$\psi_{ij} = e^{-d_{ij}/|c_{ij}|}$$

where d_{ij} is the shortest distance between the genes and c_{ij} is the Pearson correlation of their expression profiles. $\psi_{ij} < 0.05$ are set to 0. The TIF for the genes outside the pathways are generated from normal distribution with the parameters estimated from the within-pathway genes. TIF's are used as weights in a weighted Kolmogorov-Smirnov statistic.

Pathway regulation score The Pathway Regulation Score (PRS) [9] is one of the newest approaches that detect significantly deregulated pathways by exploiting both topology and fold-change data. First, the list of DEG is created according to two thresholds: fold-change and a p-value from a simple t-test. PRS for pathway p is defined as

$$PRS_p = \sum_{i=1}^{N} NS_j$$

where NS_j is the node score given as the log fold-change of a gene times number of downstream DEG. PRS is later normalized for the pathway size and the pathway-specific null distribution. The bias due to pathway size is removed by multiplying PRS by the ratio of the number of DEGs in a pathway to the total number of expressed genes. To characterize the null distribution of raw values, fold-change values of all genes are permuted and permuted scores created. The raw values are standardized by mean and SD of permuted scores. The statistical significance is assessed by gene-sampling permutation test.

CePa Another method that uses topological properties as weights in regular gene set analysis method is called Centrality-based pathway enrichment analysis [10] or CePa. The weights are based on the centrality measures for the nodes like: in-degree, out-degree, in-reach, out-reach and betweenness. The in-degree/out-degree is the number of upstream/downstream nodes directly acting on a given node. The in-reach/out-reach is the largest length of the shortest paths from a given nodes to all upstream/downstream nodes in the pathway. The betweenness is represented by the amount of information streaming through a given node. The method begins by the determination of the differentially expressed genes and mapping them to the pathways. The pathway score is then defined as

$$S_p = \sum_{i=1}^{N} w_i d_i$$

where $d_i = 1$ if the gene i is differentially expressed and $d_i = 0$ otherwise. The statistical significance is assessed by gene-sampling permutations and empirical null distribution of the pathway scores.

2.2 Simulation Study

In order to compare the performance of the methods described above a simulation study was performed. The Pancreatic cancer from KEGG [11, 12] database as implemented in `graphite` [13] package was used for the pathway topology. In the implementation a node consists of a single gene. The protein complexes are transformed into cliques of the subunits and gene families are represented as separate nodes. A hundred of data sets were generated. Each data set contains the expression profiles of 40 samples (divided into two groups of 20) and 1820 genes (70

Table 1: Type I error rates

Method	Type I error rates
TAPPA	0.060
SPIA	0.031
TopologyGSA	0.041
DEGraph	0.080
PWEA	0.055
Pathway regulation score	0.098
CePa[a]	0.033

[a]Average of all centrality measures

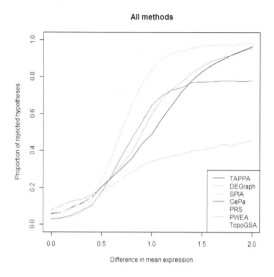

Figure 1: The statistical power of the method at 10% of DEG

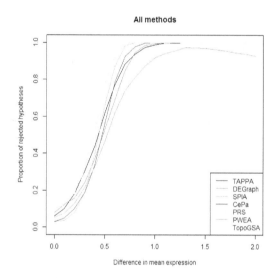

Figure 2: The statistical power of the method at 25% of DEG

from the pathway and 1750 background genes). The expression profiles of the genes related to the pathway were generated to have multivariate normal distribution with 0's means and identity covariance matrix. The univariate normal distribution with mean of 0 and standard deviation 1 was used for the background genes. The data were later modified for each of the 840 scenarios. The scenarios vary in the number of differentially expressed genes (DEG), the set of the differentially expressed genes and the size of the differential expression. The number of DEG was set to 7, 17, 35, 70 corresponding to the 10%, 25%, 50% and 100% of the pathway. The set of the DEG was 10 times randomly selected. When the proportion of the DEG raised more genes were added to the previous selection. The simulated data were subsequently modified by an addition of a constant γ to a 20 expression profiles. The constant represents the size of the differential expression and its range was set from 0 to 2 with an increment of 0.1. Nominal p-values (uncorrected for multiplicity) can be obtained from each of the gene set analysis methods. Since DEGraph assigns a p-value for each connected component, a p-value for the biggest component was taken as a representative for whole pathway. For each permutation-based p-value, 1000 random permutations were carried out and the reported p-value is the proportion of random scores higher or equal to the score observed in the orginal data. The p-values below 0.05 were considered significant.

3 Results

The first goal in the simulation study was to assess the type I error rates. The results are shown in Table 1. For CePa, the error rates were averaged across all the centrality measures. Taking the small number of the simulated datasets into account, it can be stated that all the methods are close to the target of the nominal value of 0.05.

The second goal of the simulation study was to assess statistical power as estimated by the observed proportion of the correctly rejected hypotheses. Averaging across the DEG selections, a larger effect size and/or a larger proportion of DEG leads to higher power for a given α-level.

When the proportion of the DEG is low (Figures 1 and 2), SPIA, TopologyGSA and Pathway regulation score reach the highest power. On the other hand, when the proportion of the DEG is high (50% or 100%, Figures 3 and 4), TAPPA and DEGraph perform the best.

The next step in this study was to examine the effect of the particular selections of DEG. Since the biggest differences in the power of the methods were observed for the smallest proportion of DEG (10%), only the results for this proportion are discussed further. Figure 5 presents the standard deviations of power with increasing difference in the gene expression. The variability of the power is very low for TopologyGSA and PRS method. PWEA and CePa reach plateau at approximately 1, which is also a point of maximal SD in the rest of the methods (SPIA, TAPPA and

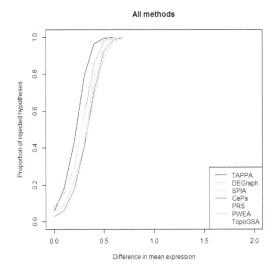

Figure 3: The statistical power of the method at 50% of DEG

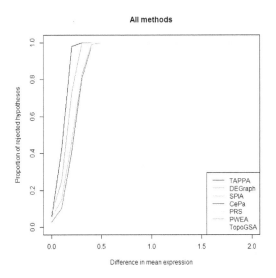

Figure 4: The statistical power of the method at 100% of DEG

DEGraph).

For SPIA, TAPPA and PRS, special situations these methods are designed for can be created. The perturbation factor from SPIA is the highest for the entry nodes of the pathway and as presented in Figure 6a, the effect of the differentially expressed entry genes is remarkable.

The difference in the gene expression between the connected nodes makes the test-statistic in TAPPA. However, no difference was observed between the pathways with unconnected and highly connected differentially expressed genes (Figure 6b). PRS employs a simple weighting scheme, in which the weight of a node depends on the number of downstream DEG. Since the variability of the power is low for PRS, the difference in the power is similar for both unconnected DEG and DEG selected along

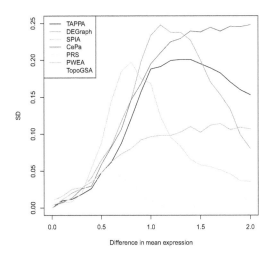

Figure 5: The standard deviation of power with increasing difference in gene expression

one path in the pathway topology (Figure 6c).

4 Discussion

Based on the results, three out of the seven approaches examined (namely PRS, TopologyGSA and SPIA) all exhibited generally very good performance in any scenario. TAPPA and DEGraph outperformed them only when the proportion of DEG was very high (50% or 100% of the genes). It should be noted that only TAPPA allows both binary and quantitative phenotypes. For binary phenotypes, Mann–Whitney test is used to evaluate the significance of association between pathway PCI and phenotype. For continuous traits, Spearman correlation is used. The performance of CePa method depends heavily on the selected centrality measure. However, when the lowest p-value of all centrality measures is assigned to a pathway (as suggested by the authors [10]), CePa shows similar power as the other best performing methods.

On the other hand, PRS and TopologyGSA are not sensitive to the positions of DEG in the pathway. Therefore, if one is interested in a special topological distribution of DEG, a different method is suggested.

The methods were compared to three examples of regular gene set analysis methods - GSEA [14] (as implemented in both limma and Category packages) and Global test [15]. The topology-based gene set methods seem to have lower power than Global test and GSEA from Category package. Only PRS at 10% DEG and TAPPA and DEGraph at 50% or 100% have higher power than the Global test. GSEA from Category package exhibits similar or even higher power than the best performing topology-based methods. The power of GSEA from limma package was lower than the most of topology-based methods. The only method with power lower than GSEA

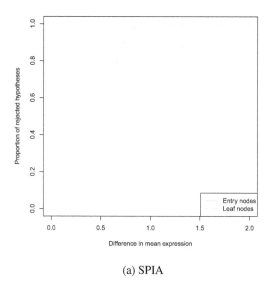

(a) SPIA

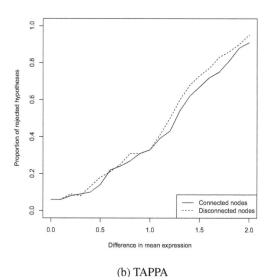

(b) TAPPA

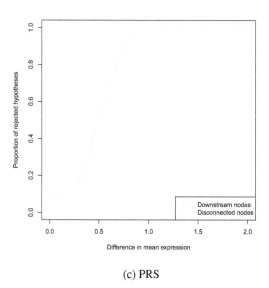

(c) PRS

Figure 6: The difference in the DEG selection

from limma was PWEA. PWEA performed generally very poorly especially when the proportion of DEG was only 10%. One of the main differences between the two GSEA implementation is in the permutations used to compute p-values. The Category package computes p-values based on permutation of the sample labels, whereas the limma package uses permutation of gene labels (same as in PWEA). The poor power of GSEA with gene permutations was also observed in [16].

5   Conclusion

In summary, when the proportion of DEG is small, Pathway regulation score, TopologyGSA and SPIA are the most powerful methods to be used. On the other hand, when the proportion of differentially expressed genes is high, TAPPA and DEGraph have higher power. TopologyGSA and Pathway regulation score are not very sensitive to the positions of differentially expressed genes in the pathway.

References

[1] P. Khatri, M. Sirota, and A. J. Butte, "Ten years of pathway analysis: Current approaches and outstanding challenges," *PLoS Comput Biol*, vol. 8, p. e1002375, 02 2012.

[2] S. Gao and X. Wang, "Tappa: topological analysis of pathway phenotype association," *Bioinformatics*, vol. 23, no. 22, pp. 3100–3102, 2007.

[3] A. L. Tarca, S. Draghici, P. Khatri, S. S. Hassan, P. Mittal, J.-s. Kim, C. J. Kim, J. P. Kusanovic, and R. Romero, "A novel signaling pathway impact analysis," *Bioinformatics*, vol. 25, no. 1, pp. 75–82, 2009.

[4] M. Massa, M. Chiogna, and C. Romualdi, "Gene set analysis exploiting the topology of a pathway," *BMC Systems Biology*, vol. 4, no. 1, p. 121, 2010.

[5] S. L. Lauritzen, *Graphical Models*. Oxford Statistical Science Series, New York, USA: Oxford University Press, July 1996.

[6] T. W. Anderson and T. W. Anderson, *An Introduction to Multivariate Statistical Analysis, 2nd Edition*. Wiley, 2 ed., Sept. 1984.

[7] L. Jacob, P. Neuvial, and S. Dudoit, "Gains in Power from Structured Two-Sample Tests of Means on Graphs," *ArXiv e-prints*, Sept. 2010.

[8] J.-H. Hung, T. Whitfield, T.-H. Yang, Z. Hu, Z. Weng, and C. DeLisi, "Identification of functional modules that correlate with phenotypic difference: the influence of network topology," *Genome Biology*, vol. 11, no. 2, p. R23, 2010.

[9] M. Al-Haj Ibrahim, S. Jassim, M. A. Cawthorne, and K. Langlands, "A topology-based score for pathway enrichment.," *J Comput Biol*, 2012.

[10] Z. Gu, J. Liu, K. Cao, J. Zhang, and J. Wang, "Centrality-based pathway enrichment: a systematic approach for finding significant pathways dominated by key genes," *BMC Systems Biology*, vol. 6, no. 1, p. 56, 2012.

[11] M. Kanehisa and S. Goto, "Kegg: Kyoto encyclopedia of genes and genomes," *Nucleic Acids Research*, vol. 28, no. 1, pp. 27–30, 2000.

[12] M. Kanehisa, S. Goto, Y. Sato, M. Furumichi, and M. Tanabe, "Kegg for integration and interpretation of large-scale molecular data sets," *Nucleic Acids Research*, vol. 40, no. D1, pp. D109–D114, 2012.

[13] G. Sales, E. Calura, and C. Romualdi, *graphite: GRAPH Interaction from pathway Topological Environment*, 2013. R package version 1.6.0.

[14] A. Subramanian, P. Tamayo, V. K. Mootha, S. Mukherjee, B. L. Ebert, M. A. Gillette, A. Paulovich, S. L. Pomeroy, T. R. Golub, E. S. Lander, and J. P. Mesirov, "Gene set enrichment analysis: A knowledge-based approach for interpreting genome-wide expression profiles," *Proceedings of the National Academy of Sciences of the United States of America*, vol. 102, no. 43, pp. 15545–15550, 2005.

[15] J. J. Goeman, S. A. van de Geer, F. de Kort, and H. C. van Houwelingen, "A global test for groups of genes: testing association with a clinical outcome," *Bioinformatics*, vol. 20, no. 1, pp. 93–99, 2004.

[16] S. Song and M. Black, "Microarray-based gene set analysis: a comparison of current methods," *BMC Bioinformatics*, vol. 9, no. 1, p. 502, 2008.

Study of the receiver and receiver-like domain relationship in cytokinin receptor of *Arabidopsis thaliana*

Vendula Hrdinová

Functional genomics and proteomics of plants
Central European Institute of Technology, Masaryk University
Kamenice 5/A2, CZ-625 00 Brno, Czech Republic

Blanka Pekárová, Tomáš Klumpler, Lubomír Janda, Jan Hejátko
Functional genomics and proteomics of plants
Central European Institute of Technology, Masaryk University
Kamenice 5/A2, CZ-625 00 Brno, Czech Republic

Abstract. Cytokinin (CK) signaling is one of the pathways mediated by multistep phosphorelay (MSP) in plants. In the MSP of *Arabidopsis thaliana*, *Arabidopsis* histidine kinases (AHKs) act as receptors initiating the pathway and interact with *Arabidopsis* histidine-containing proteins (AHPs), thus transferring the signal farther in the cascade. For the signal transduction through the cascade, the domain composition of the MSP elements is crucial. Recently it was reported that the receiver domain of one of the *Arabidopsis* sensor histidine kinases CKI1 is sufficient and necessary for the specific interaction of CKI1 with AHPs. Here we performed an extensive study of the individual domains of CK receptor AHK4 in mediating interactions with AHPs. Thorough bioinformatic analysis of the AHK4 aa sequence using similarity search was carried out to refine the precise borders of AHK4 individual domains. SMART and PROSITE databases for primary and secondary structure analysis were used to identify similarities within receiver and receiver-like domains of other AHKs and the results were manually refined. Moreover, we modeled individual structures of the receiver and receiver-like domain of AHK4 (AHK4$_{RD}$ and AHK4$_{RLD}$, respectively) employing their homology with solved structure of bacterial response regulator receiver domain CheY in order to see possible differences in the structure and to predict potential interaction interfaces. The structural predictions were used to design recombinant DNA constructs for protein-protein interaction experiments. Intriguingly, by yeast two-hybrid analysis we revealed that not only AHK4$_{RD}$ is substantial for the interaction with AHPs but we found out that the interaction can be suppressed by AHK4$_{RLD}$. We propose that AHK4$_{RLD}$ has a (negative) regulatory function in the process of molecular recognition of the downstream signaling partners and we experimentally demonstrated that this function can be provided by the heterodimerization of AHK4$_{RD}$ with AHK4RLD, either intra- or intermolecularly. The structural prediction-based model of this regulatory role will be presented.

Supported by the European Regional Development Fund (Central European Institute of Technology project no. CZ.1.05/1.1.00/02.0068), the European Social Fund (CZ.1.07/2.3.00/20.0189) and the Czech Science Foundation (P305/11/0756).

Elucidating molecular mechanisms of cytokinin action in the vascular bundle development of *Arabidopsis thaliana*

Vojtěch Didi

Functional Genomics and Proteomics of Plants
CEITEC - Central European Institute of Technology, Masaryk University
Kamenice 5, 625 00 Brno, Czech Republic

Radim Čegan[2], Mariana Benítez[3], Tereza Dobisová[1], Roman Hobza[2], Vít Gloser[4] and Jan Hejátko[1]

1 - Functional Genomics and Proteomics of Plants
CEITEC - Central European Institute of Technology, Masaryk University
Kamenice 5, 625 00 Brno, Czech Republic

2 - Department of Plant Developmental Genetics
Institute of Biophysics, The Academy of Sciences of the Czech Republic
Královopolská 135, 612 65 Brno, Czech Republic

3 - Instituto de Ecología
Universidad Nacional Autónoma de México
Mexico

4 - Department of Experimental Biology
Faculty of Science, Masaryk University
Kamenice 5, 625 00 Brno, Czech Republic

Cytokinins (CKs) belong to plant growth factors (phytohormones) and participate in numerous physiological and developmental processes such as cell division, leaf senescence, vascular bundle pattering, apical dominance, lateral root formation, chloroplast development and regulation of meristematic tissues activity. CK signalling is ensured via multistep phosphorelay (MSP). The MSP signaling pathway consists of mostly membrane-located sensor histidine kinases (HKs), histidin phosphotransfer proteins (HPts), which transfer the signal to the nucleus and response regulators (RRs). Some of these RRs act as transcriptional factors and orchestrate expression of their target genes via direct binding to the promoter sequence or through indirect regulations.

Our results show that CKs play crucial role in development of vascular bundles (VBs). We found that downregulating CK signaling or depleting endogenous CK levels affected development of specific vascular cell types and their functional properties. To elucidate molecular mechanisms underlying CK-regulated vascular tissue development, we employed next-gen transcriptional profiling. Total RNA from the apical portion of inflorescence stem from the WT and CK signaling mutant was isolated, cDNA sequencing libraries (three biological replicas from each genotype) were prepared and sequenced by Ilumina technology (HiSeq 2000). The output data were analyzed by TopHat program and almost 7000 differentially expressed genes were identified. The subsequent analysis of gene ontology (GO) via Gorilla software (cbl-gorilla.cs.technion.ac.il/) allowed us to identify developmental processes that were dominantly affected in the CK signaling mutant. The resulting model based on the aforementioned experimental and bioinformatic analyses and describing novel molecular mechanism of CK action in the vascular tissue development will be presented.

Supported by the European Regional Development Fund (Central European Institute of Technology project no. CZ.1.05/1.1.00/02.0068), the European Social Fund (CZ.1.07/2.3.00/20.0189) and the Czech Science Foundation (13-25280S).

ITAT 2013: Workshops, Posters, and Tutorials, pp. 64–68
ISBN 978-1490952086, © 2013 S. Štefanič, M. Lexa

Generovanie simulovaných testovacích dát pre genómové asociačné štúdie

Stanislav Štefanič, Matej Lexa

Fakulta informatiky, Masarykova univerzita, Botanická 68a, 60200 Brno, Česká republika, 374513@mail.muni.cz, lexa@fi.muni.cz

Abstrakt: V posledných rokoch zaznamenávame vo výskumoch ľudských chorôb prudký nárast genomového sekvenovania vzoriek jedincov a následne hromadnej detekcie genetických asociácií medzi variáciami (prevažne SNP mutácie) a presnou diagnózou. Tieto techniky vyústili do rutinného používania techník zvaných genómové asociačné štúdia (GWAS [1]). Jedná sa o štúdie, pri ktorých hľadáme asociácie medzi variáciami a fenotypom na celom genóme jedincov. Detekovanie asociácie medzi jedným SNP a konkrétnou črtou jedinca sa dnes prevádza rutinne, no drvivá väčšina biologicky relevantných vzťahov zahŕňa interakciu viacerých SNP, ktoré súčasne asociujú s danou fenotypovou črtou. Hľadanie takýchto interakcií je však kameňom úrazu v GWA štúdiách. V súčasnosti sa snažíme tento problém vyriešiť a hľadáme možnosti ako tieto interakcie odhaľovať. Pri testovaní metód a postupov, ktoré majú tieto a podobné interakcie a asociácie odhaľovať je častým a jedným z najväčších problémov nedostatok reálnych dát, u ktorých máme informáciu o všetkých neznámych vzťahoch. Preto je namieste používanie umelých testovacích dát. Zaznamenávame niekoľko pokusov o riešenie tohto problému práve cestou generovania umelých dát, ich problém však spočíva v nedostatočnej zložitosti a možnosti presného priblíženia simulovaných dát. Cieľom našej práce je tieto nedostatky odstrániť a poskytnúť možnosť generovať aj pomerne zložité simulované dáta s dostatočne presnou možnosťou priblíženia týchto dát reálnym dátam a vzťahom vyskytujúcim sa v prírode. Navrhnutá aplikácia poskytuje užívateľovi prehľadné grafické užívateľské rozhranie v ktorom nastavuje radu parametrov na základe ktorých sa budú dáta generovať. Presné nastavenia korelácií jednotlivých mutácií (SNP) a frekvencií jednotlivých alel je definované užívateľom zadanou funkciou, ktorá tieto parametre dostatočne dobre popisuje. Výstupy tejto aplikácie boli testované na metódach, ktoré odhaľujú skryté asociácie a interakcie medzi SNP navzájom a chorobou a ukryté vzťahy v týchto dátach boli správne detekované. Fungovanie aplikácie a výsledky práce ilustrujeme.

1 Úvod

Genómy jednotlivých zástupcov ľudského druhu sú z 99.9% rovnaké. Genóm každého jedinca reprezentuje celú genetickú informáciu človeka, zakódovanú ako postupnosť jednotlivých nukleotidových báz (A, C, T, G). Rozdiel medzi genetickými informáciami jednotlivých jedincov (0.1%) spôsobujú určité variácie v genóme, nazývané

mutácie. Tieto mutácie sú pre ľudský druh dôležité jednak z hľadiska evolúcie a vývoja nášho druhu (napr. tvorba imunitného systému, adaptácia na zmeny životných podmienok) na druhej strane však spôsobujú defekty a rôzne anomálie u jednotlivých členov populácie (genetické choroby). Pre označenie mutácií sa používajú pojmy polymorfizmus a SNP. Za polymorfizmus považujeme mutácie, ktoré sú rovnaké aspoň u jedného percenta zástupcov istého druhu, poprípade skúmanej vzorky jedincov [1]. Špeciálny prípad polymorfizmu je taký, kedy uvažujeme len bodové mutácie - mutácie na rovnakých pozíciach v postupnostiach báz jednotlivých individuí. V takomto prípade hovoríme o jednonukleotidovom polymorfizme, skrátene SNP [2][2]. Začali sa preto sekvenovať genetické informácie zástupcov populácie, identifikovať medzi nimi SNP, pozorovať fenotypové črty osekvenovaných ľudí a detekovať vzťahy medzi identifikovanými SNP a určitou fenotypovou charakteristikou. Základnému výskumu polymorfizmov sa venujú vedecké projekty ako sú 1000genomes [3][3], HAPMAP [4][4], vedecký inštitút NCBI [5][5] a iné. Najčastejším spôsobom skúmania vzťahu polymorfizmov a fenotypov sú štúdia génových asociácií, z nich v dnešnej dobe najviac rozšírené sú GWA štúdie [6]. Jedná sa o prístup k štúdiu asociácií medzi SNP kedy uvažujeme mutácie v celom genóme, nie iba na určitom bloku alebo časti genómu. Osekvenované alebo inak identifikované SNP sa pre ďalšie skúmanie ukladajú do súborov v špeciálnych formátoch, napríklad VCF [7]. Tieto metódy pri dostatočnom množstve pacientov spoľahlivo odhalia asociáciu jedného SNP a fenotypu. Existuje podozrenie, že väčšina biologicky a medicínsky zaujímavých asociácií nám ostáva skrytá. Dôvodom je veľké množstvo mutácií, ktoré nepôsobia izolovane, ale v interakcii s ďalšími mutáciami. Známym príkladom takejto interakcie je epistáza [8]. Postupom času vznikali metódy, ktoré sa snažili tieto interakcie detekovať, avšak dáta na ktorých by sa mali verifikovať často chýbajú. Z toho dôvodu je zaujímavé algoritmy testovať a porovnávať medzi sebou na umelých dátach, u ktorých máme informáciu o hľadaných vzťahoch.

1.1 Potreba umelých dát

Pre efektívne testovanie a porovnávanie GWAS algoritmov je vhodné generovať simulované dáta potrebného typu. Jedná sa o dáta vo formátoch VCF, poprípade MAP

---

[1] Genome-wide association studies

[2] single nucleotide polymorphism
[3] http://www.1000genomes.org/
[4] http://hapmap.ncbi.nlm.nih.gov/
[5] http://www.ncbi.nlm.nih.gov/

a PED [9], v ktorých sú zapísané jednotlivé SNP mutácie skúmanej vzorky jedincov. Hlavným problémom reálnych dát je neznalosť v nich ukrytých asociácií a interakcií. Nevieme čo je správny výstup algoritmu, ktoré vzťahy mal aplikovaný algoritmus odhaliť a tým pádom nevieme zaručiť korektnosť a efektivitu daného algoritmu. V praxi, kde sa používajú reálne dáta to tak samozrejme byť má, pretože naša snaha je nájsť algoritmus, ktorý bude interakcie odhaľovať práve na reálnych dátach a tak nám pomôže pri riešení a hľadaní SNP majúcich vplyv na určitú chorobu. Riešenie tohto problému nám ponúkajú práve simulované dáta, do ktorých dané interakcie a významné vzťahy medzi SNP zakomponujeme pri nastavovaní parametrov pre vygenerovanie dát a tak spolu s výstupmi pre testovacie algoritmy si máme možnosť uchovať aj výstupy s dátami, ktoré reprezentujú hľadané výstupy následne aplikovaných algoritmov. Ďalším problémom pri testoch na reálnych dátach je fakt, že ich získavanie je dodnes pomerne drahé a časovo náročne. Nehovoriac o fakte, že je potreba súhlasu pacientov, od ktorých tieto dáta chceme získať a následne je dobré ďalej sledovať fenotypy konkrétnych osekvenovaných jedincov. Umelé dáta môžeme generovať prakticky neobmedzene a navyše môžeme voliť rôzne stupne nastavení dát, čo nám umožňuje vykonávať veľké počty testov na veľkej vzorke dát, čím jednoduchšie potvrdíme korektnosť, resp. nespoľahlivosť skúmaných algoritmov. Naším cieľom teda bolo poskytnúť aplikáciu, ktorá umožní generovať umelé dáta simulujúce reálne dáta v prírode. Výsledkom práce je generátor predstavený v kapitole **Aplikácia**, v ktorom pri správnej voľbe parametrov môžeme dostatočne presne simulovať reálne dáta a naviac, aplikácia pracuje v relatívne dobrom čase, čo nám umožňuje viacnásobné generovanie rôzneho počtu dát s rôznymi alebo podobnými vlastnosťami, ktoré v nich chceme mať ukryté.

1.2 Existujúce simulátory

V súčasnej dobe existuje niekoľko simulátorov, ktoré dokážu generovať dáta podobné našim. Nám najpodobnejší je simulátor Hap-Sample [10][6]. Jedná sa o internetovú aplikáciu, ktorá však negeneruje simulované SNP, ale vykonáva výbery z reálnych dát pri maximamálnom zachovaní haplotypov. Využíva reálne dáta z databáz projektu HAP-MAP.
Dáta z databáz HAPMAP-u využíva taktiež program GWAsimulator [11], ktorý simuluje dáta pre štúdie typu skúmaná-kontrolná skupina alebo vzorky populácie získané z SNP čipov. Program zahŕňa LD bloky[7].
Ďalším existujúcim generátorom je HAPGEN2 [12]. Na základe zadaného referenčného haplotypu generuje vzorky LD blokov. Referenčné haplotypy používa z databáz HapMap3 a 1000G. Simuluje dáta rôznych populácií.
Posledným generátorom patriacim do skupiny podobných

programov, ktorý spomenieme++ je SDG [8], ktorý automaticky generuje databázu SNP mutácií na základe užívateľom špecifikovanej skupiny proteínov. Pre generovanie využíva databázu dbSNP [13].
Každý z týchto generátorov sa opiera o reálne dáta, ktoré čerpá z niektorej z verejne dostupných databáz. Nenarazili sme na žiaden generátor simulovaných dát, ktorý umožňuje generovanie SNP čiste na základe užívateľom definovaných asociácií a interakcií, bez potreby určitej formy reálnych dát.

2 Aplikácia

Aplikácia s názvom GeneratorSNP generuje simulované dáta v ktorých sú obsiahnuté SNP mutácie. Generovanie prebieha na základe užívateľom definovaných parametrov, medzi ktoré patria počet mutácii, počet pacientov, pomer chorých pacientov a parametre pre definíciu všetkých typov mutácií, ako sú pomery jednotlivých typov mutácií, sily korelácií, či frekvencie jednotlivých alel. Rovnako definuje aj vzťahy medzi SNP a vkladá do týchto dát významné interakcie buď medzi SNP a istou fenotypovou charakteristikou (chorobou), medzi dvomi SNP, ktoré medzi sebou korelujú alebo medzi dvoma korelujúcimi SNP, ktoré zároveň interagujú s danou fenotypovou črtou jedinca. Na základe presnej definície týchto parametrov sa následne vygeneruje tabuľka v ktorej budú zachytené všetky potrebné informácie a z ktorej sa následne zapisuje do výstupných formátov, primárne VCF.

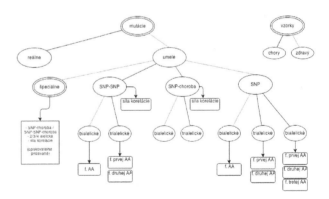

Obrázok 1: Schéma nastavenia parametrov. Čierne čiary v strome sú definované parametre, červené sú z nich automaticky dopočítavané. Elipsa reprezentuje pomer konkrétneho typu mutácie z celkového počtu všetkých mutácií, obdĺžnik reprezentuje vzorec(funkciu) na základe ktorého sa vypočítavajú určité hodnoty pre jednu konkrétnu mutáciu.

Vyberanie typu konkrétnej mutácie Pri implementácií bolo potrebné zabezpečiť, aby sa jednotlivé typy mutácií negenerovali v zhlukoch, ale boli rozvrstvené náhodne s rešpektovaním zadaných pomerov mutácií jednotlivého

---

[6]http://www.hapsample.org/
[7]linkage disequilibrium

[8]The SNP database Generator
http://www.cmbi.kun.nl/mcsis/vanhamer/program.html

typu. Riešenie tohoto problému môžeme sledovať na obrázku 1.

Generovanie prebieha tak, že sa postupne vygenerujú všetky mutácie jedna po druhej. Postupne sa vypĺňajú stĺpce tabuľky, čo znamená, že sa daná mutácia vygeneruje pre všetkých pacientov naraz. V každom kroku sa teda vypĺni konkrétna SNP mutácia a to tak, že sa v každej deliacej vetve stromu výpočtu vygeneruje náhodna hodnota z intervalu (0,1) a porovná sa s hodnotou parametru nastaveného na danej vetve. Na základe výsledku tohoto porovnania výpočet postupuje do ďalšieho uzlu a proces sa opakuje obdobným spôsobom, až sa dostane do listu stromu, v ktorom sú už známe všetky potrebné informácie o type tejto konkrétnej mutácie a môže sa vygenerovať. Postúpi sa na ďalší index a celý priebeh sa opakuje až sa vygeneruje kompletná tabuľka so všetkými SNP, ktoré užívateľ definoval. Indexy sa vyberajú postupne z randomizovaného zoznamu, čo zaručuje efektivitu výberu konkrétneho stĺpca pre danú mutáciu, ako aj to, že budú vyplnené všetky stĺpce tabuľky.

Funkcie Keďže generujeme pomerne veľký počet mutácií (klasicky 100 000) bolo sa treba vysporiadať s problémom ako efektívne nadefinovať parametre, ktoré sú pre každý konkrétny stĺpec jedinečné. Jedná sa o silu korelácie medzi SNP a chorobou, resp. SNP a SNP medzi sebou a o frekvencie jednotlivých alel v danom stĺpci tabuľky. Tri-

viálny postup by bol definovať tieto parametre napevno jednou konkrétnou hodnotou, čo by ale neodzrkadľovalo reálne hodnoty, keďže všetky stĺpce by korelovali rovnako silno a takisto zastúpenie jednotlivých alel by bolo v každom stĺpci rovnaké. Ďalším triviálnym postupom by bolo vypĺňať tieto parametre manuálne pre každú jednu mutáciu, čo je takisto nemysliteľné nadefinovať pred generovaním cez 100 000 hodnôt. Nami popisovaná aplikácia využíva pre definíciu týchto hodnôt funkcie, ktorých príklad môžeme vidieť v strednej časti obrázku 2. Užívateľ definuje vzorec tejto funkcie ako parameter všade, kde sa táto funkcionalita musí použiť, teda pre jednotlivé frekvencie alel pri daných typoch mutácií a pre korelácie SNP-SNP a SNP-choroba. Funkcia musí byť definovaná na intervale (0,1) a celý princíp spočíva v tom, že sa pri vypĺňaní konkrétneho jedného SNP vypočíta potrebná hodnota z náhodne vygenerovaného čísla z intervalu (0,1) aplikovaného na zadanú funkciu. Správnou voľbou funkcie môže užívateľ modelovať simulované mutácie presne tak ako sú zastúpené v prírode.

Spúštanie aplikácie Aplikáciu je možné spustiť dvoma spôsobmi. Primárny spôsob je generovanie hodnôt z vytvoreného grafického užívateľského rozhrania, v ktorom užívateľ nadefinuje všetky potrebné parametre a následne na ich základe vygeneruje výstupne súbory s mutáciami. Jedno nastavenie parametrov je rovné jednému generova-

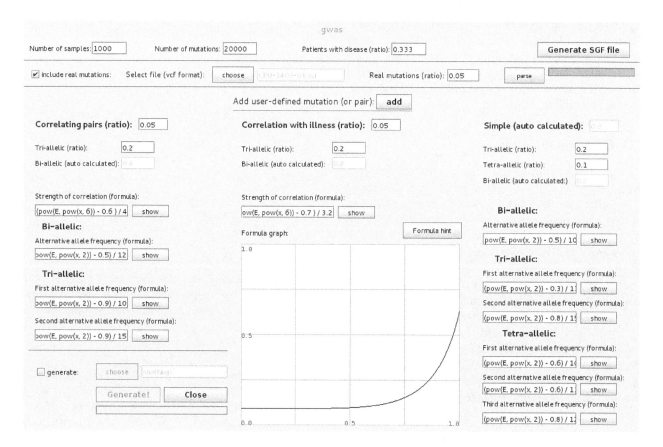

Obrázok 2: Hlavné okno aplikácie v ktorom nastavujeme potrebné parametre.

niu hodnôt. Ak spustí aplikáciu opakovane na rovnako zadaných parametroch, výstupy nebudú totožné, pretože vypĺňanie tabuľky prebieha z istého uhlu pohľadu náhodne, avšak tieto dva výstupy budú rovnaké v presnom dodržaní zadefinovaných rámcov. Hlavné okno užívateľského rozhrania, v ktorom sa definujú parametre môžeme vidieť na obrázku 2.

Hlavné okno je logicky rozčlenené do sekcií z ktorých užívateľ pochopí, ktoré parametre práve vypĺňa. Aplikácia takisto poskytuje možnosť zahrnúť do simulovaných dát aj dáta reálne, nahrané do programu zo súborov vo formáte VCF, ktoré sú k dispozícií napríklad v databáze dbSNP [13].

Druhým spôsobom je spustiť aplikáciu z prikázového riadka. Pre tieto potreby je vytvorený nami zadefinovaný formát súboru SGF [14]. Tento spôsob spúšťania je vhodný pri tandemovom generovaní dát, kedy si dopredu v súbore zapíšeme hodnoty parametrov pre viaceré generovania dát (jeden riadok = jedno generovanie) a naraz tieto dáta necháme vygenerovať bez toho, aby sme zakaždým museli vpisovať parametre do grafického rozhrania aplikácie.

3 Výsledky

Dáta vygenerované touto aplikáciou boli testované na niektorých dnes bežne používaných algoritmoch a výsledky boli viac než uspokojivé. Zakompované interakcie ukryté do týchto dát boli vo väčšine prípadov správne detekované.

Ako príklad uvádzame výsledky testovania *Testom dobrej zhody (Pearsonov chi-kvadrat test)* [15]. V prvom prípade sme do dát ukryli asociácie, ktoré sú vypísané na obrázku 4. Jedná sa o asociáciu jednej SNP a choroby, sila korelácie je vyznačená na obrázku. Výsledok testu je zobrazený na obrázku 5. Ako môžeme sledovať algoritmus správne detekoval všetky ukryté asociácie, dokonca aj tie, ktoré asociujú s chorobou s korelačným koeficientom len 0.1. Naviac sú v grafe zobrazené v poradí zodpovedajúcom silám korelácií, ktoré sme zadefinovali (najsilnejšie korelujúca hodnota je najvyššie v grafe).

```
#SNP/SNP,SNP    cor_strong
def880          0.95
def775          0.9
def700          0.8
def66           0.7
def603          0.6
def531          0.5
def445          0.4
def727          0.3
def200          0.2
def392          0.1
```

Obrázok 3: Nami zadefinované a ukryté špeciálne mutácie, ktoré asociujú s chorobou.

V druhom prípade sme do dát ukryli asociácie, ktoré sú vypísané na obrázku 6. Jedná sa o interakciu dvoch SNP

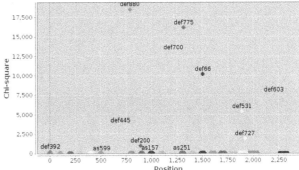

Obrázok 4: Výsledok testu. Hodnoty zobrazené na grafe zodpovedajú nami ukrytým vzťahom.

a súčasnú asociáciu s chorobou. Sila korelácie je vyznačená na obrázku. Výsledok testu je zobrazený na obrázku 7. Ako môžeme sledovať algoritmus správne detekoval všetky ukryté asociácie, dokonca aj tie, ktoré asociujú s chorobou s korelačným koeficientom len 0.1. V tomto prípade ich však v grafe nezoradil úplne presne v poradí podľa síl korelácií, ako tomu bolo v predošlom prípade. Je to spôsobené tým, že použitý testovací algoritmus nedokáže odhaľovať interakcie dvoch SNP súčasne a tak ich obe mýľne považuje za jednoduché. Následkom sú výkyvy zobrazenia v grafe, navyše slabé korelácie (menšie ako 0.2) sa nepodarilo pri všetkých testoch zobraziť.

```
#SNP/SNP,SNP    cor_strong
def258,def219   0.95
def369,def195   0.9
def392          0.9
def149,def95    0.8
def268,def829   0.7
def595          0.6
def261,def313   0.5
def154,def200   0.4
def318          0.3
def813          0.2
def257          0.1
```

Obrázok 5: Nami zadefinované a ukryté špeciálne mutácie, ktoré interagujú medzi sebou a súčasne asociujú s chorobou.

4 Diskusia

Generovanie simulovaných dát na osobnom počítači trvá pri bežne používaných hodnotách (1000 pacientov, 100 000 mutácií) v priemere 15 sekúnd. Navyše pri simulovaných dátach máme informáciu o tom, aké vzťahy a interakcie v sebe obsahujú a tak je porovnávanie algoritmov na týchto dátach rozhodne efektívnejšie, rýchlejšie a spoľahlivejšie ako ich testovanie na dátach reálnych. Po získaní

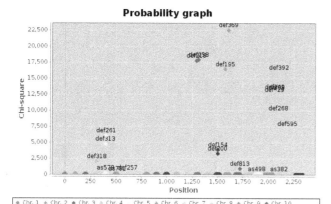

Obrázok 6: Výsledok testu. Hodnoty zobrazené na grafe zodpovedajú nami ukrytým vzťahom.

informácie o tom, že istý algoritmus preukázal spoľahlivosť a korektnosť na simulovaných dátach, je vyššia pravdepodobnosť, že po aplikovaní na reálne dáta bude tento algoritmus poskytovať správne výsledky a odhalí skryté asociácie a interakcie v prírode. Navyše aplikácia nevyžaduje pre generovanie žiadnu formu reálnych dát, avšak v prípade potreby poskytuje možnosť zahrnúť do simulovaných dát buď dáta reálne alebo vygenerované inou aplikáciou, čo je veľmi užitočným prvkom.

V ďalšom výskume plánujeme aplikáciu rozšíriť o LD bloky, kde bude jedna či viacero SNP interagovať s celým blokom. S tým súvisí aj vylepšenie závislosti SNP na chromozóme a pozícií na ktorej sa nachádza.

5　Thalamoss

Aplikácia bola primárne vytvorená pre potreby projektu THALAMOSS[9]. Tento projekt má za úlohu skúmať a identifikovať SNP mutácie, ktoré zapríčiňujú chorobu s názvom Talasémia - konkrétne β talasémiu [16]. Jedná sa o dedičné ochorenie krvi, ktoré spôsobuje poruchy tvorby bielkovinových podjednotiek β. Tým je poškodené krvné farbivo hemoglobín, čo spôsobuje problémy s viazaním kyslíka v tele a jeho prenosom. Choroba má veľmi ťažký priebeh.

5.1　Poďakovanie

Finančná podpora bola poskytnutá projektom 7.RP EÚ "THALAssaemia MOdular Stratification System for Personalized Therapy of Beta-Thalassaemia – THALAMOSS"(FP7-HEALTH-2012-INNOVATION-1 (HEALTH.2012.1.2-1) Collaborative Project).

Referencie

[1] R.C. King, W.D. Stansfield, P.K. Mulligan: *A dictionary of genetics*, 7th ed., New York: Oxford University Press, 2006.

[2] N.J. Schork, D. Fallin, S. Lanchbury: *Single nucleotide polymorphisms and the future of genetic epidemiology.* Clin Genet **58** (2000) 250–264

[3] The 1000 Genomes Project Consortium, A map of human genome variation from population-scale sequencing. *Nature* **467** (2010) 1061-1073

[4] The International HapMap Consortium, The International HapMap Project. *Nature* **426** (2003) 789-796

[5] J. McEntyre, J. Ostell, editors: *The NCBI Handbook.* Bethesda (MD): National Center for Biotechnology Information (US), 2002

[6] W.S. Bush, J.H. Moore: *Genome-Wide Association Studies.* PLoS Comput Biol, Public Library of Science **8:12** (2012) s. e1002822

[7] P. Danecek, et.al.: *The Variant Call Format and VCFtools*, USA: Bioinformatics Advance Access, 2011

[8] P.C. Phillips: *Epistasis — the essential role of gene interactions in the structure and evolution of genetic systems*, Oregon: Center for Ecology and Evolution, University of Oregon, 2008.

[9] S. Purcell, B. Neale, K. Todd-Brown, L. Thomas, M.A.R. Ferreira, D. Bender, J. Maller, P. Sklar, P.I.W. de Bakker, M.J. Daly, P.C. Sham: *PLINK: a toolset for whole-genome association and population-based linkage analysis.* American Journal of Human Genetics, 2007

[10] F.A. Wright, et al.: *Simulating association studies: a database resampling method for candidate regions or whole genome scans.* Bioinformatics **23** (2007) 2581-2588

[11] Ch. Li, M. Li: *GWAsimulator: a rapid whole-genome simulation program.* Bioinformatics **24** (2008) 140-142

[12] Z. Su, J. Marchini, P.Donnelly: *HAPGEN2: simulation of multiple disease SNPs.* Bioinformatics **27(16)** (2011) 2304-2305

[13] S.T. Sherry, M. Ward, K. Sirotkin: *dbSNP—Database for Single Nucleotide Polymorphisms and Other Classes of Minor Genetic Variation.* Genome Research **9** (1999) 677–679

[14] S. Štefanič: *Software na generování simulovaných testovacích dat pro genomové asociační studie (GWAS).* Brno: Masarykova univerzita, Fakulta informatiky, 2013

[15] D.C. Howell: *CHI-SQUARE TEST - ANALYSIS OF CONTINGENCY TABLES.* Vermont: University of Vermont, 2007

[16] R. Galanello, R. Origa: *Beta-thalassemia.* Orphanet Journal of Rare Diseases **5** (2010)

---

[9]http://thalamoss.eu/index.html

ITAT 2013: Workshops, Posters, and Tutorials, p. 69
ISBN 978-1490952086, © 2013 T. Vinař, B. Brejová

Comparative Genomics in Genome Projects
(Abstract)

Tomáš Vinař, Broňa Brejová

Faculty of Mathematics, Physics, and Informatics, Comenius University in Bratislava, Mlynská dolina, 842 48 Bratislava, Slovakia
{vinar,brejova}@fmph.uniba.sk

We will describe contributions of our research group to large international genome projects. These contributions can be divided into two categories: genome annotation and positive selection analysis.

Genome annotation. In recent years, major lowering of genome sequencing costs brought large availability of novel genome sequences. Annotation of protein coding genes is one of the basic steps in their analysis. A traditional way of annotating genes is to first create a manually curated set of high-confidence gene models, use it to train parameters a gene finding program, and then use this program to predict genes on the whole-genome scale. Retraining is required for each newly sequenced organism, unless gene finder paramters are available for a closely related species.

Unfortunately, creating these training sets is a difficult and time consuming process, limiting our ability to obtain reliable annotations for newly sequenced genomes. To address this problem, we use a variety of information, including known protein sequences (from other genomes), similarity to related genomes, and experimental evidence of transcription (RNASeq) to train a gene finder in an automated way [1]. We are using these tools in genome projects to provide an initial protein coding gene annotation that is used as a basis of further analysis [9, 10].

Positive selection analysis. Detection of positive selection is a key step in identification of genes responsible for specific phenotypic traits of a particular organism. In our earlier work [3], we have summarized an analysis framework based on codon-substitution models of Yang and Nielsen [8], and applied it to then available mammalian genomes. We have applied our methodology in the context of several vertebrate genome projects [2, 4, 5, 6]. Among other results, we have demonstrated that several functional categories (e.g. immunity, defense) are consistently enriched for positively selected genes, while other categories (e.g., genes related to basic cellular processes) are strongly conserved throughout vertebrate evolution. We have discovered several gene mutations likely responsible for lineage-specific traits and characterized differences between evolution of protein coding genes in mammals and rodents. We have demonstrated that duplicated gene clusters are generally enriched for positive selection and provided tools for analysis of genome regions accumulating segmental duplications [2, 7, 5]. We have also provided comprehensive lists of genes positively selected on individual lineages and clades that can be studied in more detail by specialists.

Outlook. With the cost of sequencing of a human-sized genome soon to be lower than the open access fee for a single publication, it is clear that sequencing efforts will continue to boom in the near future. A major effort of sequencing 10,000 vertebrate genomes currently under way will create a huge opportunity for comparative genomics. However, tools currently available are designed for comparative analysis of tens of genomes at best. Thus, there is a clear need for designing new methods that will scale to thousands of genome instead.

References

[1] B. Brejova, T. Vinar, Y. Chen, S. Wang, G. Zhao, D. G. Brown, M. Li, and Y. Zhou. Finding genes in Schistosoma japonicum: annotating novel genomes with help of extrinsic evidence. *Nucleic Acids Res*, 37(7):e52, 2009.

[2] R. A. Gibbs et al. Evolutionary and biomedical insights from the rhesus macaque genome. *Science*, 316(5822):222–224, 2007.

[3] C. Kosiol, T. Vinar, R. R. da Fonseca, M. J. Hubisz, C. D. Bustamante, R. Nielsen, and A. Siepel. Patterns of positive selection in six Mammalian genomes. *PLoS Genet*, 4(8):e1000144, 2008.

[4] R. Li et al. The sequence and de novo assembly of the giant panda genome. *Nature*, 463(7279):311–317, 2010.

[5] D. P. Locke et al. Comparative and demographic analysis of orang-utan genomes. *Nature*, 469(7331):529–533, 2011.

[6] B. H. Shaffer et al. The western painted turtle genome, a model for the evolution of extreme physiological adaptations in a slowly evolving lineage. *Genome Biol*, 14(3):R28, 2013.

[7] T. Vinar, B. Brejova, G. Song, and A. Siepel. Reconstructing histories of complex gene clusters on a phylogeny. *J Comput Biol*, 17(9):1267–1269, 2010.

[8] Z. Yang and R. Nielsen. Codon-substitution models for detecting molecular adaptation at individual sites along specific lineages. *Mol Biol Evol*, 19(6):908–917, 2002.

[9] Y. Zhou et al. The Schistosoma japonicum genome reveals features of host-parasite interplay. *Nature*, 460(7253):345–351, 2009.

[10] S. Zhu et al. Sequencing the genome of Marssonina brunnea reveals fungus-poplar co-evolution. *BMC Genomics*, 13:382, 2012.

Workshop on Computational Intelligence and Data Mining

The workshop "Computational Intelligence and Data Mining" has been organized as a part of the conference ITAT 2013. The workshop is mainly targeted at participants with research interests in evolutionary computing, artificial neural networks, and fuzzy logic. The participants were invited to submit a paper in English of up to eight pages, prepared according to the instructions at ITAT 2013 web pages. The authors of the best papers from the workshop will be invited to submit an extended version of their work to the journal Neural Network World, published by the Czech Technical University and covered in Science Citation Index Expanded and Current Contents.

A key factor influencing the overall quality of the workshop and of the final versions of the submitted papers published in these proceedings was the program committee. "Computational Intelligence and Data Mining" is grateful to 22 reviewers who read the submitted papers, and have provided competent, and in most cases very detailed, feedback to their authors. Nearly all program committee members regularly review papers for first-class international journals, and many of them are leading Czech scientists in their particular areas of computational intelligence, with an international reputation witnessed by hundreds of citations.

Each submitted paper was anonymously reviewed by at least three of the program committee members. The papers were evaluated according to a seven-grade scale from "strong reject" to "strong accept". In the end, the workshop program committee only accepted papers, where no referee suggested (even weak) rejection and the mean score of the paper was positive. This volume presents final versions of seven papers that were accepted for the workshop presentation.

Martin Holeňa
Academy of Sciences of the Czech Republic
Workshop Program Chair

Workshop Program Committee

Petr Berka, University of Economics, Faculty of Informatics and Statistics
Jan Faigl, Czech Technical University, Faculty of Electrical Engineering
František Hakl, Academy of Sciences of the Czech Republic, Institute of Computer Science
David Hartman, Charles University, Facutly of Mathematics and Physics
Jaroslav Hlinka, Academy of Sciences of the Czech Republic, Institute of ComputerScience
Martin Holeňa, Academy of Sciences of the Czech Republic, Institute of Computer Science
Ján Hric, Charles University, Facutly of Mathematics and Physics
Marcel Jiřina, Academy of Sciences of the Czech Republic, Institute of Computer Science
Jan Kalina, Academy of Sciences of the Czech Republic, Institute of Computer Science
Tomáš Kliegr, University of Economics, Faculty of Informatics and Statistics
Jiří Kléma, Czech Technical University, Faculty of Electrical Engineering
Pavel Kordík, Czech Technical University, Faculty of Information Technology
Jiří Kubalík, Czech Technical University, Faculty of Electrical Engineering
Jaromír Kukal, Czech Technical University, Faculty of Nuclear Sciences and Physical Engineering
Mirko Navara, Czech Technical University, Faculty of Electrical Engineering
Roman Neruda, Academy of Sciences of the Czech Republic, Institute of Computer Science
Tomáš Pevný, Czech Technical University, Faculty of Electrical Engineering
Petr Pošík, Czech Technical University, Faculty of Electrical Engineering
Jan Rauch, University of Economics, Faculty of Informatics and Statistics
Miroslav Šnorek, Czech Technical University, Faculty of Electrical Engineering
Martin Vejmelka, Academy of Sciences of the Czech Republic, Institute of Computer Science
Marta Vomlelová, Charles University, Facutly of Mathematics and Physics

ITAT 2013: Workshops, Posters, and Tutorials, pp. 73–76
ISBN 978-1490952086, © 2013 V. Kůrková

Representations of highly-varying functions by perceptron networks

Věra Kůrková

Institute of Computer Science, Academy of Sciences of the Czech,
vera@cs.cas.cz,
WWW home page: http://www.cs.cas.cz/ vera

Abstract: Tractability of representations of multivariable functions by perceptron networks is investigated. There are described classes of functions which cannot be tractably represented by Heaviside perceptron networks in the sense that all their representations by such networks require numbers of units or sizes of output weights depending exponentially on the number of variables d. It is shown that the concept of variational norm from approximation theory can play a role of a measure of such tractability. Existence of large sets of Boolean functions with variations depending on d exponentially is proven. The results are illustrated by an example of a class of Boolean functions defined in terms of their communication matrices.

1 Introduction

A widely-used type of a neural-network architecture is the one-hidden-layer network. Typical computational units in the hidden layer are perceptrons, radial, and kernel units. A variety of learning algorithms have been developed and successfully applied to adjust parameters of such networks (see, e.g., [8, 7] and the references therein). Recently, one-hidden-layer networks have been called shallow networks to distinguish them from deep ones, which contain more hidden layers.

Shallow networks with many types of computational units are known to be universal approximators, i.e., they can approximate up to any desired accuracy all continuous functions or $\mathscr{L}^p$-functions on compact subsets of $\mathbb{R}^d$. In particular, the universal approximation property holds for one-hidden-layer networks with perceptrons having any non-polynomial activation function [17, 23] and with radial and kernel units satisfying mild conditions [22, 20, 14], [26, p.153]. Moreover, all functions defined on finite subsets of $\mathbb{R}^d$ can be exactly represented by one-hidden-layer networks with sigmoidal perceptrons [10] or with Gaussian kernel units [21].

Proofs of the universal approximation capability of one-hidden-layer networks require potentially unlimited numbers of hidden units. These numbers representing model complexities of the networks are critical factors for practical implementations. Dependence of model complexities of shallow networks on their input dimensions, types of units, functions to be approximated, and accuracies of approximation have been studied using tools from nonlinear approximation theory. Some estimates were derived from upper bounds on rates of approximation of various

classes of multivariable functions by networks with increasing numbers of hidden units (see, e.g., [11] and references therein). On the other hand, limitations of computational capabilities of one-hidden-layer networks are less understood. Only few lower bounds on rates of approximations by such networks are known. Moreover the lower bounds are mostly non constructive and hold for types of computational units that are not commonly used [18, 19]. Also growth of sizes of weights is not well understood, it was shown that in some cases, reasonable sizes of weights are more important for successful learning than bounds on numbers of network units [4].

Recently new learning algorithms, which can be applied to deep networks, were developed (see, e.g., [5, 9]). As training networks with more than one hidden layer involves complicated nonlinear optimization procedures, generally it is more difficult than training shallow ones. Hence, it is desirable to develop some theoretical background for characterization of tasks whose computing by shallow networks requires models with considerably larger numbers of units and/or sizes of weights than computing by deep ones. Since typical neurocomputing applications deal with large numbers of variables, it is particularly important to understand how quickly model complexities of shallow networks grow with increasing input dimensions.

To contribute to such understanding, in this paper we investigate classes of multivariable functions whose representations by shallow networks are not tractable in the sense that the numbers of network hidden units or sizes of their output weights grow exponentially with increasing input dimensions. We propose to use the concept of variational norm from approximation theory as a measure of "amount of variations of a function", which was suggested by Bengio et al. [6] as a cause of difficulties in representing functions by shallow networks. We show that the size of the variational norm with respect to a dictionary of computational units reflects both the number of hidden units and sizes of output weights. We derive lower bounds on probabilistic measures of sets of real-valued Boolean functions having "large" variations. For Heaviside perceptron networks, we prove that a probability that a functions of a given Euclidean norm has a "large" variation (depending on d exponentially) grows with d exponentially, i.e., that for large dimensions in sets of functions with constant Euclidean norms most Boolean real-valued functions cannot be tractably represented by Heaviside perceptron networks. We describe a concrete class of non tractable functions in terms of properties of their communication matrices.

The paper is organized as follows. Section 2 contains basic concepts on shallow perceptron networks and Boolean functions. Section 3 proposes a mathematical formalization of the concept of a "highly-varying function", shows that it is related to large model complexities or sizes of weights in networks representing such functions, and gives estimates of probabilistic measures of sets of functions with variations depending on d exponentially. Section 4 illustrates general results by examples of Boolean functions with Hadamard communication matrices.

2 Preliminaries

One-hidden-layer networks with single linear outputs (recently called *shallow networks*) compute input-output functions from sets of the form

$$\operatorname{span}_n G := \left\{ \sum_{i=1}^{n} w_i g_i \,\middle|\, w_i \in \mathbb{R}, g_i \in G \right\},$$

where G, called a *dictionary*, is a set of functions computable by a given type of units, the coefficients w_i are called *output weights*, and n is the number of hidden units. This number is sometimes used as a measure of *model complexity*. In this paper we use the terminology "one-hidden-layer network" meaning a network with a single linear output.

We investigate growth of network complexities representing functions of increasing numbers of variables d. Let D be an infinite subset of the set of positive integers, $\mathscr{F} = \{f_d \,|\, d \in D\}$ a class of functions and $\{G_d \,|\, d \in D\}$ a class of dictionaries, such that for every $d \in D$, f_d is a function of d variables and G_d is formed by functions of d variables. We call the problem of representing the set $\mathscr{F}$ by networks from $\{\operatorname{span} G_d \,|\, d \in D\}$ *tractable* if for every $d \in D$, there exists a network in $\operatorname{span}_{n_d} G$ representing f_d as its input-output function such that n_d and absolute values of all output weights in the network grow with d polynomially. Note that different concepts of tractability were used in other contexts (see, e.g., [11]).

In this paper, we focus on representations of real-valued Boolean functions by one-hidden-layer perceptron networks. By

$$\mathscr{B}(\{0,1\}^d) := \{f \,|\, f : \{0,1\}^d \to \mathbb{R}\}$$

we denote the space of *real-valued Boolean functions of d-variables*. This space is isomorphic to the Euclidean space $\mathbb{R}^{2^d}$ and thus on $\mathscr{B}(\{0,1\}^d)$ we have the *Euclidean inner product* defined as

$$\langle f, g \rangle := \sum_{u \in \{0,1\}^d} f(u)g(u)$$

and the *Euclidean norm* $\|f\|_2 := \sqrt{\langle f, f \rangle}$. By $\cdot$ we denote the inner product on $\{0,1\}^d$, defined as $u \cdot v := \sum_{i=1}^{d} u_i v_i$.

We consider two dictionaries of computational units, which are subsets of $\mathscr{B}(\{0,1\}^d)$. The first one is the set H_d of functions on $\{0,1\}^d$ computable by *Heaviside perceptrons*, i.e.,

$$H_d := \{\vartheta(v \cdot . + b) : \{0,1\}^d \to \{0,1\} \,|\, v \in \mathbb{R}^d, b \in \mathbb{R}\},$$

where ϑ denotes the *Heaviside activation function* defined as $\vartheta(t) := 0$ for $t < 0$ and $\vartheta(t) := 1$ for $t \geq 0$. Note that H_d is the *set of characteristic functions of half-spaces*. The second dictionary P_d is closely related to H_d. It is formed by functions from $\mathscr{B}(\{0,1\}^d)$ computable by perceptrons with *signum activation function* $\operatorname{sgn} : \mathbb{R} \to \{-1,1\}$ defined as $\operatorname{sgn}(t) := -1$ for $t < 0$ and $\operatorname{sign}(t) := 1$ for $t \geq 0$. We denote

$$P_d := \{\operatorname{sgn}(v \cdot . + b) : \{0,1\}^d \to \{-1,1\} \,|\, v \in \mathbb{R}^d, b \in \mathbb{R}\}.$$

3 Highly-varying functions

In this section, we use the concept of a variational norm from approximation theory as a measure of tractability of a representation of a class of function by one-hidden-layer network.

For a subset G of a normed linear space $(\mathscr{X}, \|.\|_{\mathscr{X}})$, *G-variation (variation with respect to the set G)*, denoted by $\|.\|_G$, is defined as

$$\|f\|_G := \inf\{c \in \mathbb{R}_+ \,|\, f/c \in \operatorname{cl}_{\mathscr{X}} \operatorname{conv}(G \cup -G)\},$$

where $\operatorname{cl}_{\mathscr{X}}$ denotes the closure with respect to the norm $\|\cdot\|_{\mathscr{X}}$ on $\mathscr{X}$, $-G := \{-g \,|\, g \in G\}$, and $\operatorname{conv} G := \left\{\sum_{i=1}^{k} a_i g_i \,\middle|\, a_i \in [0,1], \sum_{i=1}^{k} a_i = 1, g_i \in G, k \in \mathbb{N}\right\}$ is the convex hull of G.

Variation with respect to a set of functions was introduced by Kůrková [13] as an extension of Barron's [2] concept of variation with respect to sets of characteristic functions. Barron focused on the set of *characteristic functions of half-spaces*, which corresponds to the dictionary of functions computable by Heaviside perceptrons. For $d = 1$, variation with respect to half-spaces coincides up to a constant with the concept of total variation from integration theory. Variational norms play an important role in estimates of approximation rates by one-hidden-layer networks (see, e.g., [3, 15, 11] and the references therein).

The following straightforward consequence of the definition of G-variation shows that in all representations of a function with "large" G-variation by networks with units from G, the number of units must be "large" or some absolute values of output weights must be "large".

Proposition 1. *Let G be a bounded subset of a normed linear space $(\mathscr{X}, \|.\|)$, then for every $f \in \mathscr{X}$, $\|f\|_G \leq \min\left\{\sum_{i=1}^{k} |w_i| \,\middle|\, f = \sum_{i=1}^{k} w_i g_i, w_i \in \mathbb{R}, g_i \in G, k \in \mathbb{N}\right\}$ and for G finite with $\operatorname{card} G = k$,*
$\|f\|_G = \min\left\{\sum_{i=1}^{k} |w_i| \,\middle|\, f = \sum_{i=1}^{k} w_i g_i, w_i \in \mathbb{R}, g_i \in G\right\}$.

Proof. The first statement follows directly from the definition and the second one holds as for G finite, conv G is closed. $\square$

Thus families of sets of d-variable functions $\{F_d \,|\, d \in D\}$ with G_d-variations growing with d exponentially cannot be tractably represented by networks with units from G_d. To describe such classes of functions, we use the following lower bound on variational norm from [16].

Theorem 2. *Let $(\mathscr{X}, \|.\|_{\mathscr{X}})$ be a Hilbert space and G its bounded subset. Then for every $f \in \mathscr{X} \setminus G^{\perp}$,*
$$\|f\|_G \geq \frac{\|f\|^2}{\sup_{g \in G} |g \cdot f|}.$$

Theorem 2 implies that functions which are "almost orthogonal" to G have large variations. Note that G-variation is a norm and thus by multiplying f by suitable constants we can obtain functions with arbitrarily large or small variations. However in neurocomputing, we are usually interested in computation of functions with similar sizes as computational units. Also in theory of circuit complexity, representations of classes of functions of fixed Euclidean norms by networks with gates computing functions with the same norms are investigated (see, e.g., [24]). In particular, representations of Boolean functions with values in $\{-1, 1\}$ by networks composed from signum perceptrons are studied. All these functions have Euclidean norms equal to $2^{d/2}$.

The maximum of the l_2-norms of the elements of the dictionary H_d formed by functions from $\mathscr{B}(\{0,1\}^d)$ computable by Heaviside perceptrons is $2^{d/2}$ and the norms of all elements of P_d are equal to $2^{d/2}$. Thus it is reasonable to explore distributions of variations of functions in the spheres $S_{2^{d/2}}^{2^d-1}$ of radii $2^{d/2}$ in $\mathscr{B}(\{0,1\}^d)$.

Consider an *angular pseudometrics* δ defined on the unit ball S^{2^d-1} in $\mathbb{R}^{2^d}$ as
$$\delta(f,g) = \arccos |f \cdot g|.$$

This pseudometrics defines the distance as the minimum of the two angles between f and g and between f and $-g$ (it is a pseudometrics as the distance of antipodal vectors is zero).

The following theorem estimates probability that a randomly chosen Boolean function of d variables with the Euclidean norm $2^{d/2}$ has variation with respect to Heaviside perceptrons larger than $\frac{1}{\cos \alpha}$.

Theorem 3. *Let d be a positive integer, μ a uniform measure on $S_{2^{d/2}}^{2^d-1}$ such that $\mu(S_{2^{d/2}}^{2^d-1}) = 1$, $\alpha \in (0, \pi/2)$, and $V_\alpha = \{f \in S_{2^{d/2}}^{2^d-1} \,|\, \|f\|_{H_d} \geq \|f\|_{P_d} \geq \frac{1}{\cos \alpha}\}$. Then*
$$\mu(V_\alpha) \geq 1 - 2^{d^2} e^{-\frac{(2^d-1)(\cos \alpha)^2}{2}}.$$

Proof. By Theorem 2, V_α contains all $f \in S_{2^{d/2}}^{2^d-1}$ satisfying for all $g \in P^d$, $|f \cdot g| \leq \cos \alpha$, i.e., all f with $\delta(f,g) = \arccos |f \cdot g| \geq \alpha$. This means that f is not contained in any of the spherical caps $C(g, \varepsilon)$ with a center $g \in P_d$ and angle

$\alpha = \arccos \varepsilon$ defined as $C(g, \varepsilon) = \{h \in S_{2^{d/2}}^{2^d-1} \,|\, h \cdot g \geq \varepsilon\}$. With d increasing, the normalized measures of the spherical caps are decreasing exponentially fast: $\mu(C(g, \varepsilon)) \leq e^{-m\varepsilon^2/2}$ (see, e.g., [1, p.11]). Schläfli [25] derived an upper bound $2^{d^2 - d\log_2 d + \mathscr{O}(d)}$ on the number of subsets of $\{0,1\}^d$ obtained by intersecting $\{0,1\}^d$ with half-spaces. Thus cardinalities of both dictionaries H_d and P_d are smaller than 2^{d^2}. Hence $\mu(V_\alpha) \geq 1 - 2^{d^2} e^{-\frac{2^d (\cos \alpha)^2}{2}}$. $\square$

Setting $\cos \alpha = (2^d - 1)^{-1/4}$, we obtain from Theorem 3 the lower bound $1 - e^{-\frac{(2^d-1)^{1/2} - 2d^2}{2}}$ on the relative size of the subset of the ball of radius $2^{d/2}$ in $\mathscr{B}(\{0,1\}^d)$ containing functions with variations with respect to half-spaces larger or equal to $(2^d - 1)^{1/4}$. So by Proposition 1, a randomly chosen real-valued Boolean function of the norm $2^{d/2}$ cannot be tractably represented by a shallow Heaviside perceptron network.

4 Examples

In the previous section, we proved that there exist "large" sets of functions with exponentially large variations. Some concrete examples of such functions can be obtained using representations of Boolean functions as communication matrices. Recall that the *communication matrix of a function* $f : \{0,1\}^d \to \{-1, 1\}$ with d even is a $2^{d/2} \times 2^{d/2}$ matrix $M(f)$ with rows and columns indexed by vectors $u, v \in \{0,1\}^{d/2}$ such that
$$M(f)_{u,v} := f(u * v),$$

where $*$ denotes the *concatenation* of two vectors in $\{0,1\}^{d/2}$ defined for $u, v \in \{0,1\}^{d/2}$ as $(u * v)_i := u_i$ for $i = 1, \ldots, d/2$ and $(u * v)_i := v_i$ for $i = d/2 + 1, \ldots, d$.

Recall that a square matrix with entries in $\{-1, 1\}$ is called *Hadamard* if each pair of its rows (columns, resp.) is orthogonal. The following theorem obtained as a reformulation of [16, Theorem 3.7] gives a lower bound on H_d-variations of functions with Hadamard communication matrices. The notation $h = \Omega(g(d))$ with two functions $g, h : \mathbb{N} \to \mathbb{R}$ means that there exist a positive constant c and $n_0 \in \mathbb{N}$ such that for all $n \geq n_o$ one has $h(n) \geq c\, g(n)$ [12].

Theorem 4. *Let d be an even integer, $f : \{0,1\}^d \to \{-1,1\}$ a function with a Hadamard communication matrix, and $f(x) = \sum_{i=1}^{m} w_i \vartheta(v_i \cdot x + b_i)$ its representation by a one-hidden-layer Heaviside perceptron network. Then $\sum_{i=1}^{m} |w_i| = \Omega(2^{2d/6})$.*

Proof. It was shown in [16, Theorem 3.7] that under the assumptions of the theorem, $\|f\|_{P_d} = \Omega(2^{d/6})$. By [15, Proposition 3], for every $h \in H_d$, $\|h\|_{P_d} \leq 1$. So $\|.\|_{P_d} \leq \|.\|_{H_d}$. The statement then follows from Proposition 1. $\square$

Theorem 4 implies that a representation of a class of d-variable Boolean functions with Hadamard communication matrices by one-hidden-layer Heaviside perceptron networks is not tractable. These functions cannot be represented by Heaviside perceptron networks with polynomially bounded numbers of units and sums of absolute values of output weights.

A paradigmatic example of a class of functions with Hadamard comunication matrices are functions $\beta_d :$ $\{0,1\}^d \to \{-1,1\}$ defined for every even positive integer d and all $x \in \{0,1\}^d$ as

$$\beta_d := (-1)^{l(x) \cdot r(x)}$$

where $l(x), r(x) \in \{0,1\}^{d/2}$ are defined for every $i = 1, \ldots, d/2$ as $l(x)_i := x_i$ and $r(x)_i := x_{d/2+i}$. When the range $\{-1,1\}$ is replaced with $\{1,0\}$, these functions compute inner product of $l(x)$ with $r(x)$ mod 2, and thus they are called 'inner product mod 2". It is well-known and easy to check that for every even integer d, the communication matrix $M(\beta_d)$ is Hadamard (see, e.g., [24]).

The functions "inner prod mod 2" were used in theory of circuit complexity as an example of a class of functions which cannot be expressed as depth-2 polynomial size circuits with weights being polynomially bounded integers [24]. Our results are stronger as they include also other functions with Hadamard communication matrices and also hold for weights which are real numbers.

Acknowledgments. This work was partially supported by GA ČR grant P202/11/1368 and an institutional support of the Institute of Computer Science RVO 67985807.

References

[1] K. Ball. An elementary introduction to modern convex geometry. In S. Levy, editor, *Falvors of Geometry*, pages 1–58. Cambridge University Press, 1997.

[2] A. R. Barron. Neural net approximation. In K. Narendra, editor, *Proc. 7th Yale Workshop on Adaptive and Learning Systems*, pages 69–72. Yale University Press, 1992.

[3] A. R. Barron. Universal approximation bounds for superpositions of a sigmoidal function. *IEEE Trans. on Information Theory*, 39:930–945, 1993.

[4] P. L. Bartlett. The sample complexity of pattern classification with neural networks: The size of the weights is more important than the size of the network. *IEEE Trans. on Information Theory*, 44:525–536, 1998.

[5] Y. Bengio. Learning deep architectures for AI. *Foundations and Trends in Machine Learning*, 2:1–127, 2009.

[6] Y. Bengio, O. Delalleau, and N. Le Roux. The curse of highly variable functions for local kernel machines. In *Advances in Neural Information Processing Systems 18*, pages 107–114. MIT Press, 2006.

[7] T. W. S. Chow and S. Y. Cho. *Neural Networks and Computing: Learning Algorithms and Applications*. World Scientific, 2007.

[8] T. L. Fine. *Feedforward Neural Network Methodology*. Springer, Berlin Heidelberg, 1999.

[9] G. E. Hinton, S. Osindero, and Y. W. Teh. A fast learning algorithm for deep belief nets. *Neural Computation*, 18:1527–1554, 2006.

[10] Y. Ito. Finite mapping by neural networks and truth functions. *Mathematical Scientist*, 17:69–77, 1992.

[11] P. C. Kainen, V. Kůrková, and M. Sanguineti. Dependence of computational models on input dimension: Tractability of approximation and optimization tasks. *IEEE Trans. on Information Theory*, 58:1203–1214, 2012.

[12] D. E. Knuth. Big omicron and big omega and big theta. *SIGACT News*, 8:18–24, 1976.

[13] V. Kůrková. Dimension-independent rates of approximation by neural networks. In K. Warwick and M. Kárný, editors, *Computer-Intensive Methods in Control and Signal Processing. The Curse of Dimensionality*, pages 261–270. Birkhäuser, Boston, MA, 1997.

[14] V. Kůrková. Some comparisons of networks with radial and kernel units. In A.E.P. Villa, W. Duch, P. Érdi, F. Masulli, and G. Palm, editors, *Neural Networks: Brain-inspired Computing and Machine Learning Research*, volume 7553 of *Lecture Notes in Computer Science*, pages II. 17–24. Springer-Verlag, Berlin, Heidelberg, 2012.

[15] V. Kůrková and M. Sanguineti. Comparison of worst-case errors in linear and neural network approximation. *IEEE Trans. on Information Theory*, 48:264–275, 2002.

[16] V. Kůrková, P. Savický, and K. Hlaváčková. Representations and rates of approximation of real–valued Boolean functions by neural networks. *Neural Networks*, 11:651–659, 1998.

[17] M. Leshno, V. Ya. Lin, A. Pinkus, and S. Schocken. Multilayer feedforward networks with a nonpolynomial activation function can approximate any function. *Neural Networks*, 6:861–867, 1993.

[18] V. Maiorov. On best approximation by ridge functions. *J. of Approximation Theory*, 99:68–94, 1999.

[19] V. Maiorov and A. Pinkus. Lower bounds for approximation by MLP neural networks. *Neurocomputing*, 25:81–91, 1999.

[20] H. N. Mhaskar. Versatile Gaussian networks. In *Proceedings of IEEE Workshop of Nonlinear Image Processing*, pages 70–73, 1995.

[21] C. A. Micchelli. Interpolation of scattered data: Distance matrices and conditionally positive definite functions. *Constructive Approximation*, 2:11–22, 1986.

[22] J. Park and I. Sandberg. Approximation and radial-basis-function networks. *Neural Computation*, 5:305–316, 1993.

[23] A. Pinkus. Approximation theory of the MLP model in neural networks. *Acta Numerica*, 8:143–195, 1999.

[24] V. Roychowdury, K. Siu, and A. Orlitsky. Neural models and spectralmethods. In *Theoretical Advances in Neural Computation and Learning*, pages 3–36. Kluwer Academic Publishers, Dodrecht, 1994.

[25] L. Schläfli. *Theorie der vielfachen Kontinuität*. Zürcher & Furrer, Zürich, 1901.

[26] I. Steinwart and A. Christmann. *Support Vector Machines*. Springer, new York, 2008.

ITAT 2013: Workshops, Posters, and Tutorials, pp. 77–85
ISBN 978-1490952086, © 2013 M. Holeňa, M. Ščavnický

ITAT

Application of Copulas to Data Mining
Based on Observational Logic

Martin Holeňa[1] and Martin Ščavnický[2]

[1] Institute of Computer Science, Academy of Sciences of the Czech Republic
Pod vodárenskou věží 2, 18207 Prague
[2] Faculty of Mathematics and Physics, Charles University
Malostranské náměstí 25, 118 00 Prague

Abstract. *The objective of the paper is a small contribution to data mining based on observational logic – introducing generalized quantifiers inspired by copulas. Fitting copulas to multidimensional data is an increasingly important method for analyzing dependencies, and the new quantifiers of observational logic assess the possibility to describe the data by a hierarchical Archimedean copula with given properties. To this end, basic concepts pertaining to copulas, Archimedean copulas and hierarchical Archimedean copulas are first recalled, together with those properties that will be needed for the definition of the new quantifiers. Since the result of assessing the possibility to describe the data by a copula depends not only on the properties of that copula, but also on the precise algorithm for fitting it to the data, we present the algorithm we have used to this end, before finally defining the new quantifiers. The paper concludes with a brief illustration of applying the proposed quantifiers to the well-known Iris data set.*

1 Introduction

One of the main directions in data mining is extracting various kinds of logical rules, such as classification rules, association rules or fuzzy rules from the available data [1, 6, 12, 20, 29, 32]. Logical rules, especially the Boolean IF ... THEN rules (Boolean implications) are considered easily understandable for humans and close to the human way of thinking. However, the semantics of Boolean logic is not rich enough to convey the diversified knowledge obtained through data mining. A very early generalization of the classical (i.e., Boolean) predicate calculus in that direction is the observational logic, elaborated in the 1970s [9]. It extends the classical predicate calculus with generalized quantifiers, assessing the results of operations with data samples. In this way, it provides a semantics that is rich enough to convey the knowledge obtained through analyzing the data.

In the first two decades after observational logic originated, only binary generalized quantifiers based on the estimation of particular probabilities and on several simple hypothesis tests were considered, both

in theory and in the implementation of a particular rules-extraction method based on observational logic, known under the acronym GUHA (General Unary Hypotheses Automaton) [8, 9]. This was due to the very important role that those two kinds of statistical methods play, as well as due to the comparatively low computational costs of evaluating formulas with such generalized quantifiers. For the latter reason, only quantifiers for binary or dichotomized data were used at that time. Moreover, all of them are based only on estimates and tests constructed by means of the 2×2-fold contingency table of the two considered variables. During the last 10-15 years, on the other hand, quantifiers based on other data analysis methods have been introduced, in particular, on general contingency tables, on estimates of joint distributions of multivariate discrete variables, on trend changes in time series, and on fuzzy hypotheses testing [15, 16, 26–28]. A survey can be found in [11], whereas much of the underlying theoretical developments of observational logic has been presented in the recent monograph [29].

The present paper follows this line of research. It proposes generalized quantifiers related to an increasingly important method of analyzing dependencies in multidimensional data – estimating the structure of joint distributions of continuous variables by means of copulas, especially by means of hierarchical Archimedean copulas. The concept of copulas as a means allowing to describe the relationship between a joint distribution and its marginals has been introduced as early as in the late 1950s [30]. However, their increasing use in data analysis is a matter of only the last 10-15 years [3, 17, 22], when the commonly available computing power has made it affordable to fit copulas even to medium-sized data.

In the next section, fundamentals of observational logic are recalled. Section 3 summarizes definitions and properties pertaining to hierarchical Archimedean copulas. In Section 4, which is the key section of the paper, three new observational quantifiers are introduced assessing the possibility to describe given data by a hierarchical Archimedean copula with given properties. Because of the limited extent of the paper, the new quantifiers are illustrated only on one data set, the well-known Iris data benchmark.

2　Observational Logic for Data Mining

Observational logic is an extension of classical monadic predicate calculus that has only unary predicates. In particular:

(i) Its language is a superset of the language of Boolean logic with unary predicates, extending that language with symbols for generalized quantifiers, which will be introduced below. Apart of those additional symbols, it has all the symbols of the original language, i.e., symbols for the unary predicates and their single variable (which can be left out due to its uniqueness), various logical connectives ($\neg, \&, \vee, \dots$), logical constants $\bar{1}$ and $\bar{0}$, and the quantifiers $\forall$ (universal) and $\exists$ (existential).

(ii) Formulas of the language containing neither any $\forall$ nor any $\exists$ are called open formulas, e.g.
`disease duration > 10 years & sex = male & ¬epileptic fits`.

(iii) If the unary predicates have been evaluated as true (1) or false (0) on some data (e.g., in the example above, if the predicates `disease duration > 10 years`, `sex = male` and `epileptic fits` have been evaluated based on the data of some patient), then any open formula can be evaluated using standard rules for the evaluation of Boolean connectives and the quantifiers $\forall$ and $\exists$

The theory of observational logic has been rigorously elaborated in [9]. Here, only the definitions of a generalized quantifier and of its evaluation will be recalled.

Definition 1. *Consider a language of Boolean logic with unary predicates, and let Q be a symbol not belonging to the symbols of that language. Let further $m \in \mathcal{N}, \varphi_1, \dots, \varphi_m$ be open formulas of the language, and Tf_Q be a 0/1-valued function on Boolean matrices with m columns, i.e.,*

$$\mathrm{Tf}_Q : \bigcup_{n \in \mathcal{N}} \{0,1\}^{n,m} \to \{0,1\}. \qquad (1)$$

Then:

a) *Q is called* generalized quantifier of arity m, *and it belongs to symbols of the language of observational logic that includes the considered language of Boolean logic, Tf_Q is called* truth function of *Q.*

b) *The formula $Q(\varphi_1, \dots, \varphi_m)$ is a formula of the considered language of observational logic. However, that formula is not called open formula, but* closed formula.

In the case of a binary generalized quantifier $\sim$, the simplified notation $\varphi_1 \sim \varphi_2$ instead of $\sim (\varphi_1, \varphi_2)$ is used.

Definition 2. *Let $m \in \mathcal{N}, \varphi_1, \dots, \varphi_m$ be open formulas, and Q be an m-ary generalized quantifier with a truth function Tf_Q. Let further $D \in \Re^{n,m}$ be a data matrix with rows $d_1, \dots, d_n$, and for $i = 1, \dots, n, j = 1, \dots, m$, let $\|\varphi_j\|_i$ be the evaluation of φ_j based on d_i according to (iii) above. Then the evaluation of $Q(\varphi_1, \dots, \varphi_m)$ based on D is the value*

$$\mathrm{Tf}_Q \begin{pmatrix} \|\varphi_1\|_1 & \cdots & \|\varphi_m\|_1 \\ \cdots\cdots\cdots\cdots\cdots\cdots\cdots \\ \|\varphi_1\|_n & \cdots & \|\varphi_m\|_{n\cdot} \end{pmatrix} \qquad (2)$$

Observe that the truth function (1) of a quantifier can be defined quite generally. Nevertheless, for all quantifiers really used in data mining, it has always been defined so as to assess the results of some operations with the data. In the early decades after observational logic originated, those operations were always either the estimation of particular probabilities, or simple hypotheses tests.

Example 1. The quantifier *founded implication* $\to_\theta$ with a threshold $\theta \in (0,1)$ corresponds to estimating the conditional probability $P_{C|A}$ of the validity of the consequent on condition of the validity of the antecedent. It underlies the restriction that the estimation is performed only if the simultaneous validity of antecedent and consequent in the data achieves at least a prescribed basic level $B \in \mathcal{N}$. Apart from this restriction, the constructed estimate is unbiased and consistent. Its truth function is defined

$$(\forall n \in \mathcal{N})(\forall x = (x_1^{(i)}, x_2^{(i)})_{i=1,\dots,n} \in \{0,1\}^{n,2})$$

$$\mathrm{Tf}_{\to_\theta}(x) = \begin{cases} 1 & \text{if } \sum_{i=1}^n x_1^{(i)} x_2^{(i)} \geq B \ \& \\ & \frac{\sum_{i=1}^n x_1^{(i)} x_2^{(i)}}{\sum_{i=1}^n x_1^{(i)}} \geq \theta, \\ 0 & \text{else.} \end{cases} \qquad (3)$$

In the case of a constant n, the validity of the observational rule $\varphi \to_\theta \psi$ is equivalent to the validity of the association rule with the same antecedent φ and consequent ψ, and with support $\frac{B}{n}$ and confidence θ, as was noticed in [10]. Hence, the extraction of association rules from data, which is very common in data mining, is actually the extraction of a specific kind of rules of observational logic.

Example 2. The quantifier *likely implication* $\to^!_{\alpha,\theta}$ with a significance level $\alpha \in (0,1)$ and a threshold $\theta \in (0,1)$ corresponds to testing the null hypothesis $P_{C|A} \leq \theta$ against the alternative $P_{C|A} > \theta$ with the binomial test [25]. Analogously to $\rightarrow_\theta$, it underlies the restriction that the test is performed only if the simultaneous validity of antecedent and consequent in the data is at least B. Its truth function is defined

$$(\forall n \in \mathcal{N})(\forall x = (x_1^{(i)}, x_2^{(i)})_{i=1,\dots,n} \in \{0,1\}^{n,2})$$

$$\mathrm{Tf}_{\rightarrow^!_{\alpha,\theta}}(x) = \begin{cases} 1 & \text{if } \sum_{i=1}^{n} x_1^{(i)} x_2^{(i)} \geq B \ \& \\ & \sum_{i=a}^{a+b} \binom{a+b}{i} \theta^i (1-\theta)^{a+b-i} \leq \alpha, \\ 0 & \text{else}, \end{cases}$$

$$(4)$$

where $a = \sum_{i=1}^{n} x_1^{(i)} x_2^{(i)}$, $b = \sum_{i=1}^{n} x_1^{(i)}$. Combining (4) with (2) implies that the rule $\varphi \rightarrow^!_{\alpha,\theta} \psi$ is true if and only if the binomial test rejects at the significance level α the hypothesis $P_{C|A} \leq \theta$, what is usually interpreted as accepting the hypothesis $P_{C|A} > \theta$.

3   Hierarchical Archimedean Copulas

Definition 3. *Let* $m \in \mathcal{N}, I = [0,1]$, *and let* $U = (U_1, \dots, U_m)$ *be a random vector on* I^m *such that the marginal distributions of* $U_1, \dots, U_m$ *are uniform. Then the joint distribution function* C *of* U *is called* copula. *Moreover, if* $\frac{\partial^m C}{\partial u_1 \dots \partial u_m}$ *exists for* u *in some open subset of* $\Re^m$, *it is called* density *of* C.

Although having been defined as joint distributions of specific random vectors, copulas are actually fundamental for the relationship between joint and marginal distributions of arbitrary random vectors, as the following theorem, which started the development of the copula theory, shows.

Theorem 1. Sklar *[30] Let* $m \in \mathcal{N}$ *and* $F_1, \dots, F_m$ *be distribution functions of one-dimensional random variables. For* $i = 1, \dots, m$, *let* $\mathrm{val}\, F_i$ *denote the value set of* F_i *and* F_i^- *the pseudoinverse of* F_i, *defined*

$$(\forall y \in [0,1])\ F_i^-(y) = \inf\{x \in \Re : F_i(x) \geq y\}. \quad (5)$$

Then there exists an m-*dimensional distribution function* H *such that* $F_1, \dots, F_m$ *are marginals of* H *if and only if there exists an* m-*dimensional copula* C *fulfilling*

$$(\forall x_1, \dots, x_m \in \Re)\ H(x_1, \dots, x_m) =$$
$$= C(F_1(x_1), \dots, F_m(x_m)). \quad (6)$$

In the positive case, C *is uniquely determined on the set* $\mathrm{val}\, F_1 \times \dots \times \mathrm{val}\, F_m$, *and is given by*

$$(\forall (u_1, \dots, u_m) \in \mathrm{val}\, F_1 \times \dots \times \mathrm{val}\, F_m)$$
$$C(u_1, \dots, u_m) = H(F_1^-(u_1), \dots, F_m^-(u_m)). \quad (7)$$

Example 3. A very often encountered example of copulas is the *product copula*, which is simply the product of input components:

$$\Pi(u_1, \dots, u_m) = \prod_{i=1}^{m} u_i. \quad (8)$$

The Sklar's theorem yields

$$(\forall x_1, \dots, x_m \in \Re)\ H(x_1, \dots, x_m) = \prod_{i=1}^{m} F_i(x_i). \quad (9)$$

Hence, Π expresses the independence of marginals.

Further important results pertaining to copulas include various results concerning their relationships to measures of dependence of random variables, most importantly the relationships of 2-dimensional copulas to measures of interdependence between two random variables. Among them, we will need the relationship to the Kendall's rank correlation coefficient.

Definition 4. *The* Kendall's rank correlation coefficient *of the random variables* X *and* Y *is the value*

$$\tau = \tau_{(X,Y)} = E\, \mathrm{sgn}((X - X')(Y - Y')), \quad (10)$$

where (X', Y') *is an independent copy of* (X, Y).

Proposition 1. *[22] Let* $I = [0,1], X$ *and* Y *be continuous random variables, and* C *be the copula corresponding to their joint distribution function according to the Sklar theorem (6). Then*

$$\tau_{(X,Y)} = 4 \int_{I \times I} C(u)\, dC(u) - 1. \quad (11)$$

In addition, we also recall several other properties of Kendall's τ.

Proposition 2. *[22] Let* X *and* Y *be continuous random variables with distribution functions* F *and* G, *respectively. Then:*
(i) $-1 \leq \tau_{(X,Y)} \leq 1$;
(ii) if X and Y are independent, then $\tau_{(X,Y)} = 0$;
(iii) if Y is almost surely an increasing function of X, then $\tau_{(X,Y)} = 1$, in particular, $\tau_{(X,X)} = 1$;
(iv) if Y is almost surely a decreasing function of X, then $\tau_{(X,Y)} = -1$, in particular, $\tau_{(X,-X)} = -1$;
(v) if σ_X is a function increasing on a set S_X such that $P(X \in S_X) = 1$ and σ_Y is a function increasing on a set S_Y such that $P(Y \in S_Y) = 1$, then $\tau_{(\sigma_X(X),\sigma_Y(Y))} = \tau_{(X,Y)}$, in particular, $\tau_{(F(X),G(Y))} = \tau_{(X,Y)}$.

Due to (i)–(iv), $\tau_{(X,Y)} > 0$ and $\tau_{(X,Y)} < 0$ can be interpreted as a positive and negative, respectively, dependence between X and Y.

In the following, we will be interested only in one particular class of copulas – hierarchical Archimedean copulas. To this end, Archimedean copulas will be introduced first.

Definition 5. *Let* $m \in \mathcal{N}, I = [0,1]$, *and*

$$\Psi = \{\psi : [0,+\infty] \to [0,1] \ \& \ \psi \ is \ continuous \ \&$$
$$\psi(0) = 1 \ \& \ \psi(+\infty) = \lim_{t \to +\infty} \psi(t) = 0 \ \&$$
$$\psi \ is \ strictly \ decreasing \ on \ [0, \inf\{t : \psi(t) = 0\}]\}.$$
$$(12)$$

Moreover, let for $\psi \in \Psi$ *be* $\psi^{-1} : I \to [0,+\infty]$ *defined*

$$(\forall u \in I) \ \psi^{-1}(u) = \inf\{t : \psi(t) = u\}. \qquad (13)$$

Then:

a) *The elements of* Ψ *are called* Archimedean generators.
b) *If* C *is an m-dimensional copula that for some* $\psi \in$
   Ψ *fulfills*

$$(\forall u_1, \ldots, u_m \in I) \ C(u_1, \ldots, u_m) =$$
$$= \psi(\psi^{-1}(u_1) + \cdots + \psi^{-1}(u_m)), \quad (14)$$

   C *is called* Archimedean copula *with generator* ψ.

Observe that a mapping $C : I^m \to I$ fulfilling (14)
is uniquely determined by its generator ψ. That mapping will be subsequently denoted C_ψ. However, the
assumption that C is a copula in Definition 5, is essential because (14) itself does not imply that the resulting C_ψ has this property. Fortunately, this assumption
can be reformulated by means of conditions on ψ because a necessary and sufficient condition on ψ for C_ψ
to be a copula is known and will be recalled below in
Theorem 2. Before, two important kinds of real functions will be introduced.

Definition 6. *Let* $a,b \in \Re \cup \{-\infty, +\infty\}, a < b, m \in$
$\mathcal{N}, m \geq 2$. *A function* $f : [a,b] \to \Re$ *is called:*

a) *m-monotone if* f *is continuous on* $[a,b]$, $f^{(k)}$ *exists*
   on (a,b) *for* $k = 1, \ldots, m-2$, $f^{(m-2)}$ *is decreas-*
   ing and convex on (a,b), *and* $(\forall k \in \{0, \ldots, m-$
   $2\})(\forall x \in (a,b)) \ (-1)^k \psi^{(k)}(x) \geq 0$;
b) *completely monotone if* f *is continuous on* $[a,b]$,
   $f^{(k)}$ *exists on* (a,b) *for every* $k \in \mathcal{N}$, *and* $(\forall k \in$
   $\mathcal{N}_0)(\forall x \in (a,b)) \ (-1)^k \psi^{(k)}(x) \geq 0$; *the set of all*
   completely monotone elements of Ψ *will be denoted*
   Ψ_∞.

This definition easily implies the following lemma.

Lemma 1. *Let* $a,b \in \Re \cup \{-\infty, +\infty\}, a < b, m \in$
$\mathcal{N}, m \geq 2$.
Then:
(i) *every completely monotone function on* $[a,b]$ *is m-*
    monotone;
(ii) *for an Archimedean copula* C_ψ *with* $\psi \in \Psi_\infty$, *the*
     density $\frac{\partial^m C_\psi}{\partial u_1 \ldots \partial u_m}$ *exists.*

Theorem 2. *[19] Let* $m \in \mathcal{N}, \psi \in \Psi$. *Then*

1. C_ψ *is a copula if and only if* ψ *is m-monotone.*
2. *In particular, a sufficient condition for* C_ψ *to be a*
   copula is $\psi \in \Psi_\infty$.

For a 2-dimensional Archimedean copula, the relationship to the Kendall's rank correlation coefficient (10)
can be expressed by means of its generator.

Proposition 3. *[17] Let* X_1 *and* X_2 *be random vari-*
ables, and let the copula corresponding to their joint
distribution function according to the Sklar theorem
(6) be Archimedean with a generator ψ *such that* $(\forall t \in$
$[0, +\infty)) \ \psi(t) > 0$. *Then*

$$\tau = \tau_\psi = 1 - 4 \int_0^\infty t(\psi'(t))^2 dt. \qquad (15)$$

Observe that Archimedean copulas include also the
above mentioned product copula, its generator is $\psi(t)$
$= \exp(-t)$. However, Archimedean generators, and
consequently also Archimedean copulas, are typically
investigated as whole families, parametrized by 1-di-
mensional or, more rarely, 2-dimensional parameters.
As will be shown, the product copula can also be actually obtained in that way.

Definition 7. *Let* $q \in \mathcal{N}, \Theta \subset \Re^q$ *and* $\psi_\Theta : [0, +\infty] \times$
$\Theta \to [0,1]$ *be such that*

$$(\forall \theta \in \Theta) \ \psi_\Theta(\cdot, \theta) \in \Psi. \qquad (16)$$

Then ψ_Θ *is called* parametrized family *of Archime-*
dean generators, and Θ *is called its* parameter set.

A number of parametrized families of Archimedean
generators can be found in [13] and [22]. Here, only two
from among those examples will be recalled.

Example 4. The *Frank family* has the parameter set
$\Theta = (-\infty, 0) \cup (0, +\infty)$ and is defined

$$(\forall t \in [0, +\infty))(\forall \theta \in \Theta) \ \psi_\Theta(t, \theta) =$$
$$= -\frac{1}{\theta} \ln(1 - (1 - e^{-\theta})e^{-t}). \quad (17)$$

If $m = 2$, then (15) yields [4, 13]

$$\tau = \tau_{\psi_\Theta(\cdot, \theta)} = 1 - \frac{4}{\theta}(1 - \frac{1}{\theta} \int_0^\theta \frac{t}{e^t - 1} dt). \qquad (18)$$

In Figure 1, the probability density of the 2-dimen-
sional Frank copula with $\theta = -3$ is shown. The density clearly indicates a negative dependence between
both components of the 2-dimensional random vector,
which is confirmed by a negative value of $\tau_{\psi_\Theta(\cdot, \theta)}$ according to (18).

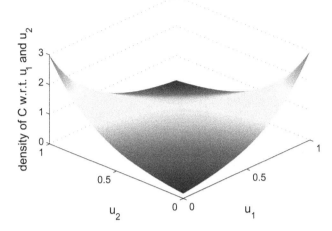

Frank copula, θ = −3

density of C w.r.t. u_1 and u_2

Fig. 1. Probability density of the 2-dimensional Frank copula with $\theta = -3$, which according to (18) corresponds to the Kendall's rank correlation coefficient $\tau_{-3} \doteq -0.307$

Example 5. The *Gumbel family* has the parameter set $\Theta = [1, +\infty)$ and is defined

$$(\forall t \in [0, +\infty))(\forall \theta \in \Theta)\ \psi_\Theta(t, \theta) =$$
$$= \exp(-t^{\frac{1}{\theta}}). \quad (19)$$

Observe that the choice $\theta = 1$ yields the product copula. If $m = 2$, then (15) leads to [4, 13]

$$\tau = \tau_{\psi_\Theta(\cdot, \theta)} = 1 - \frac{1}{\theta}. \quad (20)$$

Hence, $\tau_\theta \geq 0$, which means that the Gumbel family is unable to model a negative dependence between components of a 2-dimensional random vector, differently to the Frank family.

After all prerequisites concerning Archimedean copulas have been recalled, we now turn to hierarchical Archimedean copulas.

Definition 8. *Let $m \in \mathcal{N}$ and $(\mathcal{V}, \mathcal{E})$ be a rooted tree with a root $v_1 \in \mathcal{V}$ that has exactly m leaves, and all remaining nodes have at least 2 children; those nodes will be called forks. In connection with $(\mathcal{V}, \mathcal{E})$, the following notation will be used:*

- *for $v \in \mathcal{V}$, denote $\wedge(v)$ the set of children of v; thus according to the above assumptions, the cardinality of $\wedge(v)$ fulfils $\# \wedge (v) \geq 2$ if v is a fork, whereas $\# \wedge (v) = 0$ if v is a leaf;*
- *$\mathcal{L}$ and $\mathcal{F}$ for the sets of leaves and forks, respectively; according to the above assumptions, $\#\mathcal{L} = m$; denote further $f = \#\mathcal{F}$, and denote $v_2, \ldots, v_{f+m}$ the nodes from $\mathcal{V} \setminus \{v_1\}$ in such a way that $\mathcal{F} = \{v_1, \ldots, v_f\}, \mathcal{L} = \{v_{f+1}, \ldots, v_{f+m}\}$;*

- *for $S \subset \mathcal{V}$ and $x \in [0, 1]^{f+m}$, the simplified notation*

$$x_S = (x_{j_1}, \ldots, x_{j_{\#S}}), \ \ where \ S = \{v_{j_1}, \ldots, v_{j_{\#S}}\}, \quad (21)$$

with a further simplification $x_v = x_{\{v\}}$ for $v \in \mathcal{V}$.

Finally, let $\lambda : \mathcal{F} \to \Psi_\infty$ be a labeling of forks with completely monotone Archimedean generators such that for each $u \in [0, 1]^m$ there exists $x^u \in [0, 1]^{m+f}$ with the following two properties:
(i) $(\forall v \in \mathcal{F})\ x_v^u = C_{\lambda(v)}(x_{\wedge(v)}^u)$;
(ii) $u = x_{\mathcal{L}}^u$;
Then:

a) *if the mapping $C_{(\mathcal{V}, \mathcal{E}, \lambda)}$, defined*

$$(\forall u \in [0, 1]^m)\ C_{(\mathcal{V}, \mathcal{E}, \lambda)}(u) = x_{v_1}^u, \quad (22)$$

is an m-dimensional copula, then it is called hierarchical Archimedean copula (HAC) with the tree structure $(\mathcal{V}, \mathcal{E})$ and the labeling λ;

b) *if there exists a parametrized family of Archimedean generators $\psi_\Theta : [0, +\infty] \times \Theta \to [0, 1]$ such that*

$$(\forall v \in \mathcal{F})(\exists \theta_v \in \Theta)\ \lambda(v) = \psi_\Theta(\cdot, \theta_v), \quad (23)$$

then $C_{(\mathcal{V}, \mathcal{E}, \lambda)}$ is called homogeneous;

c) *if $(\mathcal{V}, \mathcal{E})$ is binary, then $C_{(\mathcal{V}, \mathcal{E}, \lambda)}$ is called binary;*

d) *$f(\mathcal{V}, \mathcal{E})$ is binary, $\mathcal{F} = \{v_1, \ldots, v_{m-1}\}, \wedge(v_{m-1}) \subset \mathcal{L}$, and $(\forall v \in \mathcal{F})\ v \neq v_{m-1} \Rightarrow \#(\wedge(v) \cap \mathcal{L}) = \#(\wedge(v) \cap \mathcal{F}) = 1$, then $C_{(\mathcal{V}, \mathcal{E}, \lambda)}$ is called fully nested Archimedean copula (FNAC).*

Observe that if $C_{(\mathcal{V}, \mathcal{E}, \lambda)}$ is a FNAC, then

$$C_{(\mathcal{V}, \mathcal{E}, \lambda)}(u) =$$
$$= C_{\lambda(v_1)}(u_1, C_{\lambda(v_2)}(u_2, \ldots C_{\lambda(v_{m-1})}(u_{m-1}, u_m) \ldots)). \quad (24)$$

The assumption in Definition 8 that $C_{(\mathcal{V}, \mathcal{E}, \lambda)}$ is a copula, is even more essential than the one in Definition 5 because no necessary and sufficient conditions are known that would allow to replace checking that assumption with checking some conditions on the involved Archimedean generators. The standard way of checking that $C_{(\mathcal{V}, \mathcal{E}, \lambda)}$ is a copula is expressing it as a mixture of a system of m-dimensional joint probability distributions $(G(\cdot; x)_{x \in [0, +\infty)})$ by a distribution function F on $[0, +\infty)$,

$$C_{(\mathcal{V}, \mathcal{E}, \lambda)}(u) = \int_0^{+\infty} G(u; x) dF(x), \quad (25)$$

where the marginals $G_1(\cdot; x), \ldots, G_m(\cdot; x)$ of $G(\cdot; x)$, $x \in [0, +\infty)$, are such that

$$\int_0^{+\infty} G_i(u_i; x) dF(x) = u_i \ for \ i = 1, \ldots, m. \quad (26)$$

Then $C_{(\mathcal{V},\mathcal{E},\lambda)}$ is a probability distribution due to (25), and its marginals are uniform due to (26), thus it is a copula. For finding a system of probability distributions $(G(\cdot;x)_{x\in[0,+\infty)})$ fulfilling (25)–(26), three results about completely monotone functions are useful. The first of them is the classical Bernstein theorem, the third is a direct consequence of the second.

Theorem 3. *Bernstein [2] Let $\psi : [0,+\infty] \to [0,1]$. Then ψ is the Laplace-Stieltjes transform of a distribution function F on $[0,\infty]$, i.e.*

$$(\forall t \in [0,+\infty)) \ \psi(t) = \int_0^{+\infty} e^{-tx} dF(x), \qquad (27)$$

if and only if ψ is completely monotone on $[0,+\infty]$ with $\psi(0) = 1$.

Proposition 4. *[5] Let $a,b \in \Re \cup \{-\infty,+\infty\}, a < b, g : [a,b] \to \Re, f : g([a,b]) \to \Re$. Let f be completely monotone, g be non-negative, and g' be completely monotone.*
Then the composition $f(g)$ is completely monotone.

Corollary 1. *Let $(\mathcal{V},\mathcal{E})$ be the tree structure, $\mathcal{L}$ and $\mathcal{F}$ the sets of leaves and forks from the definition of HAC. Let further $v_p \in \mathcal{F}, v_c \in \mathcal{V}$ be a child of v_p, and let the function $(\lambda(v_p)^{-1}(\lambda(v_c)))'$ be completely monotone. Finally, let $x \in (0,+\infty)$ and $\psi_{pc} : [0,+\infty] \to \Re$ be a function defined*

$$(\forall t \in [0,+\infty)) \ \psi_{pc}(t) = \exp(-x\lambda(v_p)^{-1}(\lambda(v_c)(t))). \qquad (28)$$

Then $\psi_{pc} \in \Psi_\infty$.

These results allowed to prove the only published sufficient condition for a HAC to be a copula, a condition concerning FNACs:

Proposition 5. *[18] Let $(\mathcal{V},\mathcal{E})$ be the tree, $\mathcal{L}$ and $\mathcal{F}$ be the sets of leaves and forks, respectively, and λ be the labeling of forks from the definition of HAC, and let $\mathcal{F} = \{v_1,\ldots,v_{m-1}\}$, $\mathcal{L} = \{v_m,\ldots,v_{2m-1}\}$. Let further $C_{(\mathcal{V},\mathcal{E},\lambda)} : [0,1]^m \to [0,1]$ be a mapping that fulfils (24). Finally, let $(\lambda(v_k)^{-1}(\lambda(v_{k+1})))'$ be completely monotone for $k = 1,\ldots,m-2$.*
Then $C_{(\mathcal{V},\mathcal{E},\lambda)}$ is a FNAC.

The usefulness of this result is, however, quite limited, due to the broad spectrum of possible HACs that are not FNACs. For commonly encountered parametric families ψ_Θ, the condition that $(\lambda(v_k)^{-1}(\lambda(v_{k+1})))'$ should be completely monotone is for λ fulfilling (23) equivalent to $\theta_{v_k} \leq \theta_{v_{k+1}}, k = 1,\ldots,m-2$ [14,24].

4   Some Observational Quantifiers Related to Copulas

In this section, we want the basic way of defining generalized quantifiers, i.e., assessing the results of operations with the data, to be applied in the context of HACs. In particular, they will be applied to the description of data for which some open formula φ is valid, by a HAC with given properties. The fact that the considered data should be determined by a single formula implies that we need to define unary generalized quantifiers to this end. We restrict our attention to binary HACs, and we are particularly interested in the following properties of the HAC describing the data:

(i) the copulas in the forks belong to a particular family;

(ii) the leaves corresponding to particular variables are at most a prescribed distance apart;

(iii) along the path between leaves corresponding to particular random variables, the Kendall's rank correlation coefficient (or more generally, a given measure of interdependence between random variables) achieves at least a prescribed threshold.

In connection with the last mentioned property, it is worth recalling that using ranks for the definition of generalized quantifiers was already suggested in [9].

Needless to say, the possibility to describe given data by a copula with such properties is not uniquely determined by the properties alone, but it depends also on the precise algorithm employed for HAC fitting. Therefore, we now present a greedy algorithm for fitting binary homogeneous HAC that we have used to this end. It has been inspired by proposals in [23].

Algorithm 1.
Input: A parametrized family of Archimedean generators ψ_Θ such that $(\forall \theta \in \Theta) \ \psi_\Theta(\cdot,\theta) \in \Psi_\infty$, and a data matrix $D = (d_{i,j})_{i=1,\ldots,n}^{j=1,\ldots,m} \in \Re^{n,m}$ the columns of which are realizations of m continuous variables denoted $X_m,\ldots,X_{2m-1}$, with distribution functions $F_m,\ldots,F_{2m-1}$.
Step 1. $k = m, \mathcal{F} = \mathcal{E} = \emptyset, \mathcal{L} = \{U_m,\ldots,U_{2m-1}\}$, where $U_i = F_i(X_i)$ for $i = m,\ldots,2m-1$.
Step 2. Denote $u_{i,j} = \frac{1}{n}\#\{i' : 1 \leq i' \leq n \ \& \ d_{i',j} \leq d_{i,j}\}, i = 1,\ldots,n, j = m,\ldots,2m-1$,
Step 3. For $h',\ell' \in \{k,\ldots,2m-1\} \setminus \bigcup_{i\in\mathcal{F}} \wedge(i)$ such that $h' < \ell'$, define the log-likelihood $L_{h',\ell'}$ on Θ:

$$(\forall \theta \in \Theta) \ L_{h',\ell'}(\theta) = \sum_{i=1}^n \ln \frac{\partial^2 C_{\psi(\cdot,\theta)}}{\partial u_1 \partial u_2}. \qquad (29)$$

Step 4. Select (h,ℓ) as

$$(h,\ell) = \arg \max_{(h',\ell')} \{\max_{\theta\in\Theta} L_{h',\ell'}(\theta) :$$
$$h',\ell' \in \{k,\ldots,2m-1\} \setminus \bigcup_{i\in\mathcal{F}} \wedge(i) \ \& \ h' < \ell'\} \qquad (30)$$

Step 5. Decrease $k = k - 1$.
Step 6. Define

$$U_k = C_\psi(\cdot,\theta_k)(U_h,U_\ell). \qquad (31)$$

Step 7. Put

$$\theta_k = \max_{\theta \in \Theta} L_{h,\ell}(\theta), \tag{32}$$

$$\mathcal{F} = \mathcal{F} \cup \{U_k\}, \tag{33}$$

$$\mathcal{E} = \mathcal{E} \cup \{(U_k, U_h), (U_k, U_\ell)\}, \tag{34}$$

$$\lambda(k) = \psi(\cdot, \theta_k). \tag{35}$$

Step 8. If $k > 1$, denote $u_{i,k} = C_{\psi(\cdot,\theta_k)}(u_{i,h}, u_{i,\ell})$, $i = 1, \ldots, n$, and return to Step 3.

Step 9. Else put $\mathcal{V} = \mathcal{L} \cup \mathcal{F}$ and check whether the mapping $C_{(\mathcal{V},\mathcal{E},\lambda)}$ defined by (22) is a copula, using results recalled in Section 3.

Output: Rooted tree $(\mathcal{V}, \mathcal{E})$, mapping λ, information whether the mapping $C_{(\mathcal{V},\mathcal{E},\lambda)}$ is a copula (in positive case, $C_{(\mathcal{V},\mathcal{E},\lambda)}$ is a HAC with the tree structure $(\mathcal{V}, \mathcal{E})$ and the labeling λ).

Once the HAC fitting algorithm is decided, we can define new generalized quantifiers. Taking into account the above mentioned properties of binary HAC in which we are interested, we propose the following 3 quantifiers:

1. The quantifier *HAC distance* will be denoted

$$FamilyName_{i,L,j}^{X_m,\ldots,X_{2m-1}},$$

where
   - *FamilyName* is the name of a parametrized family of Archimedean generators to which the generators labeling the forks of the fitted HAC belong,
   - $X_m, \ldots, X_{2m-1}$ are random variables from Algorithm 1,
   - $i, j \in \{m, \ldots, 2m-1\}$,
   - $L \in \mathcal{N}, L \geq 2$.

The truth function of this quantifier is defined

$$(\forall n \in \mathcal{N})(\forall x = (x^{(1)}, \ldots, x^{(n)})' \in \{0,1\}^{n,1})$$

$$\mathrm{Tf}_{FamilyName_{i,L,j}^{X_m,\ldots,X_{2m-1}}}(x) = 1 \text{ iff simultaneously} \tag{36}$$

(i) $\#\{i : x^{(i)} = 1\} \geq 1$;

(ii) according to the output of Algorithm 1, the mapping $C_{(\mathcal{V},\mathcal{E},\lambda)}$ is a copula;

(iii) the path in $(\mathcal{V}, \mathcal{E})$ between the leaves U_i and U_j has length $\leq L$.

2. The quantifier *HAC Kendall's* τ will be denoted

$$FamilyName_{i,\vartheta,j}^{X_m,\ldots,X_{2m-1}},$$

where *FamilyName*, $X_m, \ldots, X_{2m-1}$ and i, j have the same meaning as above, and $\vartheta \geq 0$. Its truth function is defined

$$(\forall n \in \mathcal{N})(\forall x = (x^{(1)}, \ldots, x^{(n)})' \in \{0,1\}^{n,1})$$

$$\mathrm{Tf}_{FamilyName_{i,\vartheta,j}^{X_m,\ldots,X_{2m-1}}} = 1 \text{ iff simultaneously} \tag{37}$$

(i) $\#\{i : x^{(i)} = 1\} \geq 1$;

(ii) according to the output of Algorithm 1, the mapping $C_{(\mathcal{V},\mathcal{E},\lambda)}$ is a copula;

(iii) for $k \in \mathcal{F}$, if k is at the path from U_i to U_j, then $\tau_{\psi_\Theta(\cdot,\theta_k)} \geq \vartheta$.

3. The quantifier *HAC distance + Kendall's* τ will be denoted

$$FamilyName_{i,L,\vartheta,j}^{X_m,\ldots,X_{2m-1}},$$

where *FamilyName*, $X_m, \ldots, X_{2m-1}$, i, j L and ϑ have the same meaning as above. Its truth function is defined

$$(\forall n \in \mathcal{N})(\forall x = (x^{(1)}, \ldots, x^{(n)})' \in \{0,1\}^{n,1})$$

$$\mathrm{Tf}_{FamilyName_{i,L,\vartheta,j}^{X_m,\ldots,X_{2m-1}}}(x) = 1 \text{ iff}$$

$$\mathrm{Tf}_{FamilyName_{i,L,j}^{X_m,\ldots,X_{2m-1}}}(x) =$$

$$= \mathrm{Tf}_{FamilyName_{i,\vartheta,j}^{X_m,\ldots,X_{2m-1}}}(x) = 1. \tag{38}$$

5   Sketchy Results from Testing the New Quantifiers

The proposed quantifiers were so far implemented only for the Frank family of Archimedean generators. The choice of this family was due to the fact illustrated in Example 4, namely that binary copulas with generators from this family can model also negative dependence between random variables. This is important, given some open formula φ, in view of the interpretation of the closed formulas $Frank_{i,\vartheta,j}^{X_m,\ldots,X_{2m-1}}\varphi$ and $Frank_{i,L,\vartheta,j}^{X_m,\ldots,X_{2m-1}}\varphi$. The condition on the Kendall's rank correlation coefficient, $\tau_{\psi_\Theta(\cdot,\theta_k)} \geq \vartheta \geq 0$ for $k \in \mathcal{F}$, is then a consequence of a positive dependence between the random variables corresponding to the children of k, but not a consequence of an inability of the copula family to model a negative dependence among them, like it would be the case, e.g., for the Gumbel family.

The implemented quantifiers were tested using 4 data sets from the UCI repository of machine learning data [31]: Iris, Seeds, Vertebral, Wine, as well as one more data set from a recent real-world application in catalysis [21]. Due to space limitation, only sketchy results for the best known among those data, the Iris data set, will be shown [7].

In Figure 2, the tree structures of three HACs fitted to data fulfilling respectively the three open formulas Setosa, Versicolor and Virginica, as well as the values of Kendall's τ in their forks, are depicted. The leaves of the trees are $X_4 =$ Sepal length, $X_5 =$ Sepal width, $X_6 =$ Petal length, $X_7 =$ Petal width. Together with the information that each of the structures indeed corresponds to a HAC, which was output from Algorithm 1, the tree structure already allows to see which formulas $Frank_{i,L,j}^{X_m,\ldots,X_{2m-1}}\varphi$ for $L =$

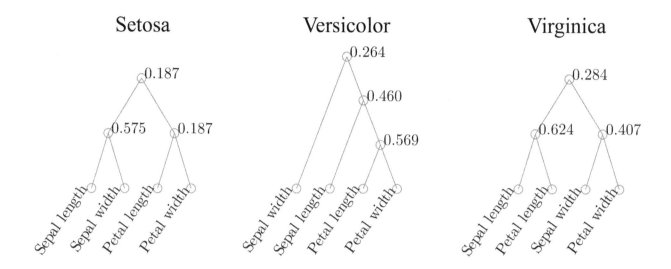

Fig. 2. The tree structure and values of Kendall's τ in forks for HACs with generators from the Frank family fitted to the `Setosa`, `Versicolor` and `Virginica` data

$1, 2, \ldots$ are valid for φ `Setosa`, `Versicolor` and `Virginica`. Taking into account the Kendall's τ, the validity, for $\vartheta \geq 0$, of the formulas $Frank_{i,\vartheta,j}^{X_m,\ldots,X_{2m-1}} \varphi$ and $Frank_{i,L,\vartheta,j}^{X_m,\ldots,X_{2m-1}} \varphi$ can also be determined. Examples of formulas with all three quantifiers are given in Table 1.

6   Conclusion

This paper continues the direction of research into data mining based on observational logic that aims at generalized quantifiers corresponding to more sophisticated operations with data. It has proposed three quantifiers related to estimating the structure of joint distributions of continuous variables by means of hierarchical Archimedean copulas. After recalling needed concepts and results from the theory of copulas, the Truth functions of the new quantifiers were defined, and their application was illustrated on the well-known Iris data benchmark.

The paper gives only the definitions of the new quantifiers, their properties are a matter of further research. One of the key ingredients of observational logic being the deducibility of new knowledge from the knowledge extracted from data [9], we are particularly interested in deducibility of formulas containing the new quantifiers from other such formulas as a consequence of properties of HACs. We also consider it important to investigate the last step of Algorithm 1, i.e., checking whether the mapping $C_{(\mathcal{V},\mathcal{E},\lambda)}$ defined by (22) indeed is a copula. It would be desirable to have, at least for homogeneous binary HACs, or for

some important subclass of them, a similar result as in Proposition 5 for FNACs.

Acknowledgment

The research reported in this paper has been supported by the Czech Science Foundation (GA ČR) grant 13-17187S.

References

1. J.M. Adamo.   *Data Mining for Association Rules and Sequential Patterns: Sequential and Parallel Algorithms.* Springer Verlag, Berlin, 2001.
2. S.N. Bernstein. Sur les fonctions absolument monotones. *Acta Mathematica*, 52:1–66, 1928.
3. U. Cherubini, E. Luciano, and W. Vecchiato. *Copula Methods in Finance.* John Wiley and Sons, New York, 2004.
4. M. Eling and D. Toplek. Modeling and management of nonlinear dependencies – copulas in dynamic financial analysis. *Journal of Risk and Insurance*, 76:651–681, 2009.
5. W. Feller. *An Introduction to Probability Theory and Its Applications. 2nd Edition.* John Wiley and Sons, New York, 1971.
6. G.D. Finn. Learning fuzzy rules from data. *Neural Computing & Applications*, 8:9–24, 1999.
7. R.A. Fisher. The use of multiple measurements in taxonomic problems. *Annals of Eugenics*, 7:179–188, 1936.
8. P. Hájek and T. Havránek. On generating of inductive hypotheses. *International Journal of Man-Machine Studies*, 9:415–438, 1977.
9. P. Hájek and T. Havránek. *Mechanizing Hypothesis Formation.* Springer Verlag, Berlin, 1978.

Table 1. Example formulas obtainable from the tree structure and values of Kendall's τ in Figure 2

$Frank_{4,2,5}^{X_4,...,X_7}$Setosa, but not $Frank_{4,2,5}^{X_4,...,X_7}$Versicolor neither $Frank_{4,2,5}^{X_4,...,X_7}$Virginica
$Frank_{4,2,6}^{X_4,...,X_7}$Virginica, but not $Frank_{4,2,6}^{X_4,...,X_7}$Setosa neither $Frank_{4,2,6}^{X_4,...,X_7}$Versicolor
$Frank_{4,3,6}^{X_4,...,X_7}$Versicolor and $Frank_{4,3,6}^{X_4,...,X_7}$Virginica, but not $Frank_{4,3,5}^{X_4,...,X_7}$Setosa
$Frank_{4,0.5,5}^{X_4,...,X_7}$Setosa, but not $Frank_{4,0.5,5}^{X_4,...,X_7}$Versicolor neither $Frank_{4,0.5,5}^{X_4,...,X_7}$Virginica
$Frank_{6,0.5,7}^{X_4,...,X_7}$Versicolor, but not $Frank_{6,0.5,7}^{X_4,...,X_7}$Setosa neither $Frank_{6,0.5,7}^{X_4,...,X_7}$Virginica
$Frank_{4,0.6,6}^{X_4,...,X_7}$Virginica, but not $Frank_{4,0.6,6}^{X_4,...,X_7}$Setosa neither $Frank_{4,0.6,6}^{X_4,...,X_7}$Versicolor
$Frank_{4,2,0.5,5}^{X_4,...,X_7}$Setosa, but not $Frank_{4,2,0.5,5}^{X_4,...,X_7}$Versicolor neither $Frank_{4,2,0.5,5}^{X_4,...,X_7}$Virginica
$Frank_{4,3,0.4,7}^{X_4,...,X_7}$Versicolor, but not $Frank_{4,3,0.4,7}^{X_4,...,X_7}$Setosa neither $Frank_{4,3,0.4,7}^{X_4,...,X_7}$Virginica
$Frank_{5,2,0.4,7}^{X_4,...,X_7}$Virginica, but not $Frank_{5,2,0.4,7}^{X_4,...,X_7}$Setosa neither $Frank_{5,2,0.4,7}^{X_4,...,X_7}$Versicolor

10. P. Hájek and M. Holeňa. Formal logics of discovery and hypothesis formation by machine. *Theoretical Computer Science*, 292:345–357, 2003.
11. P. Hájek, M. Holeňa, and J. Rauch. The guha method and its meaning for data mining. *Journal of Computer and System Sciences*, 76:34–48, 2010.
12. D.J. Hand. *Construction and Assessment of Classification Rules*. John Wiley and Sons, New York, 1997.
13. JM. Hofert. *Sampling Nested Archimedean Copulas with Applications to CDO Pricing*. PhD thesis, Ulm University, 2010.
14. J.M Hofert. A stochastic representation and sampling algorithm for nested Archimedean copulas. *Journal of Statistical Computation and Simulation*, 82:1239–1255, 2012.
15. M. Holeňa. Fuzzy hypotheses for Guha implications. *Fuzzy Sets and Systems*, 98:101–125, 1998.
16. M. Holeňa. Fuzzy hypotheses testing in the framework of fuzzy logic. *Fuzzy Sets and Systems*, 145:229–252, 2004.
17. H. Joe. *Multivariate Models and Dependence Concepts*. Chapman & Hall, London, 1997.
18. A.J. McNeil. Sampling nested archimedean copulas. *Journal of Statistical Computation and Simulation*, 78:567–581, 2008.
19. A.J. McNeil and J. Nešlehová. Multivariate Archimedean copulas, d-monotone functions and l_1-norm symmetric distributions. *The Annals of Statistics*, 37:3059–3097, 2009.
20. S. Mitra and Y. Hayashi. Neuro-fuzzy rule generation: Survey in soft computing framework. *IEEE Transactions on Neural Networks*, 11:748–768, 2000.
21. S. Moehmel, N. Steinfeldt, S. Engelschalt, M. Holeňa, S. Kolf, U. Dingerdissen, D. Wolf, R. Weber, and M. Bewersdorf. New catalytic materials for the high-temperature synthesis of hydrocyanic acid from methane and ammonia by high-throughput approach. *Applied Catalysis A: General*, 334:73–83, 2008.
22. R.B. Nelsen. *An Introduction to Copulas*. Springer Verlag, Berlin, 2006.
23. O. Okhrin, Y. Okhrin, and W. Schmid. On the structure and estimation of hierarchical Archimedean copulas. *Journal of Econometrics*, 173:189–204, 2013.
24. O. Okhrin, Y. Okhrin, and W. Schmid. Properties of hierarchical Archimedean copulas. *Statistics & Risk Modeling*, 30:21–54, 2013.
25. K.M. Ramachandran. *Mathematical Statistics with Applications*. Elsevier Science Publishers, Amsterdam, 2009.
26. J. Rauch and M. Šimůnek. Guha method and granular computing. In *Proceedings of the IEEE Conference on Granular Computing*, pages 630–635, 2005.
27. J. Rauch and M. Šimůnek. Action rules and the guha method: Preliminary considerations and results. In *IS-MIS 2009 – Foundations of Intelligent Systems*, pages 76–87. Springer Verlag, Berlin, 2009.
28. J. Rauch, M. Šimůnek, and V. Lín. Mining for patterns based on contingency tables by kl-miner – first experience. In T.Y. Lin, X. Hu, S. Ohsuga, and C.J. Liau, editors, *Data mining – Foundations and New Directions*, pages 156–163, 2003.
29. Jan Rauch. *Observational Calcucli and Association Rules*. Springer Verlag, Heidelberg, 2013.
30. A. Sklar. Fonctions dé repartition à n dimensions et leur marges. *Publications de l'Institut de Statistique de l'Universit de Paris*, 8:229–231, 1959.
31. University of California in Irwine,Machine Learning Group. Repository of machine learning databases. http://www.ics.uci.edu/ mlearn/MLRepository.html.
32. C. Zhang and S. Zhang. *Association Rule Mining. Models and Algorithms*. Springer Verlag, Berlin, 2002.

Improving the Model Guided Sampling Optimization
by Model Search and Slice Sampling

Lukáš Bajer[1,2], Martin Holeňa[2], and Viktor Charypar[3]

[1] Faculty of Mathematics and Physics, Charles University in Prague,
Malostranské nám. 25, 118 00 Prague 1, Czech Republic
bajer@cs.cas.cz
[2] Institute of Computer Science, Academy of Sciences of the Czech Republic,
Pod Vodárenskou věží 2, 182 07 Prague 8, Czech Republic
martin@cs.cas.cz
[3] Faculty of Nuclear Sciences and Physical Engineering, Czech Technical University in Prague,
Trojanova 13, 120 00 Prague 2, Czech Republic
charyvik@fjfi.cvut.cz

Abstract: Model Guided Sampling Optimization (MGSO) was recently proposed as an alternative for Jones' Kriging-based EGO algorithm for optimization of expensive black-box functions. Instead of maximizing a chosen criterion (e.g., expected improvement), MGSO samples probability of improvement of the Gaussian process model forming multiple candidates – a whole population of suggested solutions. This paper further develops this algorithm using slice sampling method and continuous local optimization of the Gaussian process model.

1 Introduction

Optimization of expensive empirical functions forms an important topic in many engineering or natural-sciences areas. For such functions, it is often impossible to obtain any derivatives or information about smoothness; moreover, there is no mathematical expression nor algorithm to evaluate. Instead, some simulation or experiment has to be performed, and the measured value or result of such experiment is the value of the objective function being considered. Such functions are also called black-box functions. They are usually very expensive to evaluate; one evaluation may cost a lot of time and money to process.

Because of the absence of the derivatives, standard continuous first- or second-order derivative optimization methods cannot be used. Further, functions of this kind are usually characterized by a high number of local optima where simple algorithms can be trapped easily. Therefore, different derivative-free optimization methods for black-box functions (often called meta-heuristics) have been proposed. Even though these methods are slow and computationaly intensive, the cost of the evaluation of the empirical objective function is always much higher, and so it is cructial to decrease the number of function evaluations as much as possible.

Evolutionary algorithms constitute a broad family of meta-heuristics that are used for black-box optimization very frequently. Some of these algorithms and techniques are designed to minimize the number of objective func-

tion evaluations All of the three following approaches use a model (of a different type in each case), which is built and updated within the optimization process.

Estimation of distribution algorithms (EDAs) [9] represent one such approach: EDAs iteratively estimate the probability distribution of selected candidate solutions (usually better than some threshold) and sample this distribution forming a new set of solutions for the next iteration.

Surrogate modelling is a technique of construction and usage of a regression model of the objective function [7]. The model (called surrogate model in this context) is then used to evaluate some of the candidate solutions instead of evaluating them with the original costly function.

Our method, *Model Guided Sampling Optimization* (MGSO), takes inspiration from both these approaches. It uses a regression model of the objective function, which also provides an error estimate. However, instead of replacing the objective function with this model for some of the evaluations, it combines its prediction and the error estimate to get a probability of reaching a better solution in a given point. Similarly to EDAs, it then samples this pseudo-distribution[1] to obtain the next set of solution candidates.

The MGSO is similar to Jones' Efficient Global Optimization (EGO) [8]. Where EGO selects a *single solution* maximizing a chosen criterion – Expected Improvement (EI) or Probability of Improvement (PoI) – the MGSO *samples* the latter criterion. Hennig in his recent work [6] examines more criteria in detail. At the same time, the GP serves as a surrogate model of the objective function for small number of the solutions. In the second version of MGSO, presented in this paper, this smooth optimization is used in every generation of the optimization whereas the previous version employed model optimization only to improve the final optimum.

This paper extends the previous brief introduction of MGSO [1]. Instead of Gibbs' sampling, it uses slice sampling introduced by Neal [10]. This enables computa-

---

[1] a function proportional to a probability distribution, it's value is given by the *probability of improvement*, see Section 2.2

tionally cheaper sampling and works even in higher dimensions where Gibbs' sampling fails. Further, the GP model is used as a surrogate model more often, which brings faster convergence in the number of function evaluations. The following section introduces methods used in the MGSO, Section 3 describes the MGSO algorithm, and Section 4 brings some preliminary results on the BBOB testing set [4].

2   Involved Methods

2.1   Gaussian Processes

Gaussian process [12] is a probabilistic model based on Gaussian distributions. This type of model was chosen because it predicts the function value in a new point in the form of univariate Gaussian distribution: the mean and the standard deviation of the function value are provided. Through the predicted mean, the GP can serve as a surrogate model, and the standard deviation is an estimate of uncertainty of the prediction in a specified point.

The GP is specified by mean and covariance functions and relatively small number of covariance function's hyper-parameters. The hyper-parameters are fitted by the maximum-likelihood method.

Let $\mathbf{X}_N = \{\mathbf{x}_i \mid \mathbf{x}_i \in \mathbb{R}^D\}_{i=1}^N$ be a set of N training D-dimensional data points with known dependent-variable values $\mathbf{y}_N = \{y_i\}_{i=1}^N$ and $f(\mathbf{x})$ be an unknown function being modelled for which $f(\mathbf{x}_i) = y_i$ for all $i \in \{1,\dots,N\}$. The GP model imposes a probabilistic model on the data: the vector of known function values $\mathbf{y}_N$ is considered to be a sample of a N-dimensional multivariate Gaussian distribution with probability density $p(\mathbf{y}_N \mid \mathbf{X}_N)$. If we take into consideration a new data point $(\mathbf{x}_{N+1}, y_{N+1})$, the new probability density is

$$p(\mathbf{y}_{N+1} \mid \mathbf{X}_{N+1}) = \frac{\exp(-\frac{1}{2}\mathbf{y}_{N+1}^\top \mathbf{C}_{N+1}^{-1} \mathbf{y}_{N+1})}{\sqrt{(2\pi)^{N+1} \det(\mathbf{C}_{N+1})}} \quad (1)$$

where $\mathbf{C}_{N+1}$ is the covariance matrix of the Gaussian distribution (for which mean is usually set to constant zero) and $\mathbf{y}_{N+1} = \{y_1,\dots,y_N,y_{N+1}\}$ (see [2] for details). This covariance can be written as

$$\mathbf{C}_{N+1} = \begin{pmatrix} \mathbf{C}_N & \mathbf{k} \\ \mathbf{k}^\top & \kappa \end{pmatrix} \quad (2)$$

where $\mathbf{C}_N$ is the covariance of the Gaussian distribution given the N training data points, $\mathbf{k}$ is a vector of covariances between the new point and training data, and κ is the variance of the new point itself.

Predictions in Gaussian processes are made using Bayesian inference. Since the inverse $\mathbf{C}_{N+1}^{-1}$ of the extended covariance matrix can be expressed using inverse of the training covariance $\mathbf{C}_N^{-1}$ and $\mathbf{y}_N$ is known, the density of the distribution in a new point simplifies to a univariate Gaussian with the density

$$p(y_{N+1} \mid \mathbf{X}_{N+1}, \mathbf{y}_N) \propto \exp\left(-\frac{1}{2}\frac{(y_{N+1} - \hat{y}_{N+1})^2}{s_{y_{N+1}}^2}\right) \quad (3)$$

with the mean and variance given by

$$\hat{y}_{N+1} = \mathbf{k}^\top \mathbf{C}_N^{-1} \mathbf{y}_N, \quad (4)$$

$$s_{y_{N+1}}^2 = \kappa - \mathbf{k}^\top \mathbf{C}_N^{-1} \mathbf{k}. \quad (5)$$

Further details can be found in [2].

The covariance $\mathbf{C}_N$ plays a crucial role in these equations. It is defined by the covariance-function matrix $\mathbf{K}$ and signal noise σ as

$$\mathbf{C}_N = \mathbf{K}_N + \sigma \mathbf{I}_N \quad (6)$$

where $\mathbf{I}$ is an identity matrix of order N. Gaussian processes use parametrized covariance functions K describing prior assumptions on the shape of the modeled function. The covariance between the function values at two data points $\mathbf{x}_i$ and $\mathbf{x}_j$ is given by $K(\mathbf{x}_i, \mathbf{x}_j)$, which forms the (i,j)-th element of the matrix $\mathbf{K}_N$ as well. In our case, we used the most common squared-exponential function

$$K(\mathbf{x}_i, \mathbf{x}_j) = \theta \exp\left(-\frac{1}{2\ell^2}(\mathbf{x}_i - \mathbf{x}_j)^\top (\mathbf{x}_i - \mathbf{x}_j)\right), \quad (7)$$

which is suitable when the modelled function is rather smooth. The closer the points $\mathbf{x}_i$ and $\mathbf{x}_j$ are, the closer the covariance function value is to 1 and the stronger correlation between the function values $f(\mathbf{x}_i)$ and $f(\mathbf{x}_j)$ is. The signal variance θ scales this correlation, and the parameter ℓ is the characteristic length-scale with which the distance of two considered data points is compared. Our choice of the covariance function was motivated by its simplicity and the possibility of finding the hyper-parameter values by the maximum-likelihood method.

2.2   Sampling

The core step of the MGSO algorithm is the sampling of the probability of improvement. This probability is, for a chosen threshold T of the function value, directly given by the predicted mean $\hat{f}(\mathbf{x}) = \hat{y}$ and the standard deviation $\hat{s}(\mathbf{x}) = s_y$ of the GP model $\hat{f}$ in any point $\mathbf{x}$ of the input space

$$\mathrm{PoI}_T(\mathbf{x}) = \Phi\left(\frac{T - \hat{f}(\mathbf{x})}{\hat{s}(\mathbf{x})}\right) = \mathrm{P}(\hat{f}(\mathbf{x}) \leqq T), \quad (8)$$

which corresponds to the value of cumulative distribution function (CDF) of the Gaussian with density (3) for the value of threshold T. Even though all the variables come from Gaussian distribution, $\mathrm{PoI}(\mathbf{x})$ is definitely not Gaussian-shaped since it depends on the threshold T and the function being modeled f – a typical example of the landscape of $\mathrm{PoI}(\mathbf{x})$ in two dimensions for the Rastrigin function is depicted in Fig. 1. The dependency on the modeled function also causes a lack of analytical marginals, derivatives or conditional probability densities.

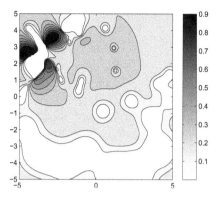

Figure 1: Probability of improvement. Rastrigin function in 2D, GP model built with 40 data points.

Gibbs' sampler. The first version of MGSO [1] used Gibbs' sampler [3]. The sampler starts at some point of the input space $\mathbf{x}_s$. Further, it moves along each dimension to a new point $\mathbf{x}'$: it cycles successively through each individual dimension x_k of $\mathbf{x}, k = 1, \ldots, D$ and samples from the conditional probability of x_k given values of the remaining $x_{j \neq k}$: for $k = 1, \ldots, D$

$$X_k \sim p(X_k \,|\, \{X_j = x_j, j \neq k\}). \tag{9}$$

As no analytical expression for these conditionals exists, piece-wise linear inverses of the empirical conditional CDF's F_k^{-1} was used to transform samples from uniform distributions

$$u_k \sim U(0,1), \quad x_k = F_k^{-1}(u_k).$$

Linear interpolation between values of the empirical CDF was computed at the 20-points grid.

Even though evaluating GP model's mean $\hat{y} = \hat{f}(\mathbf{x})$ and standard deviation $\hat{s}(\mathbf{x})$ for 20 points requires only two calls of GP model prediction, the complexity of sampling rises quickly with the number of variables D, which causes that sampling in more than three dimensions becomes extremely slow.

Slice sampling. This novel kind of sampling, brought by Neal in 2003 [10], is based on a simple and smart idea. Let f be a function proportional to the density from which sampling is desired. It starts from a starting point $(\mathbf{x}_0, f(\mathbf{x}_0))$ where a uniform single-variable sample $y \sim U(0, f(\mathbf{x}_0))$ is obtained. This value induces a subset $S = \{\mathbf{x} \in \mathbb{R}^D \,|\, f(\mathbf{x}) > y\}$, which is uniformly sampled, forming a new point $\mathbf{x}_1$. The sampler then starts again from this point $(\mathbf{x}_1, f(\mathbf{x}_1))$ and iteratively generates next samples.

The subspace S is approximated with an axis-aligned hyper-rectangle H of size $\mathbf{w} \in \mathbb{R}^D$, randomly positioned around the current point $\mathbf{x}$ and successively shrinked if a point inside H but outside S is sampled. The parameter $\mathbf{w}$ is the only parameter of this method, which should not be much smaller than a typical size of the subset S.

Larger values of $\mathbf{w}$ do not affect correctness and increase only moderatley the number of shrinking steps 13—19 in the pseudo-code Alg. 1. If the user-specified number of unsuccessful attempts of shrinking is exceeded, the slice sampling ends with an error, which possibly results in a lower number of individuals in the population during that MGSO generation.

Slice sampling has several advantages. First, it nicely scales with higher dimensionalities of the problem. Second, there is no need of conditional distributions as it is with Gibbs' sampler. Moreover, it does not require the density being normalized, which is the case of PoI. This kind of sampler is used in the second version of MGSO, described in this paper.

3   Model Guided Sampling Optimization

As it was already mentioned, the MGSO algorithm for black-box optimization has many common aspects with Jones' [8] Efficient Global Optimization algorithm. Like some of the versions of EGO, it uses the probability of improvement $\mathrm{PoI}_T^{M_i}(\mathbf{x})$ as a measure of how promising the specified point $\mathbf{x}$ is for locating the optimum. This measure is given by a chosen threshold T and the current knowledge of the function landscape modelled by the current GP model M_i. The main difference to EGO is that MGSO does not maximize this criterion, but it samples the PoI (which is proportional to a density) producing a whole population of individuals.

Algorithm 1 Slice sampling [10]

1: **Input**: f – function proportional to the density
      $\mathbf{x}_0$ – starting point, $\mathbf{x}_0 \in \mathbb{R}^D$
      $\mathbf{w}$ – scale estimates, $\mathbf{w} \in \mathbb{R}^D$
      n – required number of samples
2: **for** $k = 0, 1, \ldots, n$ **do**
3:     $y \sim U(0, f(\mathbf{x}_k))$ {height of the slice}
4:     $\mathbf{u} \sim U(0,1)^D$
5:     $\mathbf{L} \leftarrow \mathbf{x}_k - \mathbf{w} \circ \mathbf{u}$ {randomly shifted lower bound}
6:     $\mathbf{R} \leftarrow \mathbf{L} + \mathbf{w}$ {upper bound}
7:     **while** given number of tries has not been exceeded **do**
8:        $\mathbf{u} \sim U(0,1)^D$
9:        $\mathbf{x}_{k+1} \leftarrow \mathbf{L} + \mathbf{u} \circ (\mathbf{R} - \mathbf{L})$ {$\mathbf{x}_{k+1} \sim U(\mathbf{L}, \mathbf{R})$}
10:      **if** $(y < f(\mathbf{x}_{k+1}))$ **then**
11:        accept $\mathbf{x}_{k+1}$ and exit the *while* loop
12:      **end if**
13:      **for** each dimension $j = 1, \ldots, D$ **do**
14:        **if** $(x_{k+1}^j < x_k^j)$ **then**
15:          $L^j \leftarrow x_{k+1}^j$ {shrink the lower bound}
16:        **else**
17:          $R^j \leftarrow x_{k+1}^j$ {shrink the upper bound}
18:        **end if**
19:      **end for**
20:     **end while**
21: **end for**
22: **Output**: $\{\mathbf{x}_1, \ldots, \mathbf{x}_n\}$

Algorithm 2 MGSO (Model Guided Sampling Optimization)

1: **Input:** f – objective function
       N', N – sizes of the initial and standard population
       r – the number of solutions for dataset restriction
2: $S_0 = \{(\mathbf{x}_j, y_j)\}_{j=1}^{N'} \leftarrow$ generate N' initial samples and evaluate them
3: **while** no stopping condition is met, $i = 1, 2, \ldots$ **do**
4:     $M_i \leftarrow$ build a GP model and fit its hyper-parameters according to the dataset S_{i-1}
5:     $\{\mathbf{x}_j\}_{j=1}^{N} \leftarrow$ sample the $\text{PoI}_T^{M_i}(\mathbf{x})$ forming N new candidate solutions, optionally with different targets T
6:     $\mathbf{x}_k \leftarrow$ find the minimum of the GP (by local continuous optimization) and replace the nearest solution from $\{\mathbf{x}_j\}_{j=1}^{N}$ with it
7:     $\{y_j\}_{j=1}^{N} \leftarrow f(\{\mathbf{x}_j\}_{j=1}^{N})$ {evaluate the population}
8:     $S_i \leftarrow S_{i-1} \cup \{(\mathbf{x}_j, y_j)\}_{j=1}^{N}$ {augment the dataset}
9:     $(\tilde{\mathbf{x}}, \tilde{y}) \leftarrow \arg\min_{(\mathbf{x}, y) \in S_i} y$ {find the best solution in S_i}
10:     **if** any rescale condition is met **then**
11:         restrict the dataset S_i to the bounding-box $[\mathbf{l}_i, \mathbf{u}_i]$ of the r nearest solutions along the best solution $(\tilde{\mathbf{x}}, \tilde{y})$ and linearly transform S_i to $[-1, 1]^D$
12:     **end if**
13: **end while**
14: **Output:** the best found solution $(\tilde{\mathbf{x}}, \tilde{y})$

After the initial (usually uniform random) sample of the input space, its evaluation and saving to the dataset S_0, the MGSO algorithm proceeds as follows (see Alg. 2 for details; $\circ$ is a component-wise product of two vectors). First, a new GP model M_i is fitted to the current dataset S_i. The model predictive distribution guides the further optimization: the model's PoI is sampled forming the new population. The algorithm continues with evaluating the population, a new model is fitted to this augmented dataset and the process is repeated until a stopping condition (like the number of objective function evaluations) is met.

The second version of MGSO differs in two points. First, it uses the slice sampling instead of Gibb's sampler and second, a smooth model optimization (the step 6 in Alg. 2) is added: the last individual in the population is obtained by continuous local optimization of the GP model. This search, which uses the GP as a surrogate model, speeds-up the optimization process especially in the final part of the algorithm's run.

3.1 Input Space Restriction

To abstract from the search space scaling, MGSO works in an internal, linearly transformed coordinate system defined by mapping

$$scale : [\mathbf{l}, \mathbf{u}] \rightarrow [-1, 1]^D \tag{10}$$

and the transformation can be updated during the optimization. Updating restricts the learning and sampling space to the neighborhood of the so-far optimum, which

enables sampling in the situation when the PoI is non-zero only in a very small region. The lower and upper bounds $[\mathbf{l}_i, \mathbf{u}_i]$, $\mathbf{l}_i, \mathbf{u}_i \in \mathbb{R}^D$ are determined as a bounding box of the r nearest samples from the current optimum. The bounding box is expanded by 10% in order not to have training points for the GP model on the boundaries of the training region. The bounds $[\mathbf{l}_i, \mathbf{u}_i]$ can be updated each iteration i, but, in practice, they are updated only several times during one optimization run.

The value r, the initial number of samples N' and the population size N are input parameters of MGSO. As this paper is still work-in-progress, no rigorous testing for the default values of these parameters has been performed yet. For the results presented in the next section, these values have been used: $r = 15 \cdot D, N = N' = 10 \cdot D$.

The slice sampling method enables us to sample multivariate distributions much faster. Slice sampling from Matlab Statistical toolbox was used, which implements shrinking-in of all dimensions. The sampler is extended by a validity-checking of the GP model – the samples which, if added, result in ill-conditioned covariance matrix are rejected. These rejections start to occur in later phases of the algorithm run, which is a starting impulse for input space restriction and rescaling. Further, different thresholds T for $\text{PoI}_T^{M_i}$ are tested if many (N by default) such rejections arise.

4 Experimental Results and Conclusion

Preliminary testing results from our Matlab implementation[2] are comprised in this section. Because of large sampling time and low success rate of the Gibbs' sampler of the first MGSO in higher dimensions, speed of the optimization of the first and second version of MGSO is compared only in 2D testing cases. The second version of MGSO is further compared with the Covariance Matrix Adaptation Evolution Strategy (CMA-ES) [5] – the state-of-the art in the field of continuous black-box optimization methods – in 5D and 10D. The comparison of MGSO with Jones' EGO is forthcoming, but not included in this paper. More detailed evaluation of Gibbs' and slice sampling is placed in the first part of this section.

4.1 Sampling

The slice sampling has shown to be a noticeable improvement both in terms of the CPU time (for sampling and for the GP model evaluations) and the ability to provide enough samples from PoI. Illustrative results of the sampling CPU time and the number of GP model evaluations for two particular GP models in 2D and 5D are shown in Tab. 1 and sampling times and the numbers of successfully generated samples are depicted in Fig. 2.

---

[2]the source code is freely available at `http://github.com/charypar/gpeda`

Table 1: Comparison of Gibbs' and Slice sampling, results from 15 runs of sampling. Average CPU time and the number of evaluations of the GP model's PoI needed to generate 20/50 samples in 2D/5D. The differences of the CPU time per GP evaluation is mainly because of the batch evaluation of PoI for empir. CDF in Gibbs' sampler.

	Gibbs 2D	slice 2D	Gibbs 5D	slice 5D
time [s]	1.85	1.11	42.41	17.56
# GP eval.	2 402	246	20 087	2 909

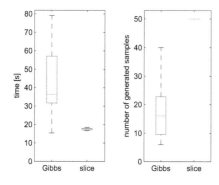

Figure 2: Computational time and the number of successfully generated samples in 5D. Results from 15 independent runs with the same GP model/PoI.

4.2 BBOB Benchmark Functions Optimization

The proposed MGSO has been tested on three different continuous benchmark functions from the BBOB testing set [4]: sphere, Rosenbrock and Rastrigin functions. Although the previous version of the algorithm [1] was practically able to optimize only two-dimensional versions of these functions, this paper provides results from 5D and 10D as well. The computational speed-up was caused mainly by the slice sampling method and partly also by the continuous model optimization step.

In two dimensions, the current version of the MGSO outperformed CMA-ES (considering budget 500 original evaluations) on both sphere and Rosenbrock functions, and it performs approximately equally well on Rastrigin function, see Fig. 3. In terms of the CPU time for the whole optimization, the CMA-ES runs in several seconds while MGSO takes several or tens of minutes to process. But as we are concerned with expensive (usually empirical-function) optimization, we suppose the cost for the MGSO search being dominated by the time and money for the original evaluations.

The MGSO scales nicely on the unimodal and symmetric sphere function. Both in 5D and 10D, a dramatically lower number of function evaluations is needed to reach threshold of the objective function values $f_\Delta = 10^{-4}$ than in the case of CMA-ES, see Fig. 4 and Fig. 5. On the Rosenbrock function, however, the number of evaluations of MGSO needed to reach $f_\Delta = 10^{-2}$ is lower in 5D,

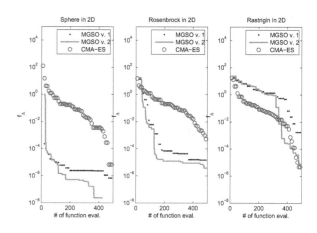

Figure 3: 2-D. Medians of the best found function values gathered from 15 independent runs. The First [1] and the second version of MGSO are compared with CMA-ES.

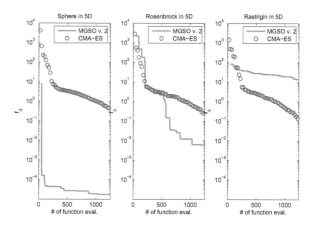

Figure 4: 5-D. Medians of the best found function values gathered from 15 runs. The second version of MGSO is compared to CMA-ES.

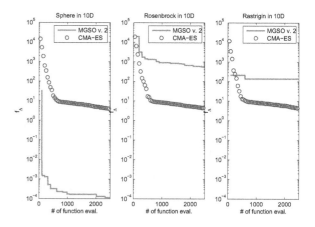

Figure 5: 5-D. Medians of the best found function values gathered from 15 runs. The second version of MGSO is compared to CMA-ES.

but CMA-ES works better in 10D. The multimodal Rastrigin function with large number of local minima is not harder than the two other functions for CMA-ES, but it is not the case of the MGSO. Our algorithm is outperformed by CMA-ES in both 5D and 10D for that benchmark function.

4.3   Conclusions and future work

Our method shows promising results in terms of the number of true objective function evaluations in the initial phase of optimization. However, there are still many issues to solve. In general, we are planning to work on improving the final local optimization in the region of the optimum either by improving MGSO itself or combining it with some other method in the final phase. Further, fitting of the hyper-parameters of the GP model will be studied, since GPML implementation[3] [11] being used is often not able to fit them to optimal values.

Future work should also test different initial sampling schemes, which affect the model quality and thus performance of the method, and perform rigorous testing of the effects of input parameters, which were set by hand for our initial experiments. A comparison with the EGO method, which was not done due to a lack of a readily available implementation, will also be performed.

The Model Guided Sampling Optimization was introduced in more detail. Several improvements of this algorithm were given and more experimental results than in the last brief work [1] were provided. The experiments show that the proposed method can successfully compete with the state-of-the art continuous black-box optimization algorithm CMA-ES in lower dimensions and on unimodal symmetric functions.

Acknowledgments

This work was supported by the Czech Science Foundation (GAČR) grants P202/11/1368 and 13-17187S, the Grant Agency of the Charles University (GAUK) 278511/2011 grant and the Grant Agency of the Czech Technical University in Prague, grant No. SGS12/196/OHK3/3T/14.

References

[1] L. Bajer, V. Charypar, and M. Holeňa. Model guided sampling optimization with gaussian processes for expensive black-box optimization. In *GECCO '13 Proceedings*, Amsterdam, Netherlands, 2013. ACM, New York.

[2] D. Buche, N. Schraudolph, and P. Koumoutsakos. Accelerating evolutionary algorithms with gaussian process fitness function models. *IEEE Transactions on Systems, Man, and Cybernetics, Part C: Applications and Reviews*, 35(2):183–194, 2005.

[3] S. Geman and D. Geman. Stochastic relaxation, Gibbs distributions, and the Bayesian restoration of images. *IEEE Transactions on Pattern Analysis and Machine Intelligence*, PAMI-6(6):721–741, 1984.

[4] N. Hansen, S. Finck, R. Ros, and A. Auger. Real-parameter black-box optimization benchmarking 2009: Noiseless functions definitions. Technical Report RR-6829, INRIA, 2009. Updated February 2010.

[5] N. Hansen and A. Ostermeier. Completely derandomized self-adaptation in evolution strategies. *Evolutionary Computation*, 9(2):159–195, June 2001.

[6] P. Hennig and C. J. Schuler. Entropy search for information-efficient global optimization. *J. Mach. Learn. Res.*, 13:1809–1837, June 2012.

[7] Y. Jin. A comprehensive survey of fitness approximation in evolutionary computation. *Soft Computing*, 9(1):3–12, Jan. 2005.

[8] D. R. Jones, M. Schonlau, and W. J. Welch. Efficient global optimization of expensive black-box functions. *Journal of Global Optimization*, 13(4):455–492, Dec. 1998.

[9] P. Larrañaga and J. A. Lozano. *Estimation of distribution algorithms: A new tool for evolutionary computation*. Kluwer, 2002.

[10] R. M. Neal. Slice sampling. *The Annals of Statistics*, 31(3):705–767, June 2003.

[11] C. E. Rasmussen and H. Nickisch. Gaussian processes for machine learning (GPML) toolbox. *J. Mach. Learn. Res.*, 11:3011–3015, Dec. 2010.

[12] C. E. Rasmussen and C. K. I. Williams. *Gaussian Processes for Machine Learning*. Adaptive computation and machine learning series. MIT Press, 2006.

---

[3]http://www.gaussianprocess.org/gpml/code/matlab/

ITAT 2013: Workshops, Posters, and Tutorials, pp. 92–99
ISBN 978-1490952086, © 2013 M. Kopp, M. Holeňa

Design and comparison of two rule-based fuzzy classifiers for computer security

Martin Kopp[1,2], Martin Holeňa[2]

[1] Faculty of Information Technology, Czech Technical University in Prague
Thákurova 9, 160 00 Prague
[2] Institute of Computer Science, Academy of Sciences of the Czech Republic
Pod Vodárenskou věží 2, 182 07 Prague

Abstract: This paper describes the design and comparison of two rule based fuzzy classifiers, which are subsequently enhanced with respect to comprehensibility. The first approach is based on random forests. The second is a specific kind of a fuzzy decision tree which is built on information granules extracted from results of a fuzzy clustering algorithm. Membership functions of fuzzy sets are fitted to the outputs of these two tree based classifiers. This gives us logical rules, which have a better comprehensibility. These two approaches are compared to each other and with a support vector machine classifier as a representative of precise classifiers. The comparison is performed on data concerning network security.

Keywords: Comprehensible classification, decision tree, fuzzy clustering, random forest, rule-based classification.

1 Introduction

There are two main lines of study in an intrusion detection: misuse detection [25] and anomaly detection [1]. Signature based misuse detection methods, of course, can recognize well known attacks only. The anomaly detection is focused on finding unusual activities [5][13][22]. This method is still less accurate in revealing known patterns, but superior in the way it can detect novelty attacks. Recently, an intrusion detection attracted many researchers from machine learning [3][14][18].

Machine learning techniques for an intrusion detection can be divided into to two groups with different goals, design of more accurate systems [17] and design or improvement of such systems to achieve better comprehensibility [19]. This paper is focused on the second goal and compares two methods, how to build up rule-based a fuzzy classifier focused on comprehensibility. The first one is based on an ensemble of decision trees [24] and referred to as the random forest method. The second one, based on information granules extracted from data by fuzzy c-means algorithm, will be called C-Fuzzy decision tree. For more information about fuzzy systems and fuzzy classification, we refer to [10][11][12].

This paper is organized as follows. Section 2 provides an overview of the random forest based method. In section 3, the C-Fuzzy decision tree method will be described, followed by the process of fitting fuzzy sets to the output in section 4. Section 5 describes experiments on the KDD 99 data set [9].

2 Random forest based method

Decision trees [23] are commonly used in machine learning and classification. Each inner node j of the tree stores a binary split function:

$$h(\mathbf{V}, \theta_j) \in \{0, 1\}, \tag{1}$$

in which $\theta = (\phi, \psi, \tau)$, where ϕ is a filter function, which chooses some features from a whole feature space $\mathbf{V}$, ψ defines a geometric primitive used to separate data (e.g. hyperplane) and τ is a vector of thresholds for inequalities used in binary tests. The leaf nodes then store class labels. The tree is built up (grown) by splitting nodes with high heterogeneity criterion such as entropy, Gini index [6] etc.

Compared to other machine learning methods, decision trees have many advantages like robustness, handling both numerical and categorical data, and finally, trees are easy to understand and interpret. In recent years, ensembles of classifiers became most popular due to their greater accuracy and generalization ability. Decision trees are no exceptions and ensembles of them are called decision forests.

In this paper we work with random decision forests. This method has been introduced in [7]. The random nature of the forest can be achieved by a random features selection or random sampling of a training dataset. These two techniques are not mutually exclusive and can be used together. For more detailed description of random forests and their application, we refer to [4].

The training of a tree is done by optimizing parameters of (1) at each split node j via:

$$\theta_j^* = \arg\max_{\theta_j} I_j \tag{2}$$

For classification, the objective function I_j takes the form of an information gain defined as:

$$I_j = H(S_j) - \sum_{i \in \{L, R\}} \frac{|S_j^i|}{|S_j|} H(S_j^i), \tag{3}$$

with S_j as a set of data points at the current node and i indexing its child nodes (left,right). The entropy for a generic set S is defined as:

$$H(S) = -\sum_{c \in C} p(c) log p(c) \tag{4}$$

where c is a class label such that $c \in C$ and C is a set of all classes. The $p(c)$ is a prior probability of c and in our implementation it is calculated as a normalized empirical histogram of labels corresponding to training points in S.

Classification forests produce a probabilistic class distribution. In fact, each tree leaf yields a posterior probability $p_t(c|\mathbf{V})$. So the forest output is typically given by:

$$p(c|\mathbf{V}) = \frac{1}{T} \sum_t^T p_t(c|\mathbf{V}) \tag{5}$$

where $t \in T$.

The properties of the forest, like accuracy and generalization, depend on several parameters:

- The forest size T.

- The maximal tree depth D.

- The proportion ρ of randomly chosen features from the whole feature space $\mathbf{V}$.

How each of them influences the forest prediction ability, will be discussed in section 5.

3 C-Fuzzy Decision tree

Standard decision trees have several limitations. At the first place, only the most discriminative attribute is chosen to be split, in each inner node. Secondly, before forests emerged, decision trees were crisp predictors. There was no membership grade or a class distribution. The cluster-oriented decision trees are a new kind of decision trees that attempt to overcome these limitations by perceiving data as a collection of information granules [20]. Information granules are almost synonym of clusters [8]. Furthermore, fuzzy granulations help to model soft bounds amongst classes, instead of crisp ones, what leads to better approximation of real bounds. It is evident now that fuzzy clusters are the central concept behind the generalized trees. They will be referred to as C-Fuzzy decision trees [21].

3.1 Overall structure of C-Fuzzy trees

The whole process of growing the tree is pretty simple and can be summarized in the following steps:

1. Run a fuzzy clustering and assign results to nodes.

2. Find a node N_i with the highest heterogeneity V_i.

3. Perform a fuzzy clustering over patterns of the node N_i.

4. Split the node N_i and assign clusters to new nodes.

5. If a stopping condition is fulfilled, end, else return to 2.

Typical stopping conditions are: a heterogeneity criterion falls under a threshold, the number of patterns assigned to the node is smaller than some value etc. When split, each node is divided to exactly c clusters. Lower values of c, like $c = 2$ or $c = 3$, produce deep trees, where higher c, like $c = 7$, produce broader trees instead.

3.2 Fuzzy clustering

A fuzzy clustering is the most important part of building the tree, it provides a full description of nodes. For the purpose of this paper, the fuzzy C-means (FCM) was selected as a well known and documented algorithm [2]. In the FCM algorithm, the clusters are build trough minimalization of some objective function. The standard objective function Q assumes the format:

$$Q = \sum_{i=1}^{c} \sum_{k=1}^{N} u_{ik}^{\gamma} d_{ik}^2 \tag{6}$$

where $U = [u_{ik}], i = 1, 2, ..., c, k = 1, 2, ..., N$ is a partition matrix, c is the number of clusters, N is the number of data points, γ is a fuzzification factor (usually $\gamma = 2$) and d_{ik} stands for the distance between the ith prototype and the kth data point. In our implementation, the data points come in the ordered pairs $(\mathbf{x}(k), y(k))$, where $\mathbf{x}(k)$ stands for the input vector of the kth data point and $y(k)$ is its corresponding output. For the clustering, these pairs are concatenated into vectors:

$$\mathbf{z}(k) = [x_1(k) x_2(k) ... x_n(k) y(k)] \tag{7}$$

where n is the number of features. This implies that the clustering is done in a $(n+1)$ dimensional space and a resulting prototype $\mathbf{f}_i$ is positioned in $\mathbf{R}^{n+1}$. The FCM algorithm starts from randomly generated prototypes and achieves optimization task by iterating following steps:

partition update

$$u_{ik} = \frac{1}{\sum_{j=1}^{c} (\frac{d_{ik}}{d_{jk}})^{2/(\gamma-1)}} \tag{8}$$

where d_{ik} is some distance of the ith prototype $\mathbf{f}_i$ and the kth data point $\mathbf{x}_k$, typically Euclidean.

prototype update

$$\mathbf{f}_i^{new} = \frac{\sum_{k=1}^{N} u_{ik}^{\gamma} \mathbf{z}_k}{\sum_{k=1}^{N} u_{ik}^{\gamma}} \tag{9}$$

If we denote the number of clusters c and split them d-times then then number of nodes will be $c*d$. But the classification is performed only in leaf nodes. There are $d(c-1)+1$ of them. Therefore, a new data point is compared to $d(c-1)+1$ prototypes and then assigned to the cluster corresponding to the most similar one.

3.3 Node splitting criterion

The tree growing process is done by splitting nodes with the highest heterogeneity criterion V_i. The heterogeneity, in this paper, is based on the variance of the data assigned to a cluster. Higher variance results in higher value of V_i. More formally, V_i is a weighted sum of distances. The prototype of the cluster in the output space is defined as:

$$\mathbf{m_i} = \frac{\sum_{(x(k),y(k)) \in \mathbf{X}_i \times \mathbf{Y}_i} u_i(\mathbf{x}(k))y(k)}{\sum_{(x(k),y(k)) \in \mathbf{X}_i \times \mathbf{Y}_i} u_i(\mathbf{x}(k))} \qquad (10)$$

where $\mathbf{x}(k)$ is the input vector of the kth data point and $y(k)$ is the corresponding output. The associated membership grade is captured by u_i. Finally the heterogeneity criterion of the ith node V_i is counted as follows:

$$V_i = \sum_{(x(k),y(k)) \in \mathbf{X}_i \times \mathbf{Y}_i} u_i(\mathbf{x}(k))(y(k) - \mathbf{m_i})^2 \qquad (11)$$

3.4 Classification

Once the tree is built up, it can be used to classify an unseen data point ($\mathbf{x}$). This task is fulfilled by computing membership grades for each leaf node as follows:

$$u_i(\mathbf{x}) = \frac{1}{\sum_{j=1}^{c} \left(\frac{||\mathbf{x} - m_i||}{||\mathbf{x} - m_j||} \right)^{2/(\gamma-1)}}, \qquad (12)$$

where $||\mathbf{x} - m_i||$ stands for the distance from the data point $\mathbf{x}$ to the prototype m_i. Higher u_i implies that the data point have higher membership grade to the cluster i.

4 Fuzzy sets fitting

This section describes how fuzzy sets were used to improve the comprehensibility of the previously described classifiers. This process will be called an enhancement by fuzzy sets. These fuzzy sets can have arbitrary membership functions with range $\langle 0, 1 \rangle$. For simplicity we decided to use fuzzy sets with Gaussian membership functions.

We want to express each class as a disjunction of its clusters, e.g. anomaly class contains one cluster for each attack type (in the ideal case). Therefore, every anomal flow should belong mostly into one specific cluster. In other words, the anomal flow is classified as specific attack type, e.g., as neptune, or port scan, or . . . .

These clusters are modelled by a conjunction of fuzzy sets. Each dimension is divided into as many fuzzy sets as is the number of clusters within the class. To improve comprehensibility, natural language terms such as: low, high, short, long . . . , can be assigned to these fuzzy sets and then we get rules, such as: This data point is anomal if x_1 is low and x_2 is short and x_3 is many or x_1 is low and x_2 is moderate and x_3 is few and x_1 is low . . . . Or we can have rules like: This data point is anomal if x_1 is close to 3 and x_2 is close to 0.5 and so on.

Outputs from a training phase for both classifiers are membership grades to fuzzy sets, but the outputs differ in the structure of the universe, on which they are defined. For the C-Fuzzy tree method, data points are spread into clusters, even data of the same class can be, and often are, split into several clusters. On the other hand, the random forest method divides data into classes only. But some classes have quite heterogeneous inputs. The reason is that in the network traffic data, with which the experiments were performed, there are many types of flows with the same label, e.g., as normal traffic. So data in these classes have to be split artificially to improve accuracy. Because of this difference, the fitting of fuzzy sets will be described separately for each method.

4.1 C-Fuzzy decision tree fitting

To this time, we have a data in clusters, which are disjoint. These clusters were created considering all features together. This suggests to model an affiliation to a class by a disjunction over the clusters of conjunctions over the features, i.e. by a disjunctive normal form (DNF). Therefore, if we denote η the predicate, which is modelled by a fuzzy set, we can write rules:

$$x \in c \; IFF \; \vee_{j \in J_c} (\eta(x_1) \wedge \; ... \; \wedge \eta(x_n)) \qquad (13)$$

where J_c is the set of clusters in the class c.

We already know the left side of these rules, membership grades, from the C-fuzzy decision tree, therefore we need to compute a truth function of DNF. In order to compute a truth function, lets recall that:

In the fuzzy logic, t-norms and t-conorms are used the same way as a Boolean product and a Boolean sum to model a conjunction and a disjunction in the standard Boolean logic.

A t-norm $\top : [0,1]^2 \to [0,1]$ is a commutative and associative function that satisfies $\top(a,1) = a$ and $a \leq b \Rightarrow \top(a,c) \leq \top(b,c)$.

A t-conorm $\bot : [0,1]^2 \to [0,1]$ is a commutative and associative function that satisfies $\bot(a,0) = a$ and $a \leq b \Rightarrow \bot(a,c) \leq \bot(b,c)$.

The two most common t-norms, minimum and algebraic product with corresponding t-conorms maximum and probabilistic sum, were used. Probabilistic sum is defined as:

$$\bot_{\text{sum}}(a,b) = a + b - (a \cdot b) \qquad (14)$$

Due to a commutativity and associativity of the probabilistic sum it can be, for an arbitrary number of inputs, computed as follows:

$$\bot_{\text{sum}}(a_1,...,a_n) = \bot(a_1,...,\bot(a_{n-1},a_n),...) \qquad (15)$$

Now the truth function of a conjunction $\text{Tf}^\wedge$ can be computed for each cluster j, for t-norm minimum:

$$\text{Tf}_j^\wedge(\mathbf{x}) = \min\{\mu_{1,j}(x_1),...\mu_{n,j}(x_n)\} \qquad (16)$$

and for algebraic product:

$$\mathrm{Tf}_j^\wedge(\mathbf{x}) = \mu_{1,j}(x_1) \cdot \ldots \cdot \mu_{n,j}(x_n), \qquad (17)$$

where μ_js are membership grades of the individual dimensions of the data point $\mathbf{x}$ to fuzzy sets, which are modelled by one dimensional Gaussians, as was mentioned above.

For each cluster, the truth function of the conjunction $\mathrm{Tf}^\wedge$ is fitted by minimizing the sum of squares error.

$$\beta_c^* = \arg\min_{\beta_c} \sum_i^N [y_i - \mathrm{Tf}^\wedge]^2 \qquad (18)$$

where $\beta = (\beta_1^\mu, \ldots, \beta_n^\mu, \beta_1^\sigma, \ldots, \beta_n^\sigma)$ are parameters of one-dimensional Gaussians in each dimension.

The truth function of a disjunction $\mathrm{Tf}^\vee$ for t-conorm maximum is evaluated by:

$$\mathrm{Tf}_c^\vee(\mathbf{x}) = \max_{j \in c} \mathrm{Tf}_j^\wedge(\mathbf{x}) \qquad (19)$$

and for t-conorm probabilistic sum:

$$\mathrm{Tf}_c^\vee(\mathbf{x}) = \perp_{\mathrm{sum}}(\mathrm{Tf}_{j \in c}^\wedge) \qquad (20)$$

4.2 Random forest fitting

This method gives a precise class prediction and membership grades for data to classes. But we need to spread heterogeneous classes into several clusters to improve accuracy of the fuzzy system. Two approaches were considered: use individual trees and fit cluster centres to some of their nodes or split classes by their discrete parameters. Later approach was selected. At first, discrete parameters were reduced to two or tree values by a one dimensional clustering. Secondly, for every possible combination of their values, the number of observations was counted and five combinations with most data were selected, which formed clusters within classes. So discrete parameters have their influence on the output, despite they are not considered in the next step. As in the previous section, a t-norm applied to Gaussians was fitted to each newly created cluster by minimizing the least squares error (18) and after that, the truth functions were evaluated in the same way. Because clustering algorithm, described above, showed a low accuracy with the current data set, we tried also the fuzzy c-means, to decide, if the weak point is in the clustering phase or in the fitting phase.

4.3 Interpretation of an example

The example rule was extracted from the KDD 99 data set by the enhanced fuzzy c-means algorithm with five clusters and two iterations. There are $d(c-1)+1 = 9$ clusters spread into two classes. To shorten the example, we have chosen four clusters only and the five most significant variables (those with the smallest variances of the fitted Gaussians, which are:

- x_1 is the duration of a flow

- x_5 is the amount of bytes sent from the source to the destination

- x_6 is the amount of bytes sent from the destination to the source

- x_{23} is the number of connections to the same host

- x_{24} is the number of connections to the same service

The data point x is considered normal if:
x_1 is close to -0.07 $\wedge$ x_5 is close to 0.04 $\wedge$ x_6 is close to 0.09 $\wedge$ x_{23} is close to -1.17 $\wedge$ x_{24} is close to -0.48 $\vee$ x_1 is close to -0.06 $\wedge$ x_5 is close to 0.35 $\wedge$ x_6 is close to 0.01 $\wedge$ x_{23} is close to -1.17 $\wedge$ x_{24} is close to -0.48 $\vee$ $\ldots$
and the data point x is considered anomal if:
x_1 is close to -0.07 $\wedge$ x_5 is close to 0 $\wedge$ x_6 is close to -0.03 $\wedge$ x_{23} is close to 0.884 $\wedge$ x_{24} is close to -0.464 $\vee$ x_1 is close to -0.11 $\wedge$ x_5 is close to 5.92 $\wedge$ x_6 is close to -0.199 $\wedge$ x_{23} is close to -1.11 $\wedge$ x_{24} is close to 2.16 $\vee$ $\ldots$,

We can use the natural language to increase the comprehensibility of the example. Fuzzy sets are divided into subsets (one subset for every cluster), we can assign the terms such as very little, or very small, to the one with the smallest mean of the Gaussian and then small, average and so on. Then we can have rules like:

The data point x is considered normal if:
x_1 is average and x_5 is average and x_6 is average and x_{23} is very small and x_{24} is small, or $\ldots$
and the data point x is considered anomal if:
x_1 is average and x_5 is average and x_6 is average and x_{23} is very big and x_{24} is small, or x_1 is average and x_5 is huge and x_6 is small and x_{23} is very small and x_{24} is huge, or $\ldots$

From this example we can assume that normal data points have an average duration, amounts of downloaded and uploaded bytes are average etc. Its evident that these anomal clusters describe two different attacks. In fact, the first cluster describes the attack called smurf, which is specific by sending a lot of ICMP packets to the broadcast address with spoofed source IP address. Then, the machine with the source IP address is overwhelmed with the ICMP response packets. This will cause a significant slowdown, or even shut-down of targeted machine. The second attack is called syn-flood or neptune. Its principle is sending a huge amount of the synchronization requests (SYN packets) to the server and then not responding to the servers reply. The attacked server have to keep all unfinished connections. This will soon cause a system break down, because of the resource depletion.

Both attacks, described above, can be recognized in the example. The very big value of x_{23} and the small value of x_{24} testify for the smurf attack, where the huge amount of

Table 1: Summary of the KDD 99 data set.

	Training set	Testing set
Attack types	smurf, neptune	satan, back, warezmaster, warezclient, pod, portsweep, ipsweep, teardrop, nmap, imap, rootkit, land, guess_passwd, ftp_write, perl, loadmodule
#instances	494.021	311.029

Table 2: Classification results for random forests based on: T - number of trees and D maximal depth of the tree.

accuracy[%]	D=5	D=10	D=15
T=4	91,17	91,33	92,81
T=8	91,07	91,31	92,46
T=12	90,99	91,27	92,50
T=16	91,19	91,49	92,60
T=20	91,15	91,57	92,58

data sent,x_5 and many requests for various services x_{24} are typical for neptune attack.

5 Experiments with the intrusion detection data

In this section, the performed experiments will be described, but first of all few words about the data set. All experiments were performed on the KDD Cup 1999 data set, which is a common benchmark for evaluating intrusion detection techniques. This data set contains more than eight million labelled network flows, therefore in our experiments a 10% sample was used. This sample, divided in the training and the testing set, was provided by the competition organizers and can be downloaded from [9]. The distribution of the data set is summarized in Table 1. The training set contains only two attacks, which are relatively easy to distinguish. But in the testing set, there is the novelty attacks and a few of them pretty tough to find. Each data point has 41 features such as: amount of transferred data, length of connection, used protocols, etc. More details can be found in [15] [16]

The goal to be achieved in further described experiments is a binary classification, in other words, to determine which network flows are anomal and which represent an ordinary behaviour. The first two experiments examine how the parameters of random forests and C-fuzzy decision trees affect their accuracy, to determine the setting of parameters of these methods for a further enhancement. Finally, the third experiment compares all methods, including the enhanced versions, with a support vector machine (SVM). The comparison in the last experiment is extended by false positive and false negative rates. The data was previously normalized to zero means and unit variances. No other preprocessing was done. The detailed description of all experiments follows.

5.1 Random forests

There are many parameters which affects properties of random forests. The major three are: T - the number of trees, D - the maximal depth of trees and the proportion of

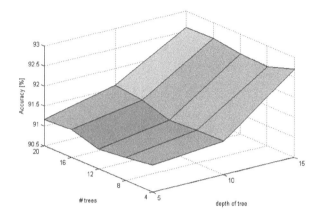

Figure 1: Classification results for random forests based on: T - number of trees and D maximal depth of the tree.

randomly chosen variables used for split ρ. Unless stated otherwise, each tree uses 30% of the training data set in the learning phase, and the proportion of random variables ρ is set to 30% too. Separate data sets were provided for the learning and the testing phase. Because of the random nature of the forest, all tests were repeated five times and results were averaged. The resulting average accuracies, are in Table 2 and Figure 1. The increasing number of trees has no effect on the precision. We assume that it is because the training set is simple, therefore it can be handled by four well trained trees only. Results shows that deeper trees performs better.

How the proportion of random variables affects the accuracy is shown on Figure 2. Twelve tests were done and the lower quartile, median and upper quartile was taken from them. The proportion of randomly chosen variables controls the diversity of grown trees: with an increasing proportion, the trees are more similar.

5.2 C-fuzzy decision trees

For C-fuzzy trees, the main two parameters are the number of clusters c and the number of splits or iterations d. As you can see in Table 3, there is only a few combinations of c and d, which yields acceptable results, e.g. the tree with five clusters performs well, but adding even one more

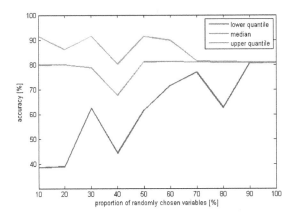

Figure 2: Classification results for random forests based on the proportion of the random variables used.

Table 3: Accuracy of C-Fuzzy decision trees based on the number of clusters c and the number of iterations d.

acc. [%]	c=2	c=3	c=4	c=5	c=6	c=7
d=1	80.52	68.14	81.51	81.44	39.24	39.16
d=2	80.52	68.08	39.27	81.46	38.50	39.24
d=3	81.53	80.70	39.37	39.19	38.32	39.14
d=4	81.33	81.07	39.36	39.19	38.43	38.37
d=5	81.25	81.28	39.36	39.28	38.42	38.37
d=6	81.24	81.50	39.45	38.50	39.20	39.11
d=7	80.48	81.50	39.34	38.50	39.20	39.17

cluster results in the huge lose of accuracy. It is evident that adding more clusters or split more often is not always the best possible option. The graphical interpretation is at Figure 3.

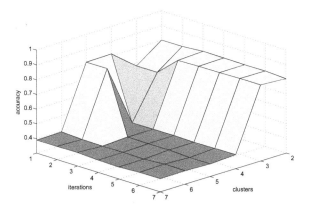

Figure 3: Accuracy of C-Fuzzy decision trees based on the number of clusters c and the number of iterations d.

Table 4: Comparison of prediction accuracy for all used methods.

	accuracy [%]	false positive[%]	false negative[%]
FT4D15	92.81	0.10	7.09
EFT4D15	75.28	0.24	24.48
EFT4D15(fcm)	84.92	0.81	14.27
CFTC2D6	81.24	0.25	18.52
CFTC5D2	81.46	0.32	18.23
ECFTC2D6	84.90	0.73	14.37
ECFTC5D2	91.23	1.03	7.74
SVM(rbf)	91.59	0.27	8.14

5.3 Comparison

In this section the final comparison is described. All previously stated methods were compared with and without enhancement by fitting membership function of fuzzy sets and with a SVM. The measures for comparison are: accuracy – the right class was determined, false positive rate – the proportion of normal data classified as anomaly, and false negative rate – the proportion of anomal data classified as normal.

For the final comparison, classifiers with the following parameters were used: the random forest with T=4 and D=15 (FT4D15), the same tree enhanced with fuzzy sets (EFT4D15) and the same enhanced tree with the fuzzy c-means algorithm used for clustering (EFT4D15fcm), C-fuzzy decision trees with c=2, c=5 and d=6, d=2 (CFTC2D6, CFTC5D2), enhanced versions of C-Fuzzy trees (ECFTC2D6,ECFTC5D2) and a SVM with the radial bases kernel. Due to a space limitation, we present results for the enhanced classifiers with t-norm algebraic product, because they are more promising. All Results are summarized in Table 4 and at Figure 4.

As was mentioned in the Introduction, there are two different types of classifiers, classifiers aiming only at precision and others aiming also at comprehensibility. There is a common trade off between the precision and the comprehensibility. Because of this, we expected that comprehensible classifiers will have lower precision than classifiers that are only precise, like SVM. Our experimental comparison shows how high the price is.

The random forest method performed very well in the standard form, even better than the SVM. But after the enhancement, the accuracy fell rapidly. The main reason is, in this case weak, clustering method. The both C-Fuzzy trees performed fairly in the standard form, but worse than the random forest or the SVM. The enhanced versions of the C-Fuzzy trees have accuracy comparable with the SVM. In this case, our enhancement improved not only comprehensibility, in the way described at Section 4.3, but even classification accuracy, slightly. All classifiers have the low false positive rate and the high false negative rate.

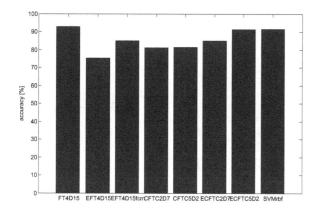

Figure 4: Comparison of all described methods.

6   Conclusion and future work

In this paper, we have described the design of random forests and C-Fuzzy tree classifiers. Then we introduced the method of the further enhancement by fuzzy sets. In experiments on the intrusion detection data, we have shown that random forests perform well in the standard form, but lose a lot of their accuracy after the enhancement when the algorithm considering only discrete variables is used. The low accuracy of this method indicates that continuous variables, at least some of them, correspond to important properties. The enhanced random forest with the fuzzy c-means performed much better, but there is still significant lost in accuracy, therefore more care should be given to the clustering phase. Our opinion is that the clusters obtained this way, contain mixed data (normal and anomal together), therefore some robust fitting algorithm should be used. On the other hand, the enhanced form of C-Fuzzy trees performed better than the standard version and even comparable to a SVM with the radial basis kernel. This indicates that C-Fuzzy trees have the ability to combine accuracy with comprehensibility based on fuzzy sets.

In the future work we would like to improve accuracy of the enhanced random forest model, extend our research to multi-class problems and test our algorithms in different domains.

Acknowledgement

The research reported in this paper has been supported by the Czech Science Foundation (GA ČR) grant 13-17187S.

References

[1] R. Bace and P. Mell. Nist special publication on intrusion detection systems. Technical report, DTIC Document, 2001.

[2] J. C. Bezdek. *Pattern Recognition with Fuzzy Objective Function Algorithms*. Kluwer Academic Publishers, Norwell, MA, USA, 1981.

[3] Ch. Chen, Y. Gong, and Y. Tian. Semi-supervised learning methods for network intrusion detection. In *Systems, Man and Cybernetics, 2008. SMC 2008. IEEE International Conference on*, pages 2603–2608. IEEE, 2008.

[4] A. Criminisi. Decision forests: A unified framework for classification, regression, density estimation, manifold learning and semi-supervised learning. *Foundations and Trends® in Computer Graphics and Vision*, 7(2-3):81–227, 2011.

[5] E. Eskin, A. Arnold, M. Prerau, L. Portnoy, and S. Stolfo. A geometric framework for unsupervised anomaly detection. In *Applications of data mining in computer security*, pages 77–101. Springer, 2002.

[6] C. Gini. Variability and mutability. *C. Cuppini, Bologna, 156p*, 1912.

[7] T. K. Ho. Random decision forests. In *Document Analysis and Recognition, 1995., Proceedings of the Third International Conference on*, volume 1, pages 278–282. IEEE, 1995.

[8] A. K. Jain, M. N. Murty, and P. J. Flynn. Data clustering: a review. *ACM computing surveys (CSUR)*, 31(3):264–323, 1999.

[9] Kdd 99 data set. http://kdd.ics.uci.edu/databases/kddcup99/kddcup99.html, 1999. Accessed: 2012-09-30.

[10] A. Klose and A. Nurnberger. On the properties of prototype-based fuzzy classifiers. *Systems, Man, and Cybernetics, Part B: Cybernetics, IEEE Transactions on*, 37(4):817–835, 2007.

[11] R. Kruse, J. E. Gebhardt, and F. Klowon. *Foundations of fuzzy systems*. John Wiley & Sons, Inc., 1994.

[12] L. I. Kuncheva. *Fuzzy classifier design*, volume 49. Physica Verlag, 2000.

[13] P. Laskov, Ch. Schäfer, and I. Kotenko. Intrusion detection in unlabeled data with quarter-sphere support vector machines. In *Proc. DIMVA*, pages 71–82, 2004.

[14] W. Lee, S. J. Stolfo, and K. W. Mok. A data mining framework for building intrusion detection models. In *Security and Privacy, 1999. Proceedings of the 1999 IEEE Symposium on*, pages 120–132. IEEE, 1999.

[15] R. Lippmann, R. K. Cunningham, D. J. Fried, I. Graf, K. R. Kendall, S. E. Webster, and M. A. Zissman. Results of the darpa 1998 offline intrusion detection evaluation. In *Recent Advances in Intrusion Detection*, volume 99, pages 829–835, 1999.

[16] R. Lippmann, J. W. Haines, D. J. Fried, J. Korba, and K. Das. The 1999 darpa off-line intrusion detection evaluation. *Computer networks*, 34(4):579–595, 2000.

[17] N. Lu, S. Mabu, and K. Hirasawa. Integrated rule mining based on fuzzy gnp and probabilistic classification for intrusion detection. *Journal of Advanced Computational Intelligence and Intelligent Informatics*, 15(5):495–505, 2011.

[18] S. Mukkamala, G. Janoski, and A. Sung. Intrusion detection using neural networks and support vector machines. In *Neural Networks, 2002. IJCNN'02. Proceedings of the 2002 International Joint Conference on*, volume 2, pages 1702–1707. IEEE, 2002.

[19] C. H. Nguyen, W. Pedrycz, T. L. Duong, and T. S. Tran. A genetic design of linguistic terms for fuzzy rule based classifiers. *International Journal of Approximate Reasoning*, 2012.

[20] W. Pedrycz and Z. A. Sosnowski. Designing decision trees

with the use of fuzzy granulation. *Systems, Man and Cybernetics, Part A: Systems and Humans, IEEE Transactions on*, 30(2):151–159, 2000.

[21] W. Pedrycz and Z. A. Sosnowski. C-fuzzy decision trees. *Systems, Man, and Cybernetics, Part C: Applications and Reviews, IEEE Transactions on*, 35(4):498–511, 2005.

[22] L. Portnoy, E. Eskin, and S. Stolfo. Intrusion detection with unlabeled data using clustering. In *In Proceedings of ACM CSS Workshop on Data Mining Applied to Security (DMSA-2001*. Citeseer, 2001.

[23] J. R. Quinlan. Induction of decision trees. *Machine learning*, 1(1):81–106, 1986.

[24] J. R. Quinlan. *C4. 5: programs for machine learning*, volume 1. Morgan kaufmann, 1993.

[25] G. Vigna and R. A. Kemmerer. Netstat: A network-based intrusion detection approach. In *Computer Security Applications Conference, 1998. Proceedings. 14th Annual*, pages 25–34. IEEE, 1998.

ITAT 2013: Workshops, Posters, and Tutorials, pp. 100–103
ISBN 978-1490952086, © 2013 V. Hubata-Vacek

Spectral analysis of EEG signals

Václav Hubata–Vacek[1]

[1]CTU in Prague, Faculty of Nuclear Sciences and Physical Engineering
Břehová 7, 115 19 Prague 1
Czech Republic
hubatvac@fjfi.cvut.cz

Abstract: Alzheimer's disease (AD) is the most common form of dementia and is characterised by loss of neurons and their synapses. This loss is caused by an accumulation of amyloid plaques between nerve cells in the brain. The affected cells can not transfer brain signals between neurons. In this paper a multi-channel signal from electroencephalograph (EEG) is analyzed. It is supposed that damaged neurons are not able to comunicate and channels are uncorrelated. The EEG signals for this analysis were obtained from Alzheimer diseased patients and healthy individuals. The coherence between channels is evaluated and tested by two-sample Wilcoxon test. For chosen channels the results are mostly significant on the level of 5%.

1 Introduction

Alzheimer's disease grows in importance with exteding age of population. Considering the disease process it is not possible to fully cure a patient with Alzheimer's disease, but early recognition may significantly extend patient's active life. The aim of this paper is to compare characteristics obtained from coherence of EEG signal channels. The coherence was obtained from Alzheimer disease patients (AD) and healthy individuals (CN). Each patient's scan consists of records from 19 electrodes. The coherence is investigated for delta, theta, alpha, and beta brain waves. It is expected that the most significant diferences are to be found in alpha zone [3], [4], [5].

2 Coherence of two signals

The coherence C_{xy}^2 gives measure of correlation of $x(t)$ and $y(t)$ signals on given frequency. Values of the coherence are from interval $< 0, 1 >$. If the correlation is close to 0, the frequencies are said to have no correlation. On the other hand, if the correlation is close to 1, the frequencies are said to have correlation. The correlation is enumerated from spectral density and cross-spectral density. At first, the enumeration of these two characteristics is described.

2.1 Spectral density

The spectral density shows power per Hertz. The power is counted from integral from second power of signal $x(t, f, \Delta f)$, where $x(t, f, \Delta f)$ is original signal $x(t)$, which

was filtered by passband on interval $< f, f + \Delta f >$. The presented formula is in the form of discrete signal

$$\psi_x^2(f, \Delta f) = \sum_{t=0}^{T} x^2(t, f, \Delta f). \qquad (1)$$

Assuming $\Delta f \to 0$, one-sided spectral density $G_x(f)$ may be evaluated in the form

$$G_x(f) = \frac{\psi_x^2(f, \Delta f)}{\Delta f}. \qquad (2)$$

Subsequently, two-sided spectral density $S_x(f)$ may be evaluated from one-sided spectral density by its reverse to negative values.

$$\begin{aligned}
S_x(f) &= G_x(f), f = 0, \\
S_x(f) &= \frac{G_x(f)}{2}, 0 < f < \infty, \\
S_x(f) &= \frac{G_x(-f)}{2}, -\infty < f < 0.
\end{aligned} \qquad (3)$$

Moreover, we can use Fourier transform to obtain spectral density in the form

$$S_x(f) = \frac{1}{T} |X(f)|^2, \qquad (4)$$

where T is length of signal and $X(f)$ is Fourier transform of signal $x(f)$. This equation uses behaviour of Fourier transform, but it is not consistent [1]. Inconsistency is visible on mean squared error (MSE)

$$\varepsilon^2 \approx \frac{G_x^2(f)}{TB_e} + \left(\frac{B_e^2 G_x''(f)}{24} \right)^2, \qquad (5)$$

where B_e is resolution frequency, which is equivalent to length of segment T_e as $B_e = 1/T_e$. The bias is growing proportionaly with increase of resolution frequency B_e. On the other hand, the variance is growing proportionaly with decrease of resolution frequency B_e. Moreover, this evaluation is not suitable for stochastic signals as the EEG [1]. The robust evaluation of spectral density $S_x(f)$ is provided by Welch method [1].

2.2 Welch method

The method splits original signal $x(t)$ to multiple signals while their spectrum is expected to be stationary. Subsequently, the spectral densities of splitted singals are averaged. The method provides robust evaluation of spectral density $S_x(f)$ of original signal $x(t)$.

2.3 Cross spectral density

Given two signals $x(t)$ and $y(t)$, the cross spectral density is defined as

$$S_{xy}(f) = \frac{1}{T} X(f) Y^*(f), \qquad (6)$$

where $Y^*(f)$ is complex conjugate number to $Y(f)$, and $X(f)$, $Y(f)$ are signals from Fourier transform of signals $x(t)$ and $y(t)$. Because of the same behaviour as spectral density, the cross spectral density is evaluated in a similar way, by averaging of splitted signal values.

2.4 Coherence function

Now we can evaluate coherence function as normed cross spectral density

$$C_{xy}(f) = \frac{S_{xy}(f)}{\sqrt{S_x(f) S_y(f)}}. \qquad (7)$$

Finally, the coherence is evaluated as squared coherence function [1]

$$C_{xy}^2(f) = \frac{|S_{xy}(f)|^2}{S_x(f) S_y(f)}, \qquad (8)$$

where $0 \leq C_{xy}^2(f) \leq 1$.

3 Evaluation process

3.1 Data

The EEG signals were obtained from two groups of patients. The first group is represented by patients with Alzheimer's disease (AD), and the second group is represented by healthy individuals (CN). The EEG data were obtained during examinations of 10 patients with moderate dementia (MMSE score 10-19). All subjects underwent brain CT, neurological and neuropsychological examinations. The CN group is a control set consisting of 10 age-matched, healthy subjects who did not suffer from any memory or other cognitive impairments. The average MMSE of the AD group is 16.2 (SD of 2.1). The age of the Alzheimer's group and the normal group is 69.4 ± 9.2 and 68.7 ± 7.7, respectively. The first group includes 5 men and 5 women, the second group is made up of 4 men and 6 women. Informed consent was obtained from all included subjects and the study was approved by the local ethics committee. All recordings were performed under similar standard conditions. The subjects were in a comfortable position, in a bed, with their eyes shut. Electrodes were positioned according to the 10-20 system of electrode placement; the recording was conducted on a 21-channel digital EEG setup (TruScan 32, Alien Technik Ltd., Czech Republic) with a 22-bit AD conversion and a sampling frequency of 200 Hz. Subjects' linked ears were used as references. Stored digitized data were zero-phase digitally filtered using a bandpass FIR filter (100 coefficients, Hamming window) of 0.5-60 Hz and a bandstop filter of 49-51 Hz. A time of recording of EEG signals varies between 6 and 10 minutes, consequently, a length of EEG signals varies between 70000 and 120000. An example of an output is depicted on the figure 1 for all 19 electrodes.

3.2 Evaluation of coherence

As previously mentioned, the Welch method was used for evaluation of spectral densities. Signals $x(t)$ and $y(t)$ were split to signals $x_m(t)$ and $y_m(t)$ of a length $N = 401$ (2 seconds). The splitted signals were balanced and multiplied by Hamming window.

$$x_{m,tr}(t) = \left(x_m(t) - \frac{1}{N} \sum_{t=1}^{N} x_m(t) \right) w(t), \qquad (9)$$

where $w(t)$ are values from Hamming window. Further, a standard MATLAB function fft was used on $x_{m,tr}(t)$ to obtain the Fourier transform $X_{m,tr}(f)$. The spectral densities for splitted signals are evaluated from the formula (4). The spectral density of signal $x(t)$ was evaluated as average of the spectral densities for splitted signals with respect to m.

The formula (6) was used in the evaluation of cross spectral density. The rest of the process is similar to evaluation of spectral density. Subsequently, the coherence is evaluated from equation (8).

The computational complexity of all pairs of signals may be very long. Optionally it is possible to use distributed computing in MATLAB to speed up the evaluation process [2].

3.3 Studied characteristics

The coherence $C_{xy}^2(f)$ is split into canals delta (0-4 Hz), theta (4-8 Hz), alpha (8-12 Hz), and beta (12-30 Hz). Mean value is measured as main characteristics of the signal. The two-sample Wilcoxon test [6] with null hypotheses and alternative hypothesis is used as

$$H_0 : F \equiv G, \qquad (10)$$

$$H_A : F \not\equiv G, \qquad (11)$$

where F is the distribution function of the measured values for AD and G is the distribution function for CN.

4 Results of testing

The coherence was evaluated for pairs of signals 2-7, 10-17, 11-12, 11-14, 11-17, 14-17 and 18-19. These channels were chosen as the most significant. The results for mean values are listed in tables 1, 2, 3, 4. As it is evident from results, the mean value of coherence is higher in CN group. This behaviour is caused by broken connections among neurons in AD patients.

In almost all cases the results are significant on the level of 5%. Values under level of significance of 3% were obtained for channels 11 and 17 in the delta and theta range and for channels 18 and 19 in the beta range. The results demonstrate that there is no prefered range. All ranges have significant channel pairs and each of them may be used for differentiation of AD and CN groups.

The results for channels 18 and 19 are depicted in the box graphs for beta channel, Figures 2 and 3.

Acknowledgment: The paper was created with the support of CTU in Prague, Grant SGS11/165/OHK4/3T/14 and Grant GAČR 13-17187S.

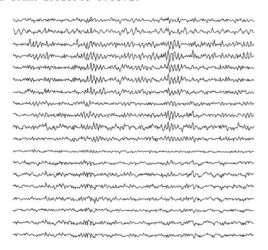

Figure 1: The EEG signals from 19 electrodes of a healthy individual (CN), record length is 5s.

Table 1: Mean value of coherence in delta range.

Channels	E(AD)	E(CN)	p_{value}
2-7	0.4584	0.7299	0.0452
10-17	0.2285	0.4715	0.1041
11-12	0.4467	0.6679	0.0890
11-14	0.2895	0.5237	0.0640
11-17	0.3486	0.6208	0.0257
14-17	0.2312	0.5271	0.0312
18-19	0.4612	0.7658	0.0312

Table 2: Mean value of coherence in theta range.

Channels	E(AD)	E(CN)	p_{value}
2-7	0.4570	0.7292	0.0452
10-17	0.2291	0.4714	0.1041
11-12	0.4468	0.6671	0.0890
11-14	0.2900	0.5234	0.0640
11-17	0.3493	0.6204	0.0257
14-17	0.2319	0.5269	0.0312
18-19	0.4608	0.7657	0.0312

Table 3: Mean value of coherence in alpha range.

Channels	E(AD)	E(CN)	p_{value}
2-7	0.4548	0.7282	0.0376
10-17	0.2298	0.4706	0.1041
11-12	0.4461	0.6649	0.0890
11-14	0.2905	0.5231	0.0757
11-17	0.3503	0.6195	0.0312
14-17	0.2328	0.5266	0.0312
18-19	0.4597	0.7659	0.0312

[2] Krupa, J., Pavelka, A., Vyšata, O., Procházka, A.: Distributed signal processing, International Conference Technical Computing Prague (2007)

[3] McBride, J., Zhao, X., Munro, N., Smith, Ch., Jicha, G., Jiang, Y.: Resting EEG Discrimination of Early Stage Alzheimer's Disease from Normal Aging Using Inter–Channel Coherence Network Graphs, Annals of Biomedical Engineering, Vol. 41, No. 6 (2013)

[4] Hsiao–Lung, Ch., Ju–His, Ch., Hon–Chung, F., Yu–Tai, T., Ling–Fu, M., Chin–Chang, H., Wen–Chun, H., Pei–Kuang, Ch., Jiun–Jie, W., Jiann–Der, L., Yau–Yau, W., Meng–Tsan, T.: Brain connectivity of patients with Alzheimer's disease by coherence and cross mutual information of electroencephalograms during photic stimulation, Medical Engineering and Physics 35 (2013)

[5] S. Tahaei, M., Jalili, M., G. Knyazeva, M.: Synchronizability of EEG-Based Functional Networks in Early Alzheimer's Disease, EEE Transactions on Neural Systems and Rehabilitation Engineering, vol. 20, no. 5, (2012)

[6] Anděl J.: Statistické metody, Matfyzpress, Praha (1998)

References

[1] Uhlíř, J., Sovka, P.: Číslicové zpracování signálů, ISBN 80-01-02613-2 (1995)

Table 4: Mean value of coherence in beta range.

Channels	E(AD)	E(CN)	p_{value}
2-7	0.4687	0.7378	0.0312
10-17	0.2880	0.4980	0.1041
11-12	0.4907	0.6739	0.1041
11-14	0.3472	0.5505	0.0757
11-17	0.4084	0.6398	0.0312
14-17	0.2955	0.5532	0.0312
18-19	0.4941	0.7763	0.0257

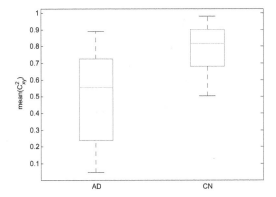

Figure 2: Box graph of mean value for channels 18-19 in beta range.

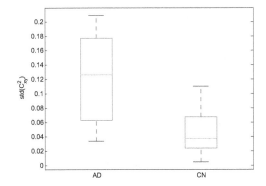

Figure 3: Box graph of standard deviation for channels 18-19 in beta range.

ITAT 2013: Workshops, Posters, and Tutorials, pp. 104–110
ISBN 978-1490952086, © 2013 J. Pejla, M. Holeňa

Using machine learning methods in a personalized reputation system

Jiří Pejla[1] and Martin Holeňa[2]

[1] Faculty of Information Technology, Czech Technical University in Prague
Thákurova 9, 160 00 Prague
jiri.pejla@gmail.com,
[2] Institute of Computer Science, Academy of Sciences of the Czech Republic
Pod Vodárenskou věží 2, 182 07 Prague
martin@cs.cas.cz

Abstract: Reputation systems become more and more important in the on-line and e-commerce communities. Example widespread on-line system where reputation could be used is information system which allows users to rate each other and express their experiences and opinions on some products or services. In this paper, we are interested in reputation of others from the perspective of one user. This reputation is called personalized and users can make use of it to find out proper information about certain products. We implement personalized reputation system for information systems using machine learning methods. Our system incorporates artificial neural networks and random forests as well as a standard heuristic method, and it has been tested on a large real world dataset.

1 Introduction

During their whole life, people must cooperate with others. Choosing friends and business partners has always been based on the trust. One wants to cooperate only with people he trusts because he is not usually disappointed by them. If we do not have enough own information and experiences with some person or company, we usually believe other people's opinions. On the opinion of majority is based the notion of reputation.

These concepts are researched in many scientific fields, e.g. Economics, Psychology, Sociology etc. We focus only on the field of Information Technology. In the Internet environment, it is very complicated to recognize whether we should trust the other party, because for instance members are often anonymous and can enter and leave a community easily (see [6]). Thanks to the reputation systems, users can easily deduce their trust to unknown partners. That is why the reputation systems are very important in the Internet communities.

There are many publications about theoretical aspects of trust and reputation, e.g. paper [3] analysed the promises and challenges of an online feedback mechanisms and paper [5] provided a survey of most known web trust and reputation systems and dealt with the problem of unfair ratings. This problem in the environment of e-marketplaces is solved in [8].

If one user has direct experience with another one, he either trusts or distrusts him. This value of trust influences the trust of his neighbours to the same user. This process is called propagation of trust and it is used as the usual method for computing the reputation of particular user (or generally, a node in a graph). A very comprehensive thesis on this topic is [6]. It deals with many computational models of trust and reputation, with personalization and contextualization. There are also experiments on centrality-based, preference-based and Bayesian estimate ratings. Unfortunately, direct propagation of distrust is not involved in this thesis. Distrust is dealt in [4], and we used formulas from this paper in our experiments.

Machine learning methods are not used very often for computation of trust. But if so, the results of experiments shows that they are more effective and accurate. For instance [1] shows that support vector machines based reputation system better recognizes malicious nodes in the mission critical networks. SVM and random forest algorithms can be used in reputation systems for spam senders behaviour analysis (see [7]). Artificial neural networks can be also used for the implementation of reputation systems (see [9]). But their paper is aimed at broker-assisting systems with subcommunities where agents do not have access to global information about history of transactions so they have to gain information from other agents. It also deals with the personalized reputation and with the problem of attacks.

To our knowledge, there are no publications about using machine learning methods for computing personalized reputation in general information systems where users can rate products or services and express their trust to other users. These information systems are very widespread and allow finding out relevant information and user experience. In the paper, a computational model of reputation is built and the accuracy of two machine learning methods is compared with the accuracy of one standard method on a real world dataset.

In the following section, the principles of used methods and their parameters are recalled. Section 3 describes the used dataset and its statistics. The key section of the paper is Section 4 where we explain our approach and all important details of implementation. Results of experiments are summarized in Section 5 and then concluded in Section 6.

2 Computing Reputation

Many ways to compute reputation have been researched. We chose one standard method for propagation of trust and distrust and two machine learning methods - artificial neural networks and random forests. These are described in the following subsections.

2.1 Propagation of Trust and Distrust

Trust and distrust can be expressed as a rating of one user by another. We used formulas from the paper [4] because it employs both sides of rating – positive (trust) and negative (distrust).

Rating is propagated using matrix multiplication. Input for this computation is a matrix of trust (denoted T) and a matrix of distrust (D), where $T_{i,j}$ (or $D_{i,j}$) means the value of trust (or distrust) from the user i to the user j. This value lies between 0 and 1. In the process of propagation, these two matrices are combined to a matrix of beliefs (B). Matrix of beliefs is equal either to T or to $T - D$.

There are four kinds of an atomic propagation, and to each, a specific operator corresponds. These four kinds are:

1. Direct propagation – operator: B

2. Transpose trust – propagation of trust in the opposite direction, operator: B^T

3. Co-citation – believe in trust from users that trust the same user, it is calculated as a backward-forward step: $B^T B$

4. Trust coupling – users that trust the same subset of users will trust each other, operator: BB^T

Every operator has a weight (vector α) and all of them are combined to a matrix C that captures all kinds of the atomic propagation:

$$C_{B,\alpha} = \alpha_1 B + \alpha_2 B^T B + \alpha_3 B^T + \alpha_4 BB^T \qquad (1)$$

Formula Parameters There are many ways of computing the propagation. We now describe specific parameters that have to be chosen before computation.

1. Weights of specific propagations ($\alpha = (\alpha_1, \ldots, \alpha_4)$) – the weights have to sum to one

2. Number of steps of the propagation (K)

3. Model to define B - there are three possibilities ($P^{(k)}$ denotes matrix where ij-th entry represents the propagation from i to j after k atomic propagations):

    (a) Trust only – values of distrust are not involved in the computation: $B = T, P^{(k)} = C_{B,\alpha}^k$

    (b) One-step distrust – the same as the trust only computation but in the end, the judgments of one's neighbours are discounted by the value of distrust to them: $B = T, P^{(k)} = C_{B,\alpha}^k \cdot (T - D)$

    (c) Propagated distrust – trust and distrust are both propagated together: $B = T - D, P^{(k)} = C_{B,\alpha}^k$

4. Type of iterating the propagation (F denotes final matrix that represents level of trust from one user to each other):

    (a) Eigenvalue propagation (EIG): $F = P^{(k)}$. Matrix exponentiation is used in this propagation. For computing the power of a matrix C this equation can be used: $C = V \cdot D \cdot V^{-1}$, where columns of V are eigenvectors of the matrix C and D is a diagonal matrix with eigenvalues of the matrix C. Thus $C^k = V \cdot D^k \cdot V^{-1}$, which can be computed effectively.

    (b) Weighted linear combinations (WLC): $F = \sum_{k=1}^K \gamma^k \cdot P^{(k)}$

5. Discount factor (γ) for penalization lengthy propagation steps – it is used only in WLC and its value have to be smaller than the largest eigenvalue of $C_{B,\alpha}$ so that the sum converges.

According to the paper [4], the best accuracy is achieved with the following parameters: one-step distrust, EIG iteration with weights $\alpha = (0.4, 0.4, 0.1, 0.1)$.

2.2 Artificial Neural Networks

Artificial neural networks (ANNs) are one of the machine learning methods that can be used for regression computing of reputation.

In this work, we used a neural network of the kind multilayer perceptron (MLP). MLP represents a string of perceptrons. A perceptron consists of a number of inputs and outputs (neurons). Inputs and outputs are connected with links and every link is assigned with the values of weight and bias. These values are optimized during training, in which the perceptron adapts its response to given inputs (learning patterns). Outputs of one perceptron (layer) are connected to inputs of the next one. Inputs of the whole system are brought to inputs of the first layer and results are obtained from outputs of the last layer. Values of output neurons are hidden except those that are in the last (output) layer. There is an activation function (e.g., sigmoid or hyperbolic tangent) connected to the hidden and the output layers, which computes the output neuron value from the input values, their weights and biases. Multilayer perceptrons are trained on learning patterns. Training is an optimization problem and we used Matlab implementation of the Levenberg-Marquardt optimization method to this purpose. Great advantage of MLPs is that they are able to approximate almost every function on the space $\mathbb{R}^k$.

Parameters

1. Number of hidden layers

2. Number of hidden neurons

3. Activation function of hidden layers, and whether it is used also in the output layer

4. Training method

2.3 Random Forests

This subsection describes random regression forests and is based on the paper [2].

A tree is an undirected graph without cycles. A decision tree contains two types of nodes – split nodes (with test function) and leaf nodes (with final answer). Input is injected into the root node and according to the result of test function in split nodes, it is sent to one of the child nodes until it arrives to the leaf node which contains the answer.

Trees are tested by sending inputs to the root of a tree and collecting results from the leaf nodes that contain results of regression. During training (an off-line phase), parameters of the split functions and the selection of final answers are optimized so as to minimize a chosen objective function. The tree is growing until the given stopping criteria are met.

Random forest is an ensemble of trees that are trained randomly. It means that trees are trained on randomly different subsets of input data or randomized node optimization is used. Individual trees have different depths and parameters of the split nodes and this improves the generalization capabilities of the resulting forest, because results are collected together from all trees. Forest training and testing can be done in parallel which is very useful for modern computer architectures.

Components

1. Forest size – number of trees

2. Split functions – are characterized by a geometric primitive that is used to separate the data, thresholds for tests, and a filter function that selects features from the input vector.

3. Objective function – with respect to this function, the parameters of a particular split node are optimized during the training phase (e.g., maximizing an information gain)

4. Randomness model – usually random training data set sampling or randomized node optimization (makes available only a small random subset of parameters of the split function).

5. Leaf prediction model – e.g., probabilistic predictor or point estimate

Table 1: Statistics of the input dataset

Statistic	Value
Number of users	9485
Number of companies	2660
Number of reviews	10030
Number of ratings between users	10766
Number of positive ratings between users	8199
Number of negative ratings between users	2567

6. Ensemble model – how to combine results from all trees, e.g., averaging

7. Stopping criteria – when to stop growing of the tree, e.g., maximum number of levels, minimum number of training points in a node, etc.

3 Used Dataset

We used a real world dataset from the company TrustYard (information system on http://www.nejremeslnici.cz/). On this website, registered users can write reviews about services that were provided to them by some craft companies or craftsmen. These reviews consist of textual description and three grades – for quality of result, ratio of price and service, and the behaviour to clients. Other users can rate this review with thumb up (positive rating) or down (negative rating). All these ratings are saved in the system database.

This dataset was anonymized (no names are included). Input data for the reputation system are split into two files – the first one contains reviews and the second one contains ratings of reviews. Basic statistics of the input dataset are introduced in Table 1. All inputs were split into two subsets. One subset was used for training the machine learning methods and searching for optimal parameters of the propagation of trust and distrust. The second subset was used for testing (comparing) all implemented methods. The testing dataset contains entries from the last three months (approximately 15% of inputs), whereas the rest of inputs is involved in training dataset. Number of the shortest paths between users in the testing and training dataset is displayed in Figure 3.

4 Proposed Design of a Reputation System

The aim of our work is to implement a personalized reputation system that provides for every user an ordered list of other users according to their reputation from the point of view of that user. This list is very useful - according to it, the system could offer to this user reviews of users that are close to him or inherit the reputation of users to companies they rated. The reviews of a user with higher reputation would be more important. And all of these reputations

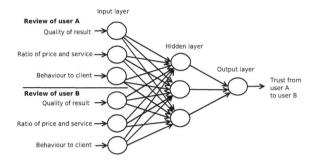

Figure 1: Schema of a neural network for the distance 1 between users

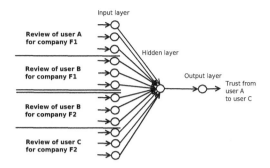

Figure 2: Schema of a neural network for the distance 2 between users

would be personalized for specific user because every user has different opinions and attitudes. This kind of reputation is more resistant to attacks (see [8]). It is also possible to compute a global reputation from this personalized reputation by simple averaging. The global reputation could be used for rewarding the most popular users or companies (e.g., access to special services in an information system) and as a personalized reputation for new users.

We want to implement a method as general as possible, so it could be used for similar systems for rating products, films, etc.

4.1 Inputs and Outputs

All used methods have the same inputs and outputs. Generally, the input to our system are reviews. We want to compute personal reputation from users' opinions. If two users rate the same company similarly, they have the same opinions and probably rate each other positively. These relations can be represented as a graph where nodes are users and edges are ratings of the same company. Edges are labelled with six values of company ratings (see Figure 1). For machine learning algorithms, we considered not only direct neighbours but also longer distances between users in that graph (see Figure 2). In the standard heuristic method, the number of steps of the propagation represents the maximal involved distance between users.

Outputs are based on ratings between users. All ratings from one user to the other one have to be combined to one resulting value of reputation. For this purpose, arithmetic mean of ratings (from -1 to 1) was used with respect to the standard heuristic method where positive value is trust and negative distrust.

4.2 Data Preparation

The main problem was how to take into account all distances between users. Number of the shortest paths between users in the testing and training dataset is displayed in Figure 3. First proposal was to implement two ANNs – first for direct neighbours (distance 1) and second for all other distances. But most inputs of the second ANN would

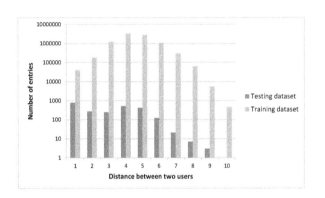

Figure 3: Number of the shortest paths between users

be zero because the number of inputs would be set to the chosen maximal number. This setting would cause large inaccuracies, so we decided to train a specialized ANN for every distance (see Figures 1 and 2).

According to Figure 3, maximal distance between two users in the graph of reviews is 10. But for this distance, there are 60 inputs (6 inputs for every edge). During training, we considered all possibilities for the number of hidden neurons between the number of inputs and the number of outputs. So in the worst case, 60 hidden neurons are used and an ANN needs approximately 60^2 training items and this cannot be satisfied. We decided to not involve all distances and use paths with maximal length of 8. With respect to the number of shorter paths, the paths of length 9 and 10 cannot affect so much the resulting reputation. A higher number of inputs is useful for ANNs and random forests because for certain users some part of rating can be more important than for the others.

There is also the problem of more paths between two users. We considered only the shortest paths. But there are also more paths of the shortest length. One user can review one company a number of times. This can be solved by choosing the last review, simple averaging the values of rating or making all combinations of paths. We chose averaging because reviews are written about different services. After averaging the reviews, there is only one review of a particular user for every reviewed company. But this does not solve the problem of multiple paths between two users because they can be connected through reviews of a different company. We considered adding user identifiers to inputs to solve it, but this would decrease the generalization of used methods. Finally, we decided to leave this paths in the same ANN and assign them the same results.

Reputation is not necessarily symmetric, so there should be two results for one path (resulting reputation from the point of view of both users). But cases in which users rate both each other are not very frequent, so we used machine learning methods with only one output. In these cases, we used the same input in reversed order and assigned it a different result.

Inputs to the standard heuristic method are only company ratings from the direct neighbours. These six values have to be combined to one input value of reputation (see Section 4.3). Standard method does not need any other data preparation because longer distances between users are taken into account by its iterations.

4.3   Experimental Setting

At first, test data were removed from the dataset. We decided to remove the last three months because of practical reasons – reputation will be computed from most recent data and this subset has an appropriate size for computation. The rest of dataset was used as a training set in 10-fold cross-validation.

Before cross-validation, training dataset was split into eight files according to the length of path between users (see Figure 3). During its splitting, these paths have to be found, which is very time-consuming. To this end, breadth-first search algorithm (BFS) was used. In addition, an appropriate result value has to be assigned to every path. This causes about 20% loss of data because for some paths the correct results are missing.

The final result was a RMSE (root-mean-square error): $\sqrt{\frac{1}{n} \sum_{i=1}^{n} (e_i - \overline{e_i})^2}$ where e_i is an observed value (the arithmetic mean of direct ratings between the involved users), $\overline{e_i}$ is an estimated value and n is the number of outputs. These errors were compared and optimal parameters were found. Finally, machine learning methods were trained on all training data and the RMSE of all methods was compared on the testing dataset with the use of optimal parameters.

Artificial Neural Networks   In ANNs, we investigated the influence of the number of hidden neurons within limits given by the number of inputs and the number of outputs. We used networks with one hidden layer. The transfer function hyperbolic tangent was used in the hidden layer and in the output layer.

Random Forests   Apart from ANNs we decided to implement random forests because of their outstanding generalization capabilities (see [2]). And we used them in the

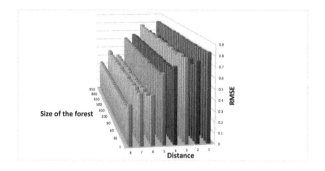

Figure 4: Training results for the random forests

same way as ANNs – we built a forest for every distance (from 1 to 8) and experimented with the size of the forest. All trees were trained randomly with the use of bagging.

Heuristic Method   As an input to the propagation method, we used our own function for comparing individual review ratings. It returns a number between -1 (if reviews are opposite) and 1 (if reviews are the same). Inputs were used only for direct neighbours. More input ratings for pair of users (different paths between the pair of users) were included in our function and then averaged. All inputs were inserted into two matrices (a matrix of trust for positive ratings and a matrix of distrust for negative ratings) with 0 representing the absence of a rating. Matrix operations as they were described in Section 2.1 were used for propagation of trust and distrust. The correct results are on the interval $\langle -1, 1 \rangle$, so the computed results have to be transformed to this interval. To this purpose, different sigmoid functions were considered, and the one best performing was used.

5   Results

All the results are absolute errors. Figure 4 represents errors on training dataset for different distances and sizes of a forest. It indicates that the size of a forest affects the resulting error much less than the distance in the graph of users. We tested 29 sizes of a forest from 1 to 1000 but the error was almost the same for every of them. Importantly, the best results were never achieved with a forest of size 1 (a tree). The worst results were computed for direct neighbours and the error was the lowest for the longest distances (concretely 8, 6 and 7). This indicates that forests need more inputs for more precise results on the used dataset.

Similar results for neural networks are shown in Figure 5. We tested the number of hidden neurons within limits given by the number of inputs and the number of outputs. The lowest error was also achieved for the longest distance (48 inputs). The worst results were computed for the distance 6. However, the number of inputs does not affect the results so much as in the case of random forests. Changing the number of neurons has the greatest impact

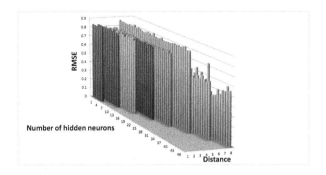

Figure 5: Training results for the neural networks

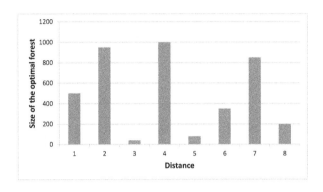

Figure 6: Optimal parameters of the random forests

if distances are long. If they are short the errors are quite similar.

Figure 6 shows the optimal sizes of forest (with the lowest error). There is no trend in these values. Errors for different sizes of forest were very similar so the optimal sizes are very different.

In Figure .7, there are optimal counts of hidden neurons for all distances. Higher number of hidden neurons gives better results for longer distances. For shorter distances, approximately 5 hidden neurons are mostly enough.

Figure 8 shows the RMSE of the used machine learning methods for different distances. Random forests almost always outperform neural networks, especially for the shortest and the longest distances. For the distance 6, neural networks clearly outperform random forests but the exact

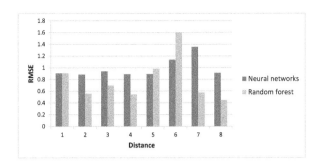

Figure 8: Testing results for the machine learning methods

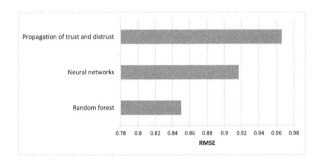

Figure 9: Comparison of the three used methods

opposite can be seen for distances 2, 3, 4, 7 and 8.

The last Figure 9 shows a final comparison of all used methods. The worst results were achieved with the method for propagation of trust and distrust. We have found out that optimal parameters of this method for the used dataset are: propagated distrust with EIG or WLC iteration with $\gamma = 0.5$ and Elliot symmetric sigmoid function for transforming the results to the correct interval. The optimal number of steps of the propagation is just 1. The machine learning methods clearly outperform the heuristic method. It can be caused by their generalization capabilities and their ability to approximate functions quite precisely. Random forests are the most accurate method on the used dataset.

6 Conclusion

In the Internet, it is more and more important to know whom should one trust or distrust. Reputation systems are the effective solution to this decision problem. Computations of a reputation are mostly based on ratings, so we focused on information systems for rating products or services. To our knowledge, this paper is the first attempt to implement and test personalized reputation system for such kind of information systems using machine learning methods.

The aim of our work was only the comparison of results of the standard method and the machine learning methods. We tested artificial neural networks and random forests on a large real world dataset. We found their optimal parameters for different distances in the social graph of users. We

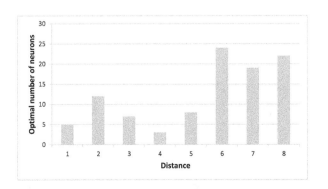

Figure 7: Optimal parameters of the neural networks

also experimented with different parameters of the standard method for propagation of trust and distrust.

Machine learning methods are more and more used for computing a reputation, e.g., in the distributed networks or broker systems, and we have shown that they are appropriate for computing a reputation also in the information systems for rating products and services. The most important finding of the paper is that the machine learning methods outperform the standard heuristic method on the used dataset.

Acknowledgement

The research reported in this paper has been supported by the Czech Science Foundation (GA ČR) grant 13-17187S.

References

[1] Akbani, R., Korkmaz, T. and Raju, G. V.: *EMLTrust: An enhanced Machine Learning based Reputation System for MANETs.* Ad Hoc Netw. **10** (2012) 435–457,

[2] Criminisi, A., Shotton, J. and Konukoglu, E.: *Decision Forests: A Unified Framework for Classification, Regression, Density Estimation, Manifold Learning and Semi-Supervised Learning.* Found. Trends. Comput. Graph. Vis. **7** (2012) 81–227

[3] Dellarocas, Ch.: *The Digitization of Word of Mouth: Promise and Challenges of Online Feedback Mechanisms.* Manage. Sci. **60** (2003) 1407–1424

[4] Guha, R., Kumar, R., Raghavan, P. and Tomkins, A.: *Propagation of trust and distrust.* ACM **WWW '04** (2004) 403–412

[5] Jøsang, A., Ismail, R. and Boyd, C.: *A survey of trust and reputation systems for online service provision.* Decis. Support Syst. **43** (2007) 618–644

[6] Mui, L.: *Computational Models of Trust and Reputation: Agents, Evolutionary Games, and Social Networks.* PhD Thesis, MIT (2002)

[7] Tang, Y., Krasser, S. He, Y., Yang, W. Alperovitch, D.: *Support Vector Machines and Random Forests Modeling for Spam Senders Behavior Analysis.* IEEE **GLOBECOM** (2008) 2174-2178

[8] Zhang, J., Cohen, R.: *Trusting advice from other buyers in e-marketplaces: the problem of unfair ratings* ACM **ICEC '06** (2006) 225–234

[9] Zong, B., Xu, F., Jiao, J. and Lü, J.: *A Broker-Assisting Trust and Reputation System Based on Artificial Neural Network.* IEEE **SMC** (2009) 4710–4715

ITAT 2013: Workshops, Posters, and Tutorials, pp. 111–117
ISBN 978-1490952086, © 2013 R. Brunetto

Probabilistic modeling of dynamic systems

Robert Brunetto

Charles University, Prague, 10 000, Czech republic,
robert@brunetto.cz,

Abstract: This article briefly introduces selected probabilistic approaches to search optimal behaviour of an agent in dynamic systems. It describes two possible extensions of Markov decision processes(MDP) which are the standard for probabilistic planning. Our uncertainty about transition probabilities is described by Markov decision processes with imprecise probabilities (MDP-IP). Missing information about actual state can be handled by Partially observable Markov decision processes (POMDP). This article compares both approaches and discusses their possible combination.

1 Introduction

Planning has a long tradition in artificial intelligence [5]. Classical planning assumes fully observable discrete deterministic environment. In some situations such as making plans for real physical robot these assumptions are not valid. When the robot decides to take an action it uses the actuators which are supposed to change the environment or the robot's position. The exact result of such actions e.g. robot's position is often nondeterministic or it depends on many unmodelled factors that can be treated as randomness. Problems where the results of actions can be described as probability distributions over robot positions are modelled using Markov decision processes (MDPs). This framework assumes that the agent fully observes new state of the world after performing the action (figure 1).

In real world this is not sufficient enough for modelling robots. It is common that exact probability distributions of actions' results are not known precisely. Markov decision processes with imprecise probabilities (MDP-IPs) framework was created to model this kind of scenarios.

The problem becomes even more complicated when the agent resp. robot does not know the exact state of the world resp. its own location. This can be modelled by so-called partially observable Markov decision processes (POMDPs). Instead of the exact starting state of agent's world resp. robot's starting location only probability distribution over the possibilities is known. This probability distribution is called belief state or only belief. Knowing this information agent chooses an action and performs it. Afterwards it does not know the exact action's result but it can sense observation which may contain some information about the new state of the agent's world. Then the agent is facing the next decision. One way to make it is to use the observation in order to calculate new belief state (denoted b) from which the same action selection pol-

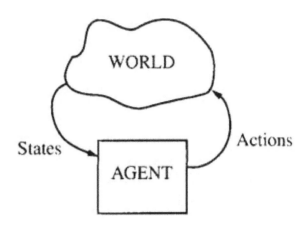

Figure 1: Agent in fully observable environment

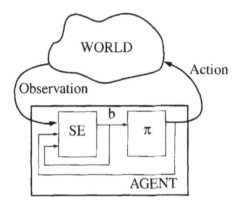

Figure 2: Agent in partially observable environment

icy (denoted π) can be reused (figure 2). The component which computes the new belief state is labeled SE for state estimator. It uses previous belief state, previous action and the observation as it's input.

Throughout this paper we use traffic example inspired by example in [1]. It models a busy intersection directed by the lights. Each car stops if there is a red light or another car in front. In the opposite case it continues through the intersection in a random direction.

1.1 Structure of following text

The following sections compare all three classes of the models mentioned above. First section after this introduction i.e. section number 2 defines MDP, MDP-IP and

POMDP formally and shows their differences on the traffic example. The next section defines policy for both fully and partially observable environments which allows us to define optimal policy for all three classes of models. Computing optimal policy is our goal. The way to achieve it is similar for all three classes of models. This article explains it and compares the calculations needed for solving all three classes of models also in section 3. The contribution of this article is the discussion of possible combination of all three model types. It can be found in the section 4.

2 Definitions

This section formally defines MDPs, POMDPs and MDP-IPs and shows their possible usage on examples.

2.1 Markov Decision processes (MDPs)

MDPs are defined as tuples of the form (S, A, R, T) where

- S is a set of states

- A is a set of actions

- R is a reward function $S \times A \to R$ telling how much the agent is rewarded for taking a given action in a given state.

- T is a transition function $S \times A \times S \to [0, 1]$ giving the probability $T(s_t, a_t, s_{t+1})$ of moving from state s_t to state s_{t+1} by executing action a_t.

In our example the set of states encodes positions of all the cars. The set of actions contains possible light combinations. Transition function would describe car movements and their probabilities. The reward function would be set up the way to minimize number of cars waiting at the intersection.

MDPs are standard framework for planning under uncertainty in fully obserable environments with known transition probabilities.

2.2 Partially observable Markov decision processes (POMDPs)

One of the reasons why modelling intersection with MDP is unrealistic is that it is not common that the sensors at the intersection could know the precise location of all cars. More typically only partial information about positions of some cars at the intersection is observed. The probabilities of receiving possible observations are defined by observation function.

POMDPs are defined as tuples of the form (S, A, R, T, Ω, O) where

- S, A, R and T are the same as in the MDP.

- Ω is a set of observations

- $O : S \times A \times \Omega \to [0, 1]$ is the observation function giving the probability of observations for given states and actions.

The difference of POMDP agent from MDP agent is the fact that the POMDP agent can not observe the state. Instead of that it only receives observation o which is randomly drawn from Ω according to probablitities given by observation function.

2.3 Markov decision processes with imprecise transition probabilities (MDP-IPs)

Another reason why modelling intersection using MDP is unrealistic is that we usually do not know the exact probabilities of cars' behaviour. It depends on the time, on the day of week, on holidays, on regional events and on other factors. Instead of searching optimal intersection behaviour for one setup of probabilities one would rather find policy always behaving reasonably. MDP-IPs can be utilized to find it. MDP-IPs are defined as tuples of the form (S,A,R,K) where

- S, A and R are defined the same way as in MDPs.

- K is a set of transition functions, $K \subseteq \{T | T : S \times A \times S \to [0, 1]\}$, i.e. set of functions which prescribes the probabilities of resulting states after performing given action from given previous state.

Delgado et al. [1] shown how to solve MDP-IPs effectively under some conditions. They assumed that K is either finite or can be expressed by finite set of linear constrains.

MDP-IPs are used in cases when the environment is fully observable but the transition function is not known precisely. In contrast to MDP the transition function is replaced by the set of possible transition functions in MDP-IPs case.

MDPs are special cases of MDP-IPs where $K = \{T\}$.

2.4 Common background

In the beginning the agent is in the state s_0. The MDP and MDP-IP frameworks assume that this state is known by the agent. The POMDP framework assume that the agent knows the probability distribution b_0 of initial states.

At each time period t the agent chooses action $a_t \in A$ accordingly to state s_t resp. belief state b_t. Perfoming this action causes the state random change to s_{t+1}. The probabilities of transitions are given by transition function T, $P(s_{t+1} | s_t, a_t) = T(s_t, a_t, s_{t+1})$.

The agent receives a reward r_t according to reward function, $r_t = R(s_{t+1}, a_t)$. Note that this reward is not observed by the agent in partially observable case. The only information agent has in partially observable case is observation o_t which is randomly drawn from the set of observations O with respect to probabilities given by observation function O, $P(o_t | s_{t+1}, a_t) = O(s_{t+1, a_t, o_t})$.

Knowing previous belief state, action performed and observation received agent can compute the next belief state using transition function T and observation function O. We denote $\tau_{O,T}(b,a,o)$ the next belief comuted this way.

$$\tau_{O,T}(b_{t-1},a_{t-1},o_t) = b_t(s') = P(s'|b_{t-1},a_{t-1},o_t) =$$
$$\frac{O(s',a_{t-1},o_t)\sum_{s\in S}T(s,a_{t-1},s')b_{t-1}(s)}{P(o_t|b_{t-1},a_{t-1})}.$$

The belief that agent's next state will be s' is calculated from the probability of observing o_t as $O(s',a_{t-1},o_t)$ multiplied by probability of reaching the state s' given by $\sum_{s\in S}T(s,a_{t-1},s')b_{t-1}(s)$. Denominator causes all believes sum to one. It is equal to $\sum_{s\in S}b_{t-1}(s)O(s,a_{t-1},o_t)$.

3 Solutions

MDP and POMDP agent's goal is to maximize expected discounted reward over infinite horizon[1] i.e. maximizing $E[\sum_{i=0}^{\infty}\gamma^i r_i]$, where γ is a so-called discount factor. It is a real number $0 < \gamma < 1$ which is used to the weight future rewards. The higher discount factor the more important future rewards are.

The MDP-IP problem is slightly different because it contains another kind of uncertainty. The transition function is not known and the its choice is not necessarily random. Hence it cannot be described by the probability theory. It doesn't make sence to consider agent's expected discounted reward. However the expected discounted reward can be considered when using one additional assumption: The assumtion that the transition function which minimizes agent's reward is chosen at every time step. Although this assumption does not necessarily needs to be true, it can be usefull. When we would teach the agent to act well under this pessimistic assumption then it would also act well when any other transition function would be used. That is the reason why we will use this assumtion from now on. We define the MDP-IP agent's goal to be also maximizing the expected discounted reward.

Policy π for MDP resp. MDP-IP is mapping $\pi : S \to A$ from states S to actions A.

POMDP agent's policy π is mapping from belief states to actions A.

MDP resp. MDP-IP agent can observe the state of the world for the whole time and it uses its policy π to choose the action at every time step.

In the POMDP case the agent does not know the exact state but it knows the belief state b which can be updated after each action a and observation o to $\tau_{O,T}(b,a,o)$. Again the POMDP-IP agent can follow its policy π at every time step.

Given policy π one can express expected discounted reward over infinite horizon as a function of initial state s resp. belief state b. We will call this function the value

function for π and denote it V_π. It can be expressed as a unique solution of the following sets of equations.

MDP case:
$$V_\pi(s) := R(s,\pi(s)) + \gamma\sum_{s'}T(s,\pi(s),s')V_\pi(s')$$
MDP-IP case:
$$V_\pi(s) := R(s,\pi(s)) + \gamma\min_{T\in K}\sum_{s'}T(s,\pi(s),s')V_\pi(s')$$
POMDP case:
$$V_\pi(b) := \sum_s b(s)[R(s,\pi(b)) +$$
$$+\gamma\sum_o V_\pi(\tau_{O,T}(b,\pi(b),o))\sum_{s'}T(s,\pi(b),s')O(s',\pi(b),o)]$$

Explanation: Agent's immediate reward $R(s,\pi(s))$ resp. expected reward $\sum_s b(s)R(s,\pi(b))$ is added to discounted (multiplication by γ) expected future reward given by $\sum_{s'}T(s,a,s')V_\pi(s')$ in the MDP case. If the probabilities are imprecise the minimalization over the transition probabilities returns the worst possible case reward. The expression is longer in the POMDP case because all possible current states and the states following are taken into account and the rewards are weighted by their probabilities which are given by observation and transition function.

These complicated expressions actually say how good each state resp. belief state is when the agent is following policy π.

Note that the recursive definition for V_π does not allow us to compute its values according to this definition directly. The values of V_π can be approximated by easy modification[2] of algorithm from section 3.3. But the algorithm for computing values of V_π is not our concern. We utilize the definition of V_π only for the definition of optimal policy.

3.1 Optimal policy

Optimal policy denoted π^* is defined as policy such that value function for π^* returns greater or equal value than any other value function does in the same state. $(\forall\pi\forall s\in S)\,V_{\pi^*}(s) > V_\pi(s)$ resp. $(\forall\pi\forall b)\,V_{\pi^*}(b) > V_\pi(b)$

Greedy policy π_V with respect to the value function V for MDP, MDP-IP is defined as:
$$\pi_V(s) = argmax_{a\in A}[R(s,a) + \gamma\sum_{s'\in S}T(s,a,s')V(s')].$$

Greedy policy π_V with respect to the value function V for POMDP is defined as:
$$\pi_V(b) = argmax_{a\in A}\sum_s b(s)[R(s,\pi(b)) +$$
$$+\gamma\sum_o V(\tau_{O,T}(b,a,o))\sum_{s'}T(s,a,s')O(s',a,o)].$$

3.2 Value functions

Optimal value function V^* is a mapping from states resp. belief states to real numbers defined as the following conditions called Bellman equations.

MDP:
$$V^*(s) = \max_{a\in A}[R(s,a) + \gamma\sum_{s\in S}T(s,a,s')V^*(s')]$$
MDP-IP:
$$V^*(s) = \max_{a\in A}\min_{T\in K}[R(s,a) + \gamma\sum_{s'\in S}T(s,a,s')V^*(s')]$$

---

[1]Sometimes maximization of expected discounted reward over finite horizon k is considered i.e. maximizing $E[\sum_{i=0}^{k}\gamma^i r_i]$. In the finite horizon it also makes sense to set $\gamma = 1$.

[2]Replace $max_{a\in A}$ by $a := \pi(s)$ resp. by $a := \pi(b)$.

POMDP:
$$V^*(b) = max_{a \in A}[\sum_{s \in S} R(s,a)b(s)+$$
$$+\gamma \sum_{o \in \Omega} P(o|a,b)V^*(\tau_{O,T}(b,a,o))]$$

In all three cases the set of equations has a unique solution [4], [1], [3]. These functions V^* can be intuitively interpreted as a functions of intial states s resp. belief states b returning expected discounted reward when the best possible action would be taken at every time step. The only difference between the definition of V^* and V_π is that the actions according to policy π were replaced by best possible actions. The functions V^* and V_π in the MDP-IP case return expected discounted reward under the assumption that the state changes according to the worst possible transition function.

Nevertheless much more important than intuitive explanation of V^* is its usefullness in the search for the optimal policy summarized by the following theorem:
$$\forall s \in S \, V^*(s) = V_{\pi^*}(s) \text{ resp. } \forall b \, V^*(b) = V_{\pi^*}(b).$$

As a collary agent can search for optimal value function V^* and use it to find the optimal policy π^* which is actually the greedy policy $\pi^* = \pi_{V^*}$ with respect to the optimal value function V^*.

3.3 Value iteration

Optimal value function can be approximated by using value iteration algorithm. In order to show only one algorithm for both fully observable and partially observable cases we denote both states and belief states by letter x. The x means state in algorithm for MDP and MDP-IP and it means belief state in the algorithm for POMDP.

> **Data**: $\varepsilon > 0$
> **Result**: count of iterations t
> V_t such that $[max_x V^*(x) - V_t(x)] < \varepsilon$
>
> $t = 0$;
> $\forall x V_0(x) = 0$;
> **repeat**
> | $t = t + 1$;
> | compute V_t from V_{t-1}
> **until** $max_x[V_t(x) - V_{t-1}(x)] < \varepsilon \frac{1-\gamma}{2\gamma}$;

The update of the value function is computed as follows:
MDP:
$$V_t(s) = max_{a \in A}[R(s,a) + \gamma \sum_{s' \in S} T(s,a,s')V_{t-1}(s')]$$
MDP-IP:
$$V_t(s) = max_{a \in A} min_T [R(s,a) + \gamma \sum_{s' \in S} T(s,a,s')V_{t-1}(s')]$$
POMDP:
$$V_t(b) = max_{a \in A} \sum_{s \in S}[R(s,a)b(s) + \gamma \sum_{o \in \Omega} P(o|a,b)V_{t-1}(b')]$$
where $b' = \tau_{O,T}(b,a,o)$

$V_1(s)$ equals the best reward agent can get after performing one action from state s. $V_1(b)$ in the POMDP case is the best expected reward agent can receive after performing one action.

$V_2(x)$ is the best expected reward agent can get after performing two actions. As t goes to infinity, $t \to \infty$, V_t approximates V^* more accurately, $V_t \to V^*$.

The value iteration algorithm stops when enough[3] precision is reached.

3.4 Update of value function for POMDPs

Although we have a formula determining the way how each belief should be updated there is still an infinite number of believes. To store and update so many values of V_t more spare representation of this value function is needed. The value function V_t has some properties which can be utilized to do so, namely the value function is piecewise linear and convex. It is sufficient to keep in memory the coefficients for each hyperplane and update only these coefficients at each step.

The belief space has $|S|$ dimensions. So each hyperplane can be represented as vector with $|S|$ elements. The set Γ of hyperplanes α represents the value function as $V_t(b) = max_{\alpha \in \Gamma}\alpha(b)$. Pineau et al. [5] shown how the value function represented as a set of hyperplanes can be updated to function from the next step which is again represented as a set of hyperplanes. It appeared that one of the key compuntional bottlenecks was a growing number of hyperplanes in Γ during time. Significant speed-up of the value iteration algorithm was achived by excluding hyperplanes which did not contribute to the maximization of above formula in any belief point.

Finding such hyperplane involves the linear optimization. Despite these speed-ups, looking for the optimal solution for POMDP is compuntionally complex. Specially it is complex when POMDP has many states hence when the belief space is many dimensional. That is motivation look for approximate solutions.

Roy et al. [6] described a scalable approach which uses the low-dimensional representations of belief space. They used a variant of Principal Components Analysis (PCA) called Exponential family PCA in order to compress certain kinds of large real-world POMDPs and in order to find good policies for these problems faster. Another way to do the update of value function approximately was introduced by Pineau et al. [5]. They speeded-up the update of the value function by doing update not over the whole belief space but only in carefully selected significant points.

4 Handling imprecise probabilities in POMDPs

There was already an attempt to combine MDP-IPs and POMDPs. Itoh et al.[2] tried to handle uncertainty about

---

[3]If the maximal difference in values from two succesive iterations is bounded by $\varepsilon \frac{1-\gamma}{2\gamma}$ then the the result V_t differs from optimal value function V^* at most by ε. See for example [3].

transtion and observation models by defining partially observable Markov decision processes with imprecise probabilities (POMDPIPs).

They searched for the solution of problems in two following cases: 1. when the sets of possible models form polytopes, 2. when the sets of possible models are finite. They shown how to solve this kind of problems effectively but they used quite different definition of optimal solution than we did. They used so-called second order believes to define probabilities over spaces of transition and observation models. Itoh et al. [2] defined POMDPIP's policy as optimal whenever the optimal policy existed for any second order belief.

This definition of optimal policy is unintuitional. Recall our transportation example. The transition models depend on holidays, regional events and other unmodelled factors. This uncertainty is encoded as a set of possible transition models. Similarly the observability can be different during the day and night.

According to definition of Itoh et al. [2] we can think of any second order belief e.g. belief such that the probability of the night observation model is 95% and the probability of the day observation model is 5% and then if we found optimal policy for this second order belief we would call it the optimal policy for the whole POMDPIP.

In many cases as in the traffic example one would like to find the policy which performs well for all (or at least for most) possible transition and observation models rather than the strategy performing well only for some specific combination of these models.

Good choice of the action to take would be the action maximizing expected value for the worst possible choice of transition and observation model i.e. action according to policy π_{V^*} where

$$V^*(b) = max_{a \in A} min_T min_O \sum_{s \in S} [R(s,a)b(s)+$$
$$+\gamma \sum_{o \in \Omega} P(o|a,b)V^*(\tau_{O,T}(b,a,o))]$$

Another possibility of overcoming imprecision of probabilities is taking expectation over all possible observation and transition models[4].

$$V^*(b) = max_{a \in A} E_T E_O \sum_{s \in S} [R(s,a)b(s)+$$
$$+\gamma \sum_{o \in \Omega} P(o|a,b)V^*(\tau_{O,T}(b,a,o))]$$

In both cases optimal value function could be approximated using the value iteration algorithm. Relation between V_t and V_{t-1} would be:

$$V_t(b) = max_{a \in A} min_T min_O \sum_{s \in S} [R(s,a)b(s)+$$
$$+\gamma \sum_{o \in \Omega} P(o|a,b)V_{t-1}(\tau_{O,T}(b,a,o))]$$

---

[4]Since any prior probabilities of observation and transitions models are given, we can regard all models as the same probable.

resp.

$$V_t(b) = max_{a \in A} E_T E_O \sum_{s \in S} [R(s,a)b(s)+$$
$$+\gamma \sum_{o \in \Omega} P(o|a,b)V_{t-1}(\tau_{O,T}(b,a,o))]$$

We are again facing similar problem to the one we previously talked about. Again the continuum of values need to be updated effectively. The approach of Pineau et al. [5] assumed convexity and piecewice linearity of value function.

The following paragraphs show that the minimization over finite transition and observation model spaces does not keep convexity of the value function.

Value function from tth time step can be seen as the expected reward the agent would get during first t steps when the world would act against it. By acting agains the agent we mean choosing the transition and observation models which are the worst for the agent. But the agent does not know its state precisely. It knows only probabalities of states given be its belief. The world chooses transitions and observations models according to this belief.

Let's ilustrate everything on a simple example. Let the set of states $S = \{s_0, s_1\}$. Because we are in this example interested in updates of value function we will for simplicity consider only one-element set of states and set of action, $\Omega = \{o_1\}, A = \{a_1\}$. Because we have only one possible observation, the agent will observe this one observation every time. So we will consider only one observation model which assigns to this observation the probability 1. However we will consider uncertainty in transition model. There will be two possible transition models T_0 and T_1. To even more simplify the consideration we let both transitions models behave deterministically. The model T_0 never changes the state i.e. the probabiliry of changing the state is 0 and the probability of staying in the same state is 1. The model T_1 always changes the state i.e. the probability of staying in the same state is 0. Futhermore let $\gamma = 0.8$ and let the reward function be defined as follows:

$$R(s_0) = 0$$

$$R(s_1) = 1$$

Because the set of states we consider has only two elements the belief space is only one dimensional. $b(s_1)$ is real number from interval $[0, 1]$ and $b(s_0)$ always equals to $1 - b(s_1)$. This allows us to show the plots of value functions. The figure 3 shows V_1 created by the first iteration of value iteration algorithm. The axis X shows $b(s_1)$. The axis Y shows the values of V_1 in b. It coresponds to the reward agent expects to receive after performing one action. It doesn't depend on chosen transition function.

However V_2 depends on transition function. The figure 4 shows how V_2 looks in POMDP with transition model T_0. The figure 5 shows how V_2 looks in POMDP with transition model T_1. If we constructed the value function

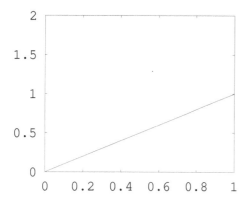

Figure 3: Function V_1

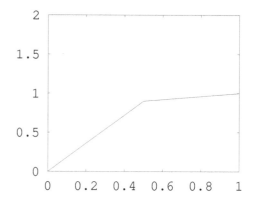

Figure 6: Influence of imprecision of transition model on V_2 when combining models by minimization.

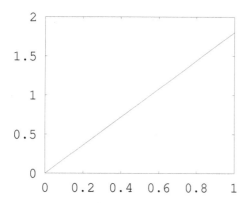

Figure 4: Function V_2 created with transition model T_0

not affect it so much. This is a difference from POMDPs, where nothing similar could happen and where the value functions were always convex.

Another aspect which is needed to be taken into consideration when representing value function approximations in computer is the question whether they are piecewice linear, because it would be harder to represent function which is not piecewice linear. This apparently relates to question which sets of transitions and observations to allow, whether to allow models which contradict each other, wheather to allow infinite sets of possible models and if so how these sets should be restricted[5].

The same questions hold also for the second proposed approach which replaced minimization by expectation.

Allowing only the sets of transition and observation models which keep some properties could lead to value functions which can be represented more easily. Otherwise novel technics for representation and effective updates of more complicated value functions will be needed to be researched. Other branches of research could consist of approximative techniques.

the way that the world chooses the worst possible model then the V_2 looks like 6. Hence it is not convex.

More generally the approximations V_t of value function can have more nonconvex parts which are alternated by convex parts.

The cause of this phoenomena is that in lower entropy belief states it can be easier to act against the agent than in high entropy beliefs in which the agent has higher chance that the choice of transition and observations models will

5   Conclusion

POMDPs combined with MDP-IPs have greater representational power than the other frameworks because they combine the most essential features for planning under uncertainty. Naturally, the main drawback of optimizing a universal plan is complexity of doing so. This article showed that value functions of POMDPs extended by imprecise probabilities are not convex. This difference from conventional POMDPs prevents the use of existing algorithms. Effective techniques for solving POMDPs with imprecise probabilities are needed to be discovered.

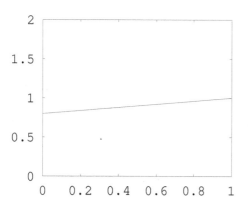

Figure 5: Function V_2 created with observation model T_1

---

[5]Interesting idea would be considering the sets of models which are convex envelopes of finite sets of models.

6 Acknowledgments

This research was supported by SVV project number 267 314.

References

[1] Delgado K. V., S. Sanner, and L. Nunes de Barros, Efficient solutions to factored MDPs with imprecise transition probabilities, *Artificial Intelligence*, 175, 1498-1527, 2011

[2] Itoh H., and K. Nakamura, Partially observable Markov decision processes with imprecise parameters, *Artficial Inteligence*, 171, 453-490, 2007

[3] Kaelbling L. P., M. L. Littman, and A. R. Cassandra, Planning and acting in partially observable stochastic domains, *Artificial Intelligence*, 101, 99-134, 1998

[4] Kolobov A., Mausam, and D. S. Weld, Discovering hidden structure in factored MDPs, *Artificial Intelligence*, 189, 19-47, 2012

[5] Pineau J., G. Gordon and S. Thrun, Anytime Point-Based Approximations for Large POMDPs, *Journal of Artificial Intelligence Research 27*, 2006

[6] Roy N., G. Gordon and S. Thrun, Finding Approximate POMDP Solutions Through Belief Compression, *Journal of Artificial Intelligence Research 23*, 2005

Poster Abstracts

ITAT 2013: Workshops, Posters, and Tutorials, p. 120
ISBN 978-1490952086, © 2013 M. Ďuriš, J. Katreniaková

Mental map models for edge drawing*

Martin Ďuriš and Jana Katreniaková

Faculty of Mathematics, Physics and Informatics, Comenius University Bratislava, Slovakia,
mato.duris@gmail.com, katreniakova@dcs.fmph.uniba.sk,

Drawing of graphs is often used for visualization of structured information. To make the drawing easy to read (and thus improve the understanding of the underlaying structures), it should fulfill some aesthetic criteria. However, the drawing of graph is mostly not just a static image. The graph can be changed over time – some vertices or edges can be changed, added or removed. The easiest way of handling the changes is to redraw the graph using the same algorithm as before. However, in this case even small changes to the graph may result in a drawing that is completely different and it is hard for the user to find correspondence between the old and new drawings. To make the new drawing readable, the user must be able to understand the changes made to the graph and rediscover the structures in the new drawing. Therefore, there should be another group of criteria – dynamic criteria, which preserve some properties of the last drawing. The concept of mental map was introduced[1] to do this for vertex placement. The mental map captures some important features of the vertex placement (e.g. relative positions up/down/left/right of vertices). It is said that the mental map is preserved between timeslices if the changes are acceptable (e.g. all relative position remain the same). There are applications where positions of vertices are fixed, for instance if they were defined by the user or the exact position of the vertices is somehow significant. In these cases, the traditional mental map is useless, since it is trivially preserved. The drawing algorithm only finds some routing of the edges. The mental map should capture key features of the edge routing. However, until now, there was no suitable model of mental map which contains also some information about the drawing of edges.

In our work, we introduce two models suitable for preserving similarity in routing of edges. We try to follow the intuitive idea of similarity of two polylines. We do not only define the mental map model, we also provide an algorithm that uses the results of the drawing algorithm to create new routing of the edges that preserves the mental map as it is defined by the model.

The first model of mental map deals with the placement of bends of the polyline. We say, that the mental map is preserved, if only a constant number of bends (from the previous edge routing) is changed. The algorithm starts with the new routing (generated by the routing algorithm) and if it does not preserve the mental map, it creates an alternative edge routing which has at most k changed bends. The algorithm tries to find the bends that must be changed

(due to obstacles in the previous routing) and there is less than k of them, it tries to make the changes in such a way to make the routing as similar as possible to the original. Otherwise, a completely new routing has to be used.

The second model is more advanced and it defines an area, where the edge can be freely routed, i.e., the drawing of the edge must fit into this area. We call this area the *corridor*. The corridor should be as small as possible to make the new drawing similar to the previous routing, however it needs to be big enough to find a valid routing. The corridor can be described as an area between two border-polylines. This makes it easy to compute whether each point from some edge routing is in the corridor and thus the routing preserves mental map. First idea can be to find some epsilon neighborhood of the original edge drawing. However the epsilon is not the same for each of the line segments which form the polyline. Some of them may be contain obstacles, the others may be free. Therefore we must build the corridor from subcorridors which correspond to line segments. We chose some borders of subcorridors to be part of the final border of corridor. The easiest way is to build the convex hull of the subcorridors, but it is too big and does not follow the idea of using a neighborhood of the polyline. Therefore, we build the borders using alpha-edges[2]. Such corridor is scalable and allows us to expand it if it is not large enough for the drawing algorithm to route the edge inside the corridor. Moreover, since the edge is directly routed using the drawing algorithm, it also preserves the static criteria.

Measuring of dynamic aesthetic criteria is hard. We proposed measurements based on geometric characteristics of the routed edges (polylines). We compared averaged distance between the edge routing before user interaction and after. Without any mental map, the average distance of the polylines is 21.86. Using mental map, the average distance is 17.07 (first model) and 10.99 (second model). If we use a widely used static criterion for edges – the length of the edge – we can see that the results of our models (especially the second one) are also good. The first model provides routing with ratio 1.2 and the second model 1.1.

Literatúra

[1] Eades P., Lai W., Misue K., and Sugiyama K.: Preserving the Mental Map of a Diagram. Proc. of Compugraphics, 91: 24–33, 1991.

[2] Edelsbrunner H., Kirkpatrick D.G., Seidel R.: On the shape of a set of points in the plane, IEEE Transactions on Information Theory 29 (4): 551–559, 1983.

*The research was supported in part by VEGA 1/1085/12

Can Software Engineers be Liberated from Petri Nets?

Hana Kubátová

Dept. of Digital Design, Faculty of Information Technology, Czech Technical University in Prague
Thákurova 9, 160 00 Praha 6, Czech Republic
hana.kubatova@fit.cvut.cz

Karel Richta

Dept. of Software Engineering, Faculty of Mathematics and Physics, Charles University in Prague
Malostranské nám.25, Praha 1, 118 00, Czech Republic
karel.richta@mff.cuni.cz

Tomáš Richta

Dept. of Intelligent Systems, Faculty of Information Technology, University of Technology in Brno
Božetěchova 2, 612 66 Brno, Czech Republic
irichta@fit.vutbr.cz

Abstract.

Petri nets are widely used for the specification of problems, in particular for describing concurrent systems. On the other hand, new versions of the UML specification precisely define the semantics of activity diagrams, and state machines, which can also be used to describe parallel systems. An interesting question is whether we can replace any Petri net machine status describing the same behavior, and vice versa.

The Problem

In our case we are in a situation where we want to describe a network of communicating agents using Petri nets. E.g. we want to define a smart home solution, which consists of a set of agents monitoring and controlling various elements, such as heating, cooling, etc. We are able to describe these agents by Petri nets, and we have a tool that can simulate designed system. On the other hand, there exist available tools that can convert description of the system by UML state diagrams to the target platform implemented as small embedded systems, or, if necessary, to transfer it directly to the hardware implemented using e.g. by FPGA.

Our aim, therefore, was the proposal of a universal procedure that can convert any description by Petri nets to an equivalent description using UML state machines. This would have allow us to simulate virtually the design of communicating agents described by Petri nets, and then transform it into an effective solution based on state diagrams.

Some beginners confuse state diagrams to activity diagrams. The difference between state machines and activity diagrams is important because these two diagrams represent two very different programming paradigms: event-driven programming (state diagrams) and structured programming (activity diagrams).

When creating state diagrams we have to constantly think about possible events. In contrast, in the activity diagrams, the events are secondary things. Natural extension of state diagrams is to allow transitions from any number of states in any number of states. This is however only useful if the system can simultaneously be in several states (regions) together, which means that each state describes only a partial aspect of the overall, global state.

The resulting formalism is known as a Petri net. The reverse procedure simulates transitions in a Petri net with branching in UML. Another extension allows the integration of diagrams, activity diagrams status (Harel). This extension supports the development of software that is both event-driven "workflow" and software-driven process model.

Conclusions

In the foregoing chapters we have shown that any Petri net can be replaced by an equivalent state machine. So it is the base idea that developers can be freed from Petri nets. It's not strict restrictions - Petri nets can be used where there is a description of the network easier to use than using the state machine description.

The conversion allows the integration of flowcharts within Harel state charts and Petri nets. This extension supports the development of software that is both event driven and workflow driven.

Acknowledgment

This work has been supported by the Ministry of Education, Youth and Sports under Research Program No. MSM 6840770014, and also by the grant project of the Czech Grant Agency (GA_CR) No. GA201/09/0990, and also by the AVAST Foundation.

References

[1] Girault, C. – Valk, R.: Petri Nets for System Engineering: A Guide to Modeling Verification, and Applications. Springer-Verlag New York, Inc., Secaucus, NJ, USA,2001.

[2] Richta, T. - Janoušek, V. - Kočí, R.: Code Generation For Petri Nets-Specified Reconfigurable Distributed Control Systems. In: *Proceedings of 15th International Conference on Mechatronics –Mechatronika 2012*. pp. 263-270. IEEE, Praha 2012.

[3] OMG (February 2009): OMG Unified Modeling Language (OMG UML), Superstructure Version 2.2. URL:
http://www.omg.org/spec/UML/2.2/Superstructure/PDF. 2009.

ITAT 2013: Workshops, Posters, and Tutorials, pp. 122–124
ISBN 978-1490952086, © 2013 R. Ostertág

About security of Digital Electronic Keys

Richard Ostertág

Department of Computer Science, Comenius University,
Mlynská dolina, 842 48 Bratislava, Slovakia
ostertag@dcs.fmph.uniba.sk
https://micro.dcs.fmph.uniba.sk/dokuwiki

Abstract: It is a common practice to equip entrance doors to apartment buildings with the Digital Electronic Key (DEK) as a way of access control. The theoretical security of DEKs is minimal, as they contain only a fixed unique 48-bit serial number, which is transferred during the identification process in plain text, using 1-Wire protocol. So the security of this solution is solely based on the assumption of intractability of practical implementation of a DEK emulator. We address this assumption and show that it is no longer valid.

1 Introduction and basic description of DEK SIET

RYS is a Slovak company that trades and develops access control and door communication systems. This company develops its own line of access control systems based on iButton (a.k.a. touch or digital electronic key – DEK) with DEK SIET operating-memory units.

These systems were designed for apartment buildings and became very popular. They are also used to provide access control in commercial or industrial settings (e.g. hotels, offices, stores, schools, server housing). [1]

We choose to discuss this system because of its popularity in Slovakia. But all conclusions apply to any system using 1-Wire protocol and serial number iButtons (i.e. we do not exploit any specific properties of this system).

1.1 Operating-memory unit

Operating-memory unit, e.g. DS-01/232 (see figure 1) is in the center of RYS access control system DEK SIET.

This unit is connected through its RELÉ1 outputs with door's electromagnet and through T1 and GND with an iButton touch probe. This unit is capable to store serial numbers of hundreds of iButtons. If a user touches the touch probe with a DEK, the iButton serial number is transferred from the DEK to the operating-memory unit. If the transferred number is stored in the unit, the unit temporarily deactivates the electromagnets and the user is allowed to enter.

We are interested in the communication between the DEK and operating-memory unit. As the DEK is a DS1990R serial number iButton® from Maxim Integrated Products, Inc, this communication uses 1-Wire protocol.

Figure 1: DS-01/232 operating-memory unit

1.2 Serial Number iButton

The DS1990R is a rugged button-shaped data carrier, which serves as an electronic registration number (see figure 2). Every DS1990R is factory lasered with a guaranteed unique 64-bit registration number that allows for absolute traceability.

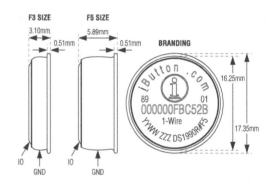

Figure 2: DS1990R serial number iButton

This 64 bit registration (or serial) number has internal structure as depicted in figure 3.

high address	MSB		LSB	low address
CRC byte	6–byte serial number			family code 01

Figure 3: Data structure of a DS1990R registration number

It contains a six-byte device-unique serial number, a

one-byte family code, and a one-byte CRC verification. All DS1990R have family code fixed to $(01)_{16}$. Other iButton devices exist, with different family codes (e.g. $(10)_{16}$ is temperature iButton), but they are not usually used in this kind of systems. Therefore every DEK can be considered as a 48 bits long factory set unique number (analogous to unique MAC addresses of network cards).

1.3 1-Wire protocol

Communication with iButton devices utilizes the 1-Wire protocol, which transfers data serially through a single data lead and a ground return. The serial transfer is done half-duplex within defined time slots. The operating-memory unit initiates the transfer by sending a command word to the iButton. They have no power source and are powered from operating-memory unit using the parasite power system on data lead. Implementation details of the protocol can be found in [2].

2 Implementation

We decided to implement iButton emulator using Arduino compatible hardware platform developed at Slovak University of Technology — Acrob [3], depicted on figure 4.

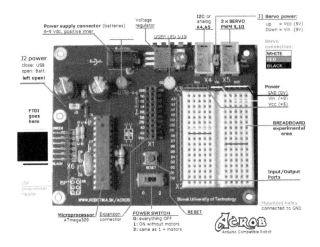

Figure 4: Acrob – an educational robotic platform

This hardware platform uses the Atmel ATmega328 microcontroller running on 16 MHz, which we programmed in C++ like language, using standard Arduino IDE [4].

We use two Acrob devices. One for emulation of the door access control system (**the reader**) and the other for iButton emulation (**the emulator**). We use the reader solely for the purpose of a more convenient development.

2.1 Hardware

The 1-Wire protocol uses only one data line. We implement this line by connecting together digital pin 12 of the emulator and the reader. This data line requires pull up resistor on the reader side, so we implement this by connecting digital pin 12 of the reader to V_{cc} using $2\,\mathrm{k}\Omega$ pull up resistor. Ground return is implemented by connecting together GNDs of the reader and the emulator.

2.2 Software

The emulator implementation consists of 289 lines of code of which 15 are in assembly language for better timing control. The code is extensively commented with references to a more in-depth documentation. The code can be accessed from our webpage [5].

The emulator contains a list of serial numbers, and when it is running, it is cyclically sending each programmed serial number in an endless loop.

The reader implementation is straightforward as we can use OneWire library. It has only 49 lines of simple code (again, please see [5]).

3 The brute force attack

To emulate the iButton, we need to know its serial number. If we have a physical access to the iButton, then we can read it in less than 5 ms. Also it is possible to glimpse the serial number, as it is engraved on the iButton surface. But physical access is not always possible.

Then we can use the brute force attack. If serial numbers of iButtons are long enough, then this kind of attack can be infeasible. If we omit predictable parts of serial numbers, we have to find six bytes. Our empirical observations suggest that serial numbers are allocated in sequence. All keys we have seen so far had zeros in two most significant bytes of these six bytes. Therefore for a brute force attack it would be sufficient to try all 2^{32} serial numbers of the above mentioned form. If we assume 5 ms as an upper bound to try one serial number, we will need for a successful brute force attack $5\,\mathrm{ms} \times 2^{32}/60/60/24/7 \approx 35.5$ weeks in the worst case.

4 Conclusions

We have developed an iButton emulator and showed that using a 289 lines long program anybody with access to an Arduino compatible device can emulate any chosen DS1990R iButton. Cost (around 30.00 €) and time needed for this attack (with known serial number) are negligible.

In the future, we plan to test our DEK emulator on real door entry systems and try to develop a miniaturized version with the size similar to the iButton. We will also try to speed up the brute force attack by narrowing down unknown bits of the serial number by further empirical observations of distribution of the real serial numbers used in the wild. Also, when attacking large apartment building, we can take into our advantage the fact, that it is sufficient to find any valid key to obtain access into building.

This work was supported by VEGA grant 1/0259/13.

References

[1] RYS: Access control and door entry systems. (`http://www.rys.sk/html_eng/english.htm`) [Online; accessed 1-July-2013].

[2] Maxim Integrated Products, Inc.: Book of iButton standards (application note 937). `http://www.maximintegrated.com/app-notes/index.mvp/id/937` (2002) [Online; accessed 1-July-2013].

[3] Balogh, R.: Acrob - an educational robotic platform. AT&P Journal Plus **10** (2010) 6–9 ISSN 1336-5010. `http://ap.urpi.fei.stuba.sk/balogh/pdf/10ATPplusAcrob.pdf` [Online; accessed 1-July-2013].

[4] Arduino: Arduino software. (`http://arduino.cc/en/main/software`) [Online; accessed 1-July-2013].

[5] Ostertág, R.: The iButton emulator source code. (`https://micro.dcs.fmph.uniba.sk/iButton.zip`) [Online; accessed 1-July-2013].

ITAT 2013: Workshops, Posters, and Tutorials, pp. 125–126
ISBN 978-1490952086, © 2013 R. Ostertág

Performance counters as entropy source in Microsoft Windows OS

Richard Ostertág

Department of Computer Science, Comenius University,
Mlynská dolina, 842 48 Bratislava, Slovakia
ostertag@dcs.fmph.uniba.sk
https://micro.dcs.fmph.uniba.sk/dokuwiki

Abstract: In cryptography we often need to generate random numbers. Many programming languages provide build-in functions for generating random numbers, but these have to be deterministic as all algorithms running on deterministic machines, and that implies predictability. This problem can be avoided if we use a true hardware source of entropy. But even on systems without such dedicated hardware, one can use system events to collect entropy. We study and analyze Microsoft Windows OS performance counters as such source.

1 Introduction

To implement a nondeterministic random bit generator, we need a nondeterministic source (for example thermal noise or nuclear decay). But this requires specialized hardware, which may not be available. On computers without a hardware entropy source, programmers try to obtain entropy using existing peripherals. Modern UNIX and Windows operating systems have OS-level random number generators based on the timing of kernel I/O events [1].

But sometimes we need to implement our own entropy source, e.g. because we use system without I/O intensive peripherals (no disk, no network, etc.), or we do not trust the system proprietary implementation[1], or if the system does not provide any.

In our quest for a good entropy source on Microsoft Windows, we choose to use the performance counter facility of this operating system.

2 Performance counters

Performance counters monitor system components (processors, memory, network I/O, etc.). Microsoft Windows provides different types of performance counters, including counters that count the number of items and those that measure the average time required to perform an operation. Performance counters are divided into categories, such as Cache, Memory, LogicalDisk or Objects. Each category contains different counters identified by their names (e.g. in category Objects we have counters with

names like Mutexes or Events). One counter can have multiple instances, for example counter "Bytes Received/sec" in "Network Interface" category have an instance for every network card in the system. Also many counters have a "general", summarizing instance like _Total[2] or Default.

Overall, our Microsoft Windows installation contains 2,266 performance counters. All of them will be further analyzed in the next section.

3 Evaluation

We evaluate the sequences of counter values using the Shannon entropy (H_1) [2] and the min-entropy (H_∞) [3]. Let p_i be the probability that the output of a counter producing a k-bit outcome will be equal to i, where $0 \le i < 2^k$. Then H_1 and H_∞ are defined as follows:

$$H_1 = -\sum_{i=0}^{2^k-1} p_i \log_2 p_i \qquad H_\infty = \min_{i=0}^{2^k-1} -\log_2 p_i$$

Shannon entropy measures the average amount of bits needed to describe the counter outcome, whereas min-entropy measures the probability that an attacker can guess the outcome with a single guess. The min-entropy is always less than or equal to Shannon entropy.

For a perfect random counter p_i is 2^{-k} and the Shannon entropy and min-entropy of the output are both equal to k bits, and all possible counter outcomes are equally probably. The information present in the output on average cannot be represented in a sequence shorter than k bits, and an attacker cannot guess the output with probability greater than 2^{-k} [1].

For all counters we gathered 10,000 samples of theirs raw values (long) with 20 ms delay between samples. The system was otherwise idle (user did not use the system, but typical services and background applications were running). We then excluded all counters with zero Shannon entropy. The remaining 326 counters had entropy ranging from 0.00147303 to 13.2877.

Then we switched from raw data collection to "mangled" data collection. For every raw long l_i collected we xor-ed all it's bits to get $f(l_i)$.

$$f(a) = a_{63} \oplus a_{62} \oplus \ldots \oplus a_0, \text{ where } a = (a_{63}a_{62}\ldots a_0)_2$$

---

[1] We have tried to study Microsoft Windows implementation of the OS-level entropy gathering algorithm, but we did not find any source code or in-depth specification, only a vague description, which has been insufficient for analysis.

[2] If we later do not mention an instance of a counter, we have this "general" instance on mind.

Then eight such bits $f(l_1), f(l_2), \ldots, f(l_8)$ from eight longs $l_1, l_2, \ldots, l_8$ were grouped into one byte $m(l_1, \ldots, l_8)$.

$$m(l_1, l_2, \ldots, l_8) = \left(f(l_1) f(l_2) \ldots f(l_8) \right)_2$$

This way we again collected 10,000 byte samples from every (non-zero entropy) counter with 20 ms delay between raw samples on an otherwise idle system. Then we selected only counters with entropy and min-entropy of at least 7, resulting in 62 counters.

We also wanted to evaluate stability of entropy and thus we introduce floating entropy. Floating entropy is calculated as a mean of entropies of consecutive overlapping windows of length 1,000 with step one. Standard deviation of floating entropy is standard deviation of entropies of all windows.

Only counters with floating Shannon entropy of at least 7.8 and standard deviation less than 0.017 and floating min-entropy at least 6.55 proceeded to the next round. This way we had obtained 16 promising counters listed in table 1.

Category	Name
LogicalDisk	**% Idle Time**
PhysicalDisk	**% Idle Time**
Process	Elapsed Time
Process	IO Other Operations/sec
Processor	**% C3 Time**
Processor	C3 Transitions/sec
Processor	% Idle Time
Processor	% Privileged Time
Processor Information	**% C3 Time**
Processor Information	**DPCs Queued/sec**
Processor Information	**% Priority Time**
Synchronization	**AcqShrdLite/sec**
Synchronization	IPI Send Broadcast Req./sec
System	**System Calls/sec**
Thread	**Context Switches/sec**
Thread	**% Processor Time**

Table 1: Promising performance counters based on the first experiment. Counters passing also thresholds of the second experiment are highlighted.

We further analyzed these promising counters by sampling them on another personal computer. Shannon and min-entropies from this second experiment are shown in figure 1.

In last round we excluded "Process, IO Other Operations/sec", "Processor, % Privileged Time" and "Synchronization, IPI Send Broadcast Requests/sec" as theirs min-entropy, this time, was below threshold of 7 bits. "Process, Elapsed Time" and "Processor, C3 Transitions/sec" and "Processor, % Idle Time" counters were also disqualified, because they had standard deviation of floating Shannon entropy greater than 0.019.

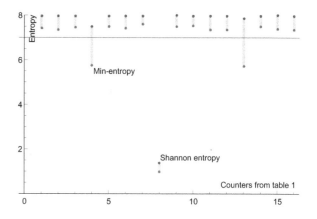

Figure 1: Shannon and min-entropies of counters in table 1 evaluated on a different computer.

The remaining ten counters had entropy (Shannon and min) of at least 7, floating Shannon entropy of at least 7.79 with standard deviation less than 0.019 and floating min-entropy of at least 6.5 with standard deviation less than 0.16 in two experiments on different computers. In the second experiment we have slightly relaxed thresholds to account for small disturbance in measured properties.

4   Conclusions

We have analyzed 2,266 performance counters of Microsoft Windows operating system and have found among them ten promising counters, highlighted in table 1, with high and stable entropy.

In future, we plan to study correlation between selected counters (e.g. we expect that LogicalDisk and PhysicalDisk will be highly correlated) with the aim to exclude redundant counters. Also we plan to test behavior of these counters on different versions of Microsoft Windows. We also want to study influence of virtualization of underlying OS on these counters and their other properties like the Markov-Rényi min entropy.

This work was supported by VEGA grant 1/0259/13.

References

[1] Hamburg, M., Kocher, P., Marson, M.E.: Analysis of Intel's Ivy Bridge digital random number generator. http://cryptography.com/public/pdf/Intel_TRNG_Report_20120312.pdf (2012) [Online; accessed 1-July-2013].

[2] Shannon, C.E.: A mathematical theory of communication. The Bell System Technical Journal **27** (1948) 379–423, 623–656

[3] Barker, E.B., Kelsey, J.M.: Recommendation for Random Number Generation Using Deterministic Random Bit Generators. US Department of Commerce, National Institute of Standards and Technology, Computer Security Division, Information Technology Laboratory (2012)

Tutorial Materials

ITAT 2013: Workshops, Posters, and Tutorials, pp. 128–135
ISBN 978-1490952086, © 2013 M. Hodoň, J. Miček, O. Karpiš, P. Ševčík

Bezdrôtové siete senzorov a aktuátorov - od teórie k aplikáciám

Michal Hodoň

Katedra Technickej kybernetiky,
Fakulta riadenia a informatiky,
Žilinská univerzita v Žiline,
Univerzitná 8215/1, 010 26 Žilina

Juraj Miček, Ondrej Karpiš, Peter Ševčík

Katedra Technickej kybernetiky,
Fakulta riadenia a informatiky,
Žilinská univerzita v Žiline,
Univerzitná 8215/1, 010 26 Žilina

Abstract. *V súčasnosti sa často stretávame s pojmami „Prevasive Computing, Mobile Computing, Ubiquitous Computing (Ubicomp), Ambient Intelligence, Smart Dust, Internet of Things", ktoré naznačujú, že v najbližšej dobe je možné očakávať ďalší masívny prienik prostriedkov a systémov informačných technológií do všetkých oblastí ľudskej spoločnosti. Zariadenia schopné snímať parametre prostredia budov, monitorovať aktivitu jednotlivca, monitorovať a ovládať technické systémy, umožňovať vyžiadanú asistenciu pri náročnejších činnostiach a mnohé ďalšie sa dnes stávajú realitou. Väčšina týchto zariadení je schopná vzájomnej komunikácie a priamo, alebo prostredníctvom prístupových zariadení sú integrované do siete Internet. Narastá množstvo dostupných informácií. Čas na získanie relevantných dát je dnes mimoriadne krátky. Menia sa paradigmy spracovania dát. Každým dňom sa rozširujú aplikačné oblasti prostriedkov informačných technológií. To čo nebolo ešte včera realizovateľné je dnes komerčne používané.*

Jednou z oblastí, ktorá už dnes predstavuje úspešne využívanú technológiu je oblasť bezdrôtových senzorických sietí, (Wireless Sensor Network, WSN). Práve bezdrôtovým sieťam senzorov je venovaný tento príspevok. Na základe predchádzajúceho vývoja je možné predpokladať, že v najbližšom desaťročí sa počet aplikácií WSN mnohonásobne zvýši. Aj z tohto dôvodu je príspevok venovaný popisu WSN, možnostiam ich využitia a niektorým otázkam spojeným s návrhom prvku siete, siete senzorov a možných aplikácií. V druhej časti príspevku sú uvedené úspešné i menej úspešné aplikácie popisovanej technológie, ktoré vznikli na našom pracovisku.

1 Úvod

V posledných rokoch sa bezdrôtovým sieťam senzorov venuje stále väčšia pozornosť. Uvedený stav súvisí najmä:

- s pokrokmi technológie v oblasti výroby mikroelektronických systémov, ktorá umožňuje integrovať v jednom obvode výkonný systém spracovania dát,
- s pokrokmi v oblasti snímačov, najmä vývoj nových snímacích prvkov na báze mikro-elektoro-mechanických systémov, MEMS,
- s pokrokmi v oblasti komunikačných technológií, spoľahlivé digitálne RF-komunikačné systémy krátkeho dosahu s nízkou energetickou náročnosťou,
- s pokrokmi v oblasti zdrojov energie a systémov zberu energie z okolia.

Je zrejmé, že pokiaľ technologické možnosti výroby základných komponentov WSN nedosiahli kritickú hranicu, nebolo možné očakávať široké nasadzovanie technológií WSN v rôznych aplikačných oblastiach. Napriek tomu je možné spomenúť jednu oblasť aplikácií, kde ekonomické hľadiská nehrajú dominantnú úlohu. Je to vojenská oblasť, v ktorej je možné sledovať snáď prvé nasadenie WSN na monitorovanie pohybu vojsk. Spomeňme systém označovaný ADSID (Air Delivered Seismic Intrusion Detector), ktorý bol používaný jednotkami US Air Force vo vietnamskej vojne. Pre zaujímavosť pripomeňme, že každý senzor bol približne 120 cm dlhý, jeho priemer mal cca 23 cm a vážil 17 kg. Senzor obsahoval citlivý seizmometer, ktorý bol schopný zaznamenávať vibrácie spôsobené pohybujúcimi sa vozidlami a osobami. Senzory boli rozmiestnené popri známej Ho Či Min-ovej ceste. Zaznamenané informácie boli vysielané priamo do lietadiel, ktoré lietali nad monitorovanou oblasťou. Pripomeňme tiež systém používaný na monitorovanie pohybu ponoriek v 50-tych rokoch minulého storočia. Systém s označením SOSUS, Sound Sourveillance System, bol vyvinutý pre armádne účely USA a využíval sieť hydrofónov rozmiestnených v Atlantickom a Tichom oceáne. Dnes je táto sieť používaná na sledovanie podmorského života a vulkanickej aktivity.

No až technologické pokroky v poslednom období podnietili vznik nových zaujímavých ekonomicky efektívnych aplikácií.

Bezdrôtová sieť senzorov pozostáva z priestorovo rozložených autonómnych snímacích prvkov, ktoré navzájom komunikujú. Sú rozmiestnené v monitorovanej oblasti a priebežne vyhodnocujú stav sledovaného objektu. Pojem objekt chápeme v najširšom slova zmysle a môže predstavovať strážený priestor, diagnostikovanú výrobnú linku, dopravný prostriedok, či živú bytosť. V súčasnosti podľa [1] až 99% inštalovaných senzorov komunikuje prostredníctvom vodičov. Predpokladá sa, že v nasledujúcich 10-tich rokoch budú WSN predstavovať nie viac než 10 % všetkých inštalovaných senzorov. V súlade s [1] a [2] uveďme, že pri využití WSN klesajú oproti tradičným riešeniam finančné náklady na inštaláciu a údržbu.

Európska komisia podporila výskumnú a vývojovú činnosť, ako aj nové aplikácie WSN v rámci siedmeho rámcového programu (7FP) v oblasti informačno-komunikačných technológií, 7FP-ICT. Pre roky 2007 až 2013 je celkový objem financií na úrovni 50 mld. €. V poslednom období 2010 až 2012 podporila EK výskum WSN najmä prostredníctvom prvej výzvy „Pervazívne a dôverné siete a obslužná infraštruktúra". Na podporu výskumu v rámci spomenutej výzvy vyčlenila EK finančný objem 625 mil. €. V rámci 6-tej výzvy „Informačno-komunikačné technológie pre nízko-uhlíkovú ekonomiku" bol definovaný cieľ 6.7 „Spolupracujúce systémy pre energeticky efektívnu a udržateľnú mobilitu", ktorý je venovaný aj využitiu WSN v oblasti dopravy a je podporený finančným objemom 40 mil. €. V rámci podpory medzinárodnej spolupráce EÚ-Brazília bol vyčlenený finančný objem 5 mil. € na podporu spoločných výskumných aktivít v 5-tich špecifikovaných oblastiach, medzi ktoré patria i problémové okruhy z oblasti „WSN pri monitorovaní a riadení zložitých a rozsiahlych systémov". Táto výzva bola smerovaná na vývoj nových metód parametrizácie, autokonfigurácie, adaptivity, autolokalizácie, optimalizácie, prevádzky v prostredí s vysokou úrovňou rušenia a mnohých ďalších, ktoré by mali byť implementované v pokročilých bezdrôtových sieťach senzorov. Ďalšie výzvy ako napr. podpora medzinárodnej spolupráce EÚ-Japonsko alebo výzvy súvisiace s programom Horizon 2020 sú smerované na riešenie rôznych čiastkových problémov sietí WSN.

Pripomeňme, že najväčší finančný objem (625 mil. € z celkových 2 422 mil. € venovaných 7FP ICT pre roky 2010 - 2012) bol vyčlenený práve na riešenie problémov dotýkajúcich sa výskumu WSN. Za predpokladu, že vyčlenené finančné prostriedky budú účelne využité môžeme v najbližšom období očakávať mimoriadne významný pokrok v oblasti vývoja WSN a tvorby nových efektívnych aplikácií s prienikom do komerčných oblastí.

Záverom je možné konštatovať, že problematika WSN sa dostáva do popredia záujmu aj v európskom výskumnom priestore o čom svedčia mnohé zaujímavé aplikácie [3], [4], [5].

2 Aplikačné oblasti

Bezdrôtové siete senzorov, ako priestorovo distribuované siete tvorené relatívne jednoduchými vzájomne spolupracujúcimi prvkami majú veľký aplikačný potenciál vo vojenských, priemyselných, dopravných, environmentálnych a mnohých ďalších oblastiach.

V nasledujúcich rokoch je možné očakávať ich významné rozšírenie za predpokladu, že budú úspešne doriešené niektoré otázky súvisiace s komunikačnými protokolmi a ich štandardizáciou, efektívnymi zdrojmi energie, ktoré budú schopné zabezpečiť až 20 rokov autonómnej prevádzky uzlov siete a ďalšími pokrokmi v oblasti technológie výroby nízkopríkonových mikroelektronických prvkov.

Ako už bolo spomenuté v úvode jedna z prvých aplikačných oblastí bola tvorená vojenskými aplikáciami (Military). Práve vo vojenskej oblasti sa vyskytuje množstvo úloh spojených s monitorovaním územne rozľahlých oblastí, pričom ekonomické hľadiská zavádzania nových technológií nie sú až natoľko prioritné ako v iných odvetviach hospodárstva.

Spomeňme aspoň systémy navádzania a sledovania cieľa, systémy na detekciu pohybu a identifikáciu druhu bojových prostriedkov, monitorovanie bojového poľa (battlefield surveillance) aplikácie WSN v súvislosti s monitorovaním a ovládaním mínových polí, detekciu nukleárnych, biologických a chemických útokov (nuclear, biological and chemical attack detection) a mnohé ďalšie, [6].

Ďalšie zaujímavé aplikácie WSN je možné nájsť pri monitorovaní a ochrane životného prostredia. Monitorovanie prostredia patrí dnes snáď medzi najčastejšie aplikácie bezdrôtových sietí senzorov. Práve tieto aplikácie si vyžadujú použitie veľkého počtu lacných snímacích prvkov, ktoré je možné jednoducho rozmiestniť do sledovanej oblasti. Ako najčastejšie aplikácie je možné uviesť monitorovanie pohybu ľadovcov, monitorovanie a ochrana lesa pred požiarmi, nepovoleným výrubom, pytliakmi, varovné systémy pred záplavami a ďalšími prírodnými katastrofami, sledovanie zmien mikroklímy, intenzity slnečného žiarenia a množstvo ďalších zaujímavých aplikácií.

Ďalšou perspektívnou aplikačnou oblasťou bezdrôtových senzorických sietí je oblasť starostlivosti o zdravie, záchrana služba a asistenčné systémy (e-Helath). Je zrejmé, že s využitím technológií WSN je možné zvýšiť súčasnú úroveň monitorovania pacientov, ako aj úroveň zdravotnej starostlivosti. Ako príklad uveďme monitorovanie vitálnych funkcií pacientov v nemocnici. Tieto monitorovacie systémy umožňujú pohyb pacienta pri zachovaní všetkých funkcií statických systémov. Pripomeňme oblasť starostlivosti o staršiu generáciu, prípadne o ľudí s telesným postihnutím, ktorým moderné technológie dovoľujú zvýšiť kvalitu života. V tejto oblasti by bolo možné nájsť mnoho zaujímavých a inšpiratívnych príkladov.

S využitím technológie WSN sa dnes často stretneme v dopravných aplikáciách. Pri monitorovaní a riadení dopravy sú zdroje informácií priestorovo rozptýlené v rozľahlej oblasti. Komplexný prehľad o stave dopravy je možné získať len na základe informácií získaných z veľkého počtu vhodne rozmiestnených snímačov. Problematika monitorovania a riadenia dopravy preto prirodzenie smeruje aj do oblasti aplikácií senzorických sietí.

Spomeňme ešte aplikácie WSN technológií v priemysle. V priemyselných aplikáciách sa najčastejšie stretávame s úlohami monitorovania výroby, pri riadení skladového hospodárstva, prípadne dnes už častejšie, s riadením technologických procesov. Pripomeňme, že v prípade aplikácií v riadení technologických procesov sa často stretávame s pojmami „bezdrôtová sieť senzorov a akčných členov", „Wireless Sensor and Actuator Networks" – WSAN, prípadne tiež „priemyselná bezdrôtová sieť senzorov",„Industrial Wireless Sensor Networks", IWSN.

Poznamenajme, že popísané aplikácie tvoria len malú oblasť celého aplikačného priestoru WSN. Neboli spomenuté viaceré aplikačné oblasti, s ktorými sa dnes v praxi často stretneme – automatizácia budov, monitorovanie produktovodov, zabezpečovacie systémy, poľnohospodárstvo a mnohé ďalšie.

3 Základné problémy

Je zrejmé, že bezdrôtová sieť senzorov je tvorená veľkým množstvom uzlov „nodov", ktoré sú rozmiestnené v monitorovanej oblasti. Senzorické uzly bývajú rozmiestnené náhodne, alebo do vopred definovaných pozícií. Každý z prvkov siete musí spĺňať často protichodné požiadavky. Veľký výpočtový výkon pri minimálnej cene a spotrebe energie, dlhá životnosť pri obmedzených zdrojoch energie, schopnosť presnej autolokalizácie pri minimálnej cene riešenia a mnoho ďalších. Je potrebné dosiahnuť požadované užívateľské vlastnosti pri minimálnych nákladoch na realizáciu a prevádzku siete. V závislosti od konkrétnej aplikácie sa stretneme s rôznymi požiadavkami kladenými na sieť senzorov. No vo všeobecnosti je najčastejšie potrebné riešiť nasledujúce problémy:

- komunikácia: štandardizácia komunikačných protokolov,
- časová synchronizácia,
- lokalizácia,
- životnosť: energetická náročnosť,
- spoľahlivosť,
- bezpečnosť.

Problém spoľahlivej komunikácie medzi prvkami siete je jednou zo základných úloh, ktoré je potrebné riešiť. V súčasnosti existuje pomerne veľa sofistikovaných protokolov, ktoré pri nízkej energetickej náročnosti prijímačov/vysielačov dokážu zabezpečiť spoľahlivý prenos informácií s dostatočnou priepustnosťou. Poznamenajme, že v procese návrhu WSN je potrebné rešpektovať obmedzenia vyplývajúce z európskych normalizačných a tých štátnych telekomunikačných autorít, kde sa bude WSN používať.

Problém efektívnej časovej synchronizácie je problém, ktorý sa vyskytuje vo väčšine distribuovaných systémov spracovania dát. V mnohých aplikáciách od presnosti časovej synchronizácie technických prostriedkov priamo závisí presnosť dosiahnutých výsledkov. Ako príklad uveďme sledovanie pohybujúcich sa objektov na základe emitovaného hluku, všetky úlohy lokalizácie na báze vyhodnotenia TOA (Time of Arrive) a pod. Ďalším vážnym dôsledkom nepresnej synchronizácie je nárast spotreby komunikačného podsystému v celej WSN. Poznamenajme, že v prípade časového multiplexu musí byť prijímač senzorického uzla aktivovaný s predstihom maximálnej synchronizačnej chyby pred zahájením komunikácie.

Presnosť lokalizácie senzorov je primárnym problémom vo viacerých aplikáciách WSN (sledovanie objektov, v aplikáciách zdravotnej starostlivosti a iných.). Problém autolokalizácie každého uzla siete sa vyskytne v tzv. neštruktúrovaných sieťach, v ktorých sú senzory rozmiestnené náhodne, prípadne ak sú senzory súčasťou mobilných objektov. V týchto prípadoch je potrebné zabezpečiť aby každý senzor bol schopný získať aktuálnu informáciu o svojej polohe.

Životnosť, chápaná ako čas prevádzky senzorov bez zásahu obsluhy je pri využívaní napájacích článkov daná ich kapacitou a spotrebou energie. Je zrejmé, že v tomto prípade je možné životnosť zvýšiť zvýšením kapacity energetických zdrojov, alebo znížením spotreby zariadenia. Ďalšia možnosť je napájať senzor zo systému schopného získať energiu z okolia (Energy Harvesting). Dnes sa stretávame s mikrokontrolérmi ktorých spotreba v aktívnom režime je pod hodnotou $100\mu A/MHz@3V$. Z jednej batérie o kapacite 1000 mAh môže byť procesorová jednotka v prevádzke až 1 rok. V reálnych aplikáciách sa mikrokontrolér často nachádza v úspornom režime so spotrebou cca. sto krát nižšou, potom sa limitujúcim faktorom stáva spotreba komunikačného modulu, prípadne proces samovybíjania batérie. Poznamenajme, že aj v oblasti zdrojov energie, či už primárnych článkov, alebo nabíjateľných sa v poslednom období stretávame s výrazným zlepšením parametrov, najmä so zvýšením energetickej hustoty a so znížením samovybíjacieho prúdu.

Spoľahlivosť bezdrôtovej siete senzorov predstavuje významný problém, ktorý bol analyzovaný vo viacerých vedeckých a odborných prácach [7], [8]. Spoľahlivosť patrí stále medzi najčastejšie dôvody prečo nie je možné využiť WSN v priemyselných aplikáciách. Pod pojmom spoľahlivosť WSN budeme v zmysle všeobecnej definície spoľahlivosti rozumieť schopnosť zachovávať si funkčné vlastnosti v danom čase pri definovaných podmienkach činnosti. V bezdrôtových sieťach snímačov sa stretávame s vysokou mierou redundancie systému. Táto skutočnosť umožňuje i pri nižšej spoľahlivosti jednotlivých komponentov siete dosiahnuť požadovanej úrovne spoľahlivosti celej siete.

Bezpečnosť siete je široký pojem, ktorý zahŕňa problematiku autentifikácie, integrity, dôvernosti apod. Bezpečnosť WSN je ďalšia dnes často diskutovaná otázka. Väčšina autorov sa zhoduje v názore, že WSN je vďaka obmedzeným zdrojom (nízky výpočtový výkon, obmedzená kapacita pamätí, nespoľahlivé komunikačné linky, a pod.) mimoriadne zraniteľná. Je zrejmé, že čím väčší objem informácií je prenášaný sieťou, tým je bezpečnostné riziko prenosu vyššie. Z tohto pohľadu by bolo najvhodnejšie spracovávať snímané informácie priamo v mieste ich vzniku a sieťou WSN sprostredkovávať prenos len výsledných, značne komprimovaných dát (fúzia rozhodnutí). Takto sa však potlačí jedna z výhod WSN, ktorá vyplýva z možnosti použiť metódy kolaboratívneho spracovania signálov. Ďalší zaujímavý problém je aj problém autentifikácie, najmä pri ad-hoc sieťach, kde všetky prvky siete sú rovnocenné a sieť neobsahuje tzv. „certifikačnú autoritu". Je možné reálne predpokladať, že aj v ďalšom období bude problematike bezpečnosti venovaná zvýšená pozornosť.

Uvedené okruhy problémov z oblasti bezdrôtových sietí senzorov nepopisujú vyčerpávajúcim spôsobom ich analýzu a metódy riešenia. Mali len poukázať na šírku problémov, ktoré sprevádzajú vývoj nových aplikácií WSN. V celom príspevku nebolo spomenutých mnoho tém, ktoré sú z teoretického i praktického hľadiska zaujímavé a aktuálne, preto niektoré aspoň vymenujeme. Sú to nasledujúce témy:

- distribuované spracovanie signálov,
- kooperatívne spracovanie signálov,
- adaptivita siete,
- parametrizácia siete,
- inherentný šum a možnosti jeho potlačenia a mnohé ďalšie.

Každá zo spomenutých tém v sebe skrýva mnoho problémov, ktorých riešenia sú zaujímavé ako z teoretického, tak i praktického hľadiska. Oblasť WSN preto poskytuje dostatok priestoru pre zaujímavú výskumnú, vývojovú, realizačnú i experimentálnu prácu.

4   Prehľad vybratých aplikácií WSN

Problematika návrhu a realizácie rôznych prvkov WSN je na Katedre technickej kybernetiky (KTK) riešená od roku 2008, kedy bol navrhnutý prvý senzor pre monitoring rôznych parametrov dopravy v rámci riešenej problematiky inteligentných dopravných systémov. Od tej doby bolo realizovaných viacero zaujímavých prototypov z rôznych aplikačných oblastí, orientovaných primárne na monitoring parametrov dopravy a životného prostredia. Okrem toho bolo vyvinutých zopár prototypov aj pre oblasť Military i e-Health.

Pri praktickej realizácii senzorov bolo nutné okrem základných problémov popísaných vyššie riešiť aj ďalšie vlastnosti parametrizácie senzorov, ako sú výpočtový výkon senzora, cena, energetická nenáročnosť/životnosť senzora, bezpečnosť komunikácie, odolnosť voči poruchám, a pod.

Mnohé z uvedených požiadaviek si navzájom odporujú. Zvyšovaním výpočtového výkonu narastá energetická náročnosť, ako aj cena senzora. Zvýšenie zabezpečenia prenosu vyžaduje väčší výpočtový výkon. Zvýšená odolnosť voči poruchám zvyčajne negatívne ovplyvňuje cenu produkcie. Nie je teda možné vyvinúť dostatočne univerzálny prvok, ktorý bude optimálny z hľadiska všetkých uvedených požiadaviek. Naviac je potrebné pripomenúť, že rôzne aplikácie kladú rôznu váhu na splnenie jednotlivých požiadaviek. Problematika návrhu senzorických prvkov je popísaná v [10]. Autori navrhujú pri vývoji využívať triedu všeobecne použiteľných modulov a aplikačne orientovaných nosičov nosných dosiek - modulov (carriers) a takto dosiahnuť vysoký stupeň univerzálnosti a možnosti používať vyvinuté systémy v čo najširšej množine rôznych aplikácií. Odhliadnuc od hardvérovej platformy a druhu aplikácie každý sensor node WSN musí byť schopný realizovať tri základné funkcie - zber, predspracovanie a posielanie dát. Zber dát sa vykonáva v časti sensor node, ktorú nazveme podsystém zberu dát.

Podsystém zberu dát je časť sensor node, ktorá je mimoriadne závislá od požiadaviek konkrétnej aplikácie. Táto časť obsahuje snímacie prvky, ktoré snímajú tie veličiny, ktoré sú relevantné pre riešenie danej úlohy. Je zrejmé, že iné snímacie prvky sú potrebné pre snímanie parametrov cestnej dopravy, iné pre telemonitoring pacientov v zdravotnom zariadení a celkom iné pri monitorovaní sopečnej aktivity. Z tohto dôvodu je obtiažne špecifikovať univerzálne vlastnosti a parametre podsystému na zber dát. Každá aplikácia vyžaduje do istej miery špeciálny, originálny prístup k jej návrhu. Preto sa v praktických aplikáciách stretávame so skutočnosťou, že práve podsystém na zber údajov sa v rámci pilotného projektu špeciálne vyvíja podľa požiadaviek aplikácie.

Na nasledovných prototypoch je možné získať predstavu o aplikačných možnostiach využitia senzorov pre WSN:

4.1   KTK node pre monitoring akustických emisií a vibrácií v dopravných systémoch

Popisovaný senzor bol vyvinutý z dôvodov experimentálneho overovania nových metód kolaboratívneho spracovania signálov najmä vo frekvenčnom rozsahu do 15 kHz pre akustické emisie a do 1000 Hz vibrácie a chvenie so zameraním na energetickú efektívnosť. Zámerom bolo, po umiestnení senzora v blízkosti monitorovanej komunikácie, na základe emitovaného zvuku vozidiel určiť hustotu premávky na danej komunikácii. Senzor bol realizovaný na báze 32-bitového MCU ST32F100, snímací subsystém bol tvorený mikrofónom MCE100, predzosilňovačom, antialising filtrom druhého rádu a zosilňovačom s riaditeľným ziskom v rozsahu 1 až 352. Výstup zo zosilňovača bol privedený na vstup analógovo číslicového prevodníka integrovaného do puzdra MCU. Na snímanie vibrácií bol použitý 3-osí akcelerometer MMA8453 s možnosťou komunikácie prostredníctvom I2C s 12 a 8-bitovým výstupom. Spotreba akcelerometra v aktívnom režime je do 225 uA v závislosti od vibrácií, spotreba využitého MCU v tzv. „Run móde" je okolo 4.6 mA@8MHz. Množinu snímačov bolo možné rozšíriť prostredníctvom aplikačného konektora. Pamäťový subsystém bol kvôli možnosti uchovania veľkého objemu dát rozšírený o mikroSD kartu. Za účelom experimentálnych prác s rôznymi komunikačnými modulmi bol na základnej doske senzora umiestnený konektor, prostredníctvom ktorého bolo možné k základnému modulu pripojiť komunikačnú jednotku, v našom prípade to boli moduly XBee PRO v pásme 2.4 GHz. Senzor bol realizovaný na dvojvrstvovej doske plošných spojov s rozmermi 38 x 45 mm, obr.1. Na monitorovanie a riadenie WSN bol vyvinutý modul, ktorý sa pripája k personálnemu počítaču prostredníctvom konektora USB, obr.1 dole.

Obr.1 Vyvinutý node s USB modulom

Senzor bol o.i. využitý aj na hodnotenie kvality cestnej siete v rámci Žilinského kraja, keď po nainštalovaní do testovacieho vozidla zaznamenával na integrovanú SD kartu hodnotu vibrácií a hluku vozidla pri prechode cez testovanú komunikáciu.Viac informácií je možné nájsť v [13].

4.2 KTK node pre lokalizáciu snajpera

Miernou modifikáciou architektúry vyššie popísaného KTK nodu bol vyvinutý senzor pre oblasť Military využitý na riešenie problému lokalizácie snajpera v neznámych bojových podmienkach. Riadiaca jednotka senzora bola postavená na využití 32-bitového MCU STM32F100 s jadrom ARM Cortex M3. Snímací subsystém bol zložený z elektrótového mikrofónu pre nahrávanie akustických signálov a z 3-osého, 12/8-bitového akcelerometra MMA8453 určeného na snímanie vibrácií. Na riešenie lokalizačných a synchronizačných problémov bol aplikovaný integrovaný GPS modul LR9552LP.

Na verifikáciu funkčnosti systému bolo uskutočnené meranie lokalizácie výbuchu svetlice, ktorý bol riadene realizovaný 60m od senzorov. Tromi senzormi, A, B a C, umiestnenými so súradnicami (v metroch) A [0,0], B [36,0], C [17.1,-3.8] vzhľadom k senzoru A bolo realizovaných 10 meraní lokalizácie epicentra výbuchu svetlice na základe porovnávania časov prijatia jednotlivých signálov (Time Difference of Arrival - TDOA). Zaznamenané dáta sa ukladali na SD-kartu pričom boli neskôr spracované off-line. Priemerná chyba lokalizácie epicentra výbuchu bola 0.6m. Viac informácií je možné nájsť v [11].

Obr. 3 Vyvinutý prototyp senzoru pre lokalizáciu snajpera

Modifikáciou riadiaceho softvéru senzoru je možné zmeniť jeho aplikačné využitie na ochranu/monitoring rôznych území, ako napr. v [14], kde bol senzor využitý na ochranu zalesnených území pred nelegálnou ťažbou dreva zhotovením WSN pre detekciu zvuku motorovej píly (Obr. 4 a 5).

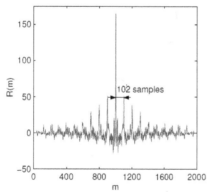

Obr. 4 Autokorelačná sekvencia analyzovaného zvuku motorovej píly

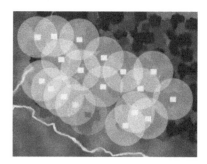

Obr. 5 Rozmiestnenie senzorov v zalesnenom území

4.3 KTK node pre snímanie parametrov mechanického kmitania

Ďalší snímač navrhnutý na KTK bol určený na snímanie parametrov mechanického kmitania v podmienkach železničnej dopravy. Účelom merania bolo nájsť frekvenčné pásmo s najväčšou energiou vibrácií, aby bolo možné navrhnúť vibračný generátor s rezonančnou frekvenciou v strede uvedeného pásma a súčasne posúdiť veľkosť získanej energie pri prijateľných rozmeroch generátora. Navrhnutý snímač vibrácií bol schopný zaznamenať vibrácie vo frekvenčnom rozsahu 0 až 1kHz s predpokladaným meraným rozsahom maximálne do 6g. Snímač bol napájaný lítium-polymer 3.6 V/1850 mAh akumulátora umožňujúceho nepretržitú prevádzku snímača cca. 10 hodín. Ako riadiaca jednotka bol využitý MCU AT91SAM7S64 integrovaný spolu s dvoma 64MB FLASH pamäťami AT45DB321C, GPS modulom LEA-4S, snímačom vibrácií MMA7260 i modulom na SD pamäťovú kartu. Na obr.6 je uvedená bloková schéma navrhnutého snímača vibrácií.

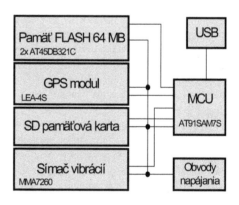

Obr.6 Bloková schéma senzoru pre snímanie vibrácií

Pomocou uvedeného snímača boli uskutočnené merania na troch typoch vlakových súprav. Na trase Prievidza-Handlová-Remata bolo uskutočnené meranie v motorovom vozni 810. Meranie na zmodernizovanej motorovej jednotke 813-913 bolo realizované na trase Handlová-Prievidza. Tretie meranie sa uskutočnilo v rýchliku R 604 Dargov na elektrifikovanej trati medzi stanicami Nové Mesto nad Váhom a Bratislava. Vo všetkých troch prípadoch boli merané vibrácie v troch osiach, pričom bola použitá frekvencia vzorkovania 5 kHz. Snímač vibrácií bol využitý na získanie a uchovanie dát reprezentujúcich vibrácie, ktoré vznikajú počas jazdy vlaku. Na základe získaných údajov je možné získať informácie o frekvenčnom rozložení energie signálu za účelom návrhu ptimálnej rezonančnej frekvencie mikrogenerátorov. Ďalšou možnosťou je použiť snímač na vyhodnotenie kvality železničného zvršku, alebo na kontrolu kvality odpruženia železničných vozňov.

4.4 KTK node pre klasifikáciu vozidiel

Vyvinutý senzor bol určený na detekciu a určenie typu vozidla na základe emitovaného magnetického poľa vozidla využitím senzora LSM303 obsahujúceho magnetometer i akcelerometer. Ako riadiaca jednotka bol využitý 32-bitový MCU STM32F100RB, ako komunikačná jednotka bol využitý už zmienený X-bee modul alternovaný RFM70, oba pracujúce v 2.4GHz pásme ISM. Ako alternatíva bol v [15] využitý aj modul MRF24J40MA (Microchip). Namerané dáta mohli byť ukladané na SD kartu i priamo do počítača cez USB rozhranie. Vyvinutý prototyp je zobrazený na obr. 7.

Vyvinutý senzor bol využitý na viacero experimentálnych meraní, počnúc analýzou jeho citlivosti a rozlišovacej schopnosti vzhľadom k jeho umiestneniu voči testovanej komunikácii, cez analýzu vplyvu rozličných rýchlostí testovaného vozidla na výsledky merania emitovaného magnetického poľa až po návrh a otestovanie metódy pre klasifikáciu typu a rýchlosti vozidiel prechádzajúcich po monitorovanej komunikácii. Metóda bola otestovaná v rámci merania uskutočneného na začiatku obce Nedožery-Brezany, 28. marca 2012 v časovom rozmedzí medzi 16:00 - 16:18. Počas merania bolo uskutočnené aj komparatívne meranie kamerou, ktorou boli zaznamenané nasledovné dáta - 131 osobných automobilov, 4 dodávky, 4 nákladné autá, 2 autobusy a jeden bicykel, čo dalo dokopy 142 vozidiel. Z dát nameraných senzorom bolo možné rozlíšiť 148 vozidiel, z ktorých 8 bolo detegovaných ako protiidúcich a ďalších 5 malo slabý korelačný koeficient, čo nám dalo celkový výsledok 135 vozidiel reprezentujúci 91% úspešnosť. Viac informácií o vyvinutom senzore i metóde pre klasifikáciu vozidiel je možné nájsť v [12].

Obr. 7 Vyvinutý prototyp senzora pre klasifikáciu vozidiel

4.5 KTK node pre monitoring prostredia

Senzor bol navrhnutý na báze 32-bitového MCU ST32L151C vybaveného s ARM-Cortex M3 jadrom s nízkou spotrebou 214μA/MHz nakoľko bolo zariadenie primárne určené pre použitie na miestach bez prívodu elektriny. Snímací subsystém bol tvorený už zmeneným

senzorom LSM303DLM, slotom pre SD kartu a komunikačným modulom MRF24J40MA pracujúcom v ISM pásme 2.405 - 2.48 GHz. Napájanie systému bolo riešené cez Li-Pol akumulátory, alternatívne i cez superkapacitory, využívajúce technológie solárneho napájania i termogenerátora pre svoje nabíjanie.

Senzor je určený pre snímanie magnetického poľa, vibrácií i akustického signálu okolia, čo umožňuje jeho všestranné využitie v rôznych odvetviach hospodárstva. Viac informácií o danom senzore ako aj o spôsoboch jeho napájania je možné nájsť v [16], [17], i [18].

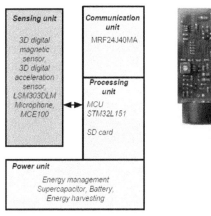

Obr. 8 Vyvinutý prototyp senzora pre monitoring prostredia

4.6 KTK node pre Body Area Network

V rámci oblasti e-Helath bola navrhnutá a vyvinutá špeciálna sieť BAN (Body Area Network) pre monitoring vitálnych funkcií pacienta súvisiacich s analýzou príznakov stresu. Sieť pozostáva z niekoľkých senzorov merajúcich teplotu, vlhkosť/potenie (senzor HIH-6131-021-001) ako aj tep pacienta (oximeter), a zo smartfónu ako riadiacej jednotky doplnenej o prenosové rozhranie pripojené cez USB. Prenosové rozhranie je určené na prepojenie systému smartfónu s ostatnými senzormi využívajúc nízkopríkonový MCU CC2511F32RSP (Texas Instruments) integrujúci full-speed USB kontroler i proprietárne rádio pre 2.4 GHz 802.15.6 IEEE štandard CC2500. S dôvodu väčšieho počtu periférií bol na senzorovej časti využitý ako riadiaci MCU CC2545. TDMA (Time Division Multiple Access) bol využitý ako metóda prístupu na komunikačný kanál, samotná komunikácia prebiehala na báze Chritianovho algoritmu. Viac informácií je možné nájsť v [19] a [20].

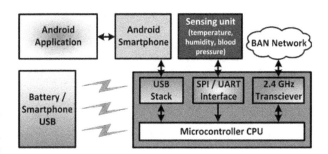

Obr. 9 Bloková schéma vyvinutej BAN

Obr.10 Vyvinutý prototyp senzora pre BAN

4.7 WSN pre navigáciu vozidiel v neprehľadných križovatkách

Prototyp špeciálnej WSN pre riešenie problému neprehľadných križovatiek je aktuálne vyvíjaný pre potreby použitia na miestach bez prívodu elektrickej energie. Systém pozostáva z viacerých senzorov umiestnených pozdĺž monitorovanej cestne komunikácie v rozstupoch zaručujúcich včasnú detekciu vozidla i reakciu naň. Scnzory sú založené na využití MCU MSP430F2232 s ultranízkou spotrebou, sub-1GHz RF prijímača/vysielača CC1101 pracujúceho v ISM pásme 868 MHz a digitálneho 3-osého magnetometra MAG3110. Systém je schopný autonómnej prevádzky po dobu minimálne 180 dní a je stavaný na detekciu automobilov pohybujúcich sa rýchlosťou najviac 50 km/h, maximálna rýchlosť automobilov v mestskej prevádzke. TDMA bol aj v tomto prípade využitý ako metóda prístupu na komunikačný kanál. Viac informácií o danom systéme je možné nájsť v [21].

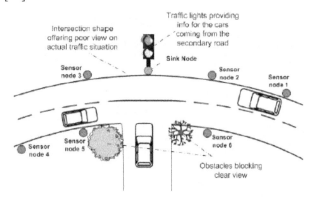

Obr. 9 Návrh rozmiestnenia senzorov vyvíjanej WSN pre navigáciu vozidiel v neprehľadnej križovatke

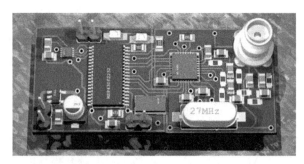

Obr. 10 Renderovaný 3D model prototypu senzora vyvíjanej WSN pre navigáciu vozidiel v neprehľadnej križovatke

5 Záver

V oblasti vývoja aplikácií WSN je možné rozpoznať dva základné smery. Jeden smer vedie k sieťovaniu výrobných strojov, technológií a komerčných zariadení z dôvodov lepšej diagnostiky a monitorovania, efektívnejšieho využitia energií a výrobných kapacít, jednoduchšieho a účinnejšieho ovládania a riadenia, ako aj zvýšenia užívateľského komfortu. Druhý smer vedie k sieťovaniu ľudí z dôvodov zvýšenia kvality zdravotnej starostlivosti, osobnej bezpečnosti, zvýšenia komfortu života, ako aj uľahčenia života handicapovaným osobám. Je možné predpokladať, že nasadenie WSN v druhej oblasti zákonite prinesie i zmeny v sociálnych vzťahoch spoločnosti a umožní využívanie WSN na hranici súčasných etických noriem. Ľudia už dnes pociťujú stratu osobnej slobody a oprávnene požadujú zvýšenie kontroly nad využívaním moderných informačných tcchnológií. Ako každá nová technológia aj technológia WSN sa dá využiť v prospech ľudí, no súčasne sa otvára priestor aj na jej zneužitie.

Napriek uvedeným problémom je možné konštatovať, že prienik technológie WSN do rôznych oblastí bude i naďalej pokračovať.

Poďakovanie

Tento príspevok vznikol aj vďaka podpore cez Európsky fond regionálneho rozvoja v rámci operačného programu Výskum a vývoj pre projekt ITMS 26220120050: Centrum excelentnosti pre systémy a služby inteligentnej dopravy II.

"Podporujeme výskumné aktivity na Slovensku/Projekt je spolufinancovaný zo zdrojov EÚ"

Literatúra

[1] P. Harrop: Wireless Sesor Networks 2009-2019, IDTechEx, 2008

[2] P. Harrop, R. Das: Wireless Sesor Networks 2010-2020, IDTechEx, 2010

[3] K. Romer, F. Mattern: The Design Space of Wireless Sensor Networks, IEEE Wireless Communications 12, 2004

[4] A. Herms, E. Nett, S. Schemmer: Real-Time Mesh Networks for Industrial Applications, Proceedings of the 17th World Congress IFAC, Korea 2008

[5] D. Christin, P. S. Mogre, M. Hollick: Survey on Wireless Sensor Network Technologies for Industrial Automation: The Security and Quality of Service Perspectives, Future Internet 2010, ISSN 1999-5903

[6] P. Kuckertz et al.: Sniper Fire Localization Using Wireless Sensor Networks and Genetic Algoritm Based Data Fusion

[7] H. M. F. AboEiFotoh, E. S. ElMallah, H. S. Hassanin: On The Reliability of Wireless Sensor Networks, IEEE ICC, 2006

[8] M. Cinque, D. Controneo, G. De Caro, M. Pelella: Reliability Requirements of Wireless Sensor Networks for Dynamic Structural Monitoring, Proceedings of Workshop on Applied Software Reliability, Philadelphia, USA 2006

[9] J. Miček: Bezdrôtové senzorické siete-súčasnosť, perspektívy, aplikácie, ATP Journal, 7, 8, 9, 10, 2011, ISSN 1335-2237

[10] P. Dutta, et al.: A Building Block Approach to Sensornet Systems, In Proc. SenSys 08, 2008, North Carolina, USA.

[11] O. Karpiš, J. Miček: Sniper localization using WSN 2011. In: ICMT´11. - Brno : University of Defence, 2011. - ISBN 9788072317875. - S. 1063-1068.

[12] O. Karpiš: Sensor for Vehicles Classification. In Proceedings of the Federated Conference on Computer Science and Information Systems pp. 785–789, ISBN 978-83-60810-51-4.

[13] J. Miček, J. Kapitulík: Wireless sensors networks in road transportation applications. IEEE Perspective Technologies and Methods in MEMS Design (MEMSTECH), 11-14 May 2011, Lviv, Ukraine.

[14] J. Papán, M. Jurečka a J. Púchyová: WSN for Forest Monitoring to Prevent Illegal Logging. Proceedings of the Federated Conference on Computer Science and Information Systems pp. 809–812, ISBN 978-83-60810-51-4.

[15] O. Karpiš: Solar-cell based powering of a node for traffic monitoring IOSR Journal of Engineering, Vol. 3, Issue 4 (April. 2013), pp. 28-32), e-ISSN: 2250-3021, p-ISSN: 2278-8719.

[16] J. Miček, J. Kapitulík: WSN sensor node for protected area monitoring. Proceedings of the Federated Conference on Computer Science and Information Systems pp. 803–807, ISBN 978-83-60810-51-4.

[17] J. Miček, J. Kapitulík: Wireless Sensor Node for Traffic Monitoring: Analysis and Design. European International Journal of Science and Technology, Vol. 2, No. 1, February 2013, pp.85-97, ISSN: 2304-9693

[18] M. Kochláň, P. Ševčík: Supercapacitor power unit for an event-driven wireless sensor node. Proceedings of the Federated Conference on Computer Science and Information Systems pp. 791–796, ISBN 978-83-60810-51-4

[19] M. Kochláň, M. Hodoň, J. Púchyová: Vital functions monitoring via Sensor Body Area Network with smartphone network coordinator. In: MEMSTECH´ 2013, 16-20 April 2013, Polyana, Ukraine, pp.143-147, ISBN 978-617-607-424-3.

[20] M. Hodoň, J. Púchyová, M. Kochláň: Smartphone-Based Body Area Network for Stress Monitoring: Radio Interference Investigation. Communications: scientific letters of the University of Žilina, ISSN 1335-4205, v tlači.

[21] M. Hodoň, J. Miček, M. Chovanec: Wireless Sensor Networks for Intelligent Transportation Systems. IEEE CommSoft newsletter: No. 2, 2012, v tlači.

Index